JACKSONIAN AND ANTEBELLUM AGE

Other titles in the Perspectives in American Social History series

PERSPECTIVES IN
AMERICAN SOCIAL HISTORY

Jacksonian and Antebellum Age

People and Perspectives

Mark R. Cheathem, Editor
Peter C. Mancall, Series Editor

Santa Barbara, California · Denver, Colorado · Oxford, England

Library of Congress Cataloging-in-Publication Data

Jacksonian and antebellum age : people and perspectives / Mark R. Cheathem, editor.
     p. cm.
     Includes bibliographical references and index.
     ISBN 978-1-59884-017-9 (hard copy : alk. paper) — ISBN 978-1-59884-018-6 (ebook)   1. United States—History—1815–1861.   2. United States—Social conditions—To 1865.   3. Jackson, Andrew, 1767–1845—Influence.   I. Cheathem, Mark Renfred.

     E338.J33 2008
     973.5—dc22

                                                                        2007026736

12 11 10 09 08   1 2 3 4 5 6 7 8 9 10

Senior Production Editor: Vicki Moran
Editorial Assistant: Sara Springer
Production Manager: Don Schmidt
Media Editor: Karen Koppel
Media Resources Coordinator: Ellen Brenna Dougherty
Media Resources Manager: Caroline Price
File Manager: Paula Gerard

ABC-CLIO, Inc.
130 Cremona Drive, P.O. Box 1911
Santa Barbara, California 93116-1911

This book is also available on the World Wide Web as an ebook. Visit www.abc-clio.com for details.

This book is printed on acid-free paper ∞

Manufactured in the United States of America

Contents

Series Introduction

S ocial history is, simply put, the study of past societies. More specifically, social historians attempt to describe societies in their totality, and hence often eschew analysis of politics and ideas. Though many social historians argue that it is impossible to understand how societies functioned without some consideration of the ways that politics works on a daily basis or what ideas could be found circulating at any given time, they tend to pay little attention to the formal arenas of electoral politics or intellectual currents. In the United States, social historians have been engaged in describing components of the population which had earlier often escaped formal analysis, notably women, members of ethnic or cultural minorities, or those who had fewer economic opportunities than the elite.

Social history became a vibrant discipline in the United States after it had already gained enormous influence in Western Europe. In France, social history in its modern form emerged with the rising prominence of a group of scholars associated with the journal *Annales Economie, Societé, Civilisation* (or *Annales ESC* as it is known). In its pages and in a series of books from historians affiliated with the École des Hautes Études en Sciences Sociale in Paris, brilliant historians such as Marc Bloch, Jacques Le Goff, and Emanuel LeRoy Ladurie described seemingly every aspect of French society. Among the masterpieces of this historical reconstruction was Fernand Braudel's monumental study, *The Mediterranean and the Mediterranean World in the Age of Philip II,* published first in Paris in 1946 and in a revised edition in English in 1972. In this work Braudel argued that the only way to understand a place in its totality was to describe its environment, its social and economic structures, and its political systems. In Britain the emphasis of social historians has been less on questions of environment, per se, than in a description of human communities in all their complexities. For example, social historians there have taken advantage of that nation's remarkable local archives to reconstruct the history of the family and details of its rural past. Works such as Peter Laslett's *The World We Have Lost*, first printed in 1966, and the multi-authored *Agrarian History of England and Wales*, which began to appear in print in 1967, revealed that painstaking work could reveal the lives and habits of individuals who never previously attracted the interest of biographers, demographers, or most historians.

Social history in the United States gained a large following in the second half of the twentieth century, especially during the 1960s and 1970s. Its development sprang from political, technical, and intellectual impulses deeply embedded in the culture of the modern university. The politics of civil rights and social reform fueled the passions of historians who strove to tell the stories of the underclass. They benefited from the adoption by historians of statistical analysis, which allowed scholars to trace where individuals lived, how often they moved, what kinds of jobs they took, and whether their economic status declined, stagnated, or improved over time. As history departments expanded, many who emerged from graduate schools focused their attention on groups previously ignored or marginalized. Women's history became a central concern among American historians, as did the history of African Americans, Native Americans, Latinos and others. These historians pushed historical study in the United States farther away from the study of formal politics and intellectual trends. Though few Americanists could achieve the technical brilliance of some social historians in Europe, collectively they have been engaged in a vast act of description, with the goal of describing seemingly every facet of life from 1492 to the present.

The sixteen volumes in this series together represent the continuing efforts of historians to describe American society. Most of the volumes focus on chronological areas, from the broad sweep of the colonial era to the more narrowly defined collections of essays on the eras of the Cold War, the Baby Boom, and America in the age of the Vietnam War. The series also includes entire volumes on the epochs that defined the nation, the American Revolution and the Civil War, as well as volumes dedicated to the process of westward expansion, women's rights, and African American history.

This social history series derives its strength from the talented editors of individual volumes. Each editor is an expert in his or her own field who selected and organized the contents of his or her volume. Editors solicited other experienced historians to write individual essays. Every volume contains first-rate analysis complemented by lively anecdotes designed to reveal the complex contours of specific historical moments. The many illustrations to be found in these volumes testify too to the recognition that any society can be understood not only by the texts that its participants produce but also by the images that they craft. Primary source documents in each volume will allow interested readers to pursue some specific topics in greater depth, and each volume contains a chronology to provide guidance to the flow of events over time. These tools—anecdotes, images, texts, and timelines—allow readers to gauge the inner workings of America in particular periods and yet also to glimpse connections between eras.

The articles in these volumes testify to the abundant strengths of historical scholarship in the United States in the early years of the twenty-first century. Despite the occasional academic contest that flares into public notice, or the self-serving cant of politicians who want to manipulate the nation's past for partisan ends—for example, in debates over the second amendment to the United States Constitution and what it means about potential limits to the rights of gun ownership—the articles here all reveal the vast increase in knowledge of the American past that has taken place over the last half century. Social historians do not dominate history faculties in American colleges and universities, but no one could deny them a seat at the intellectual table. Without their efforts, intellectual, cultural, and political historians would be hard pressed to understand why certain ideas circulated when they did, why some religious movements prospered or foundered, how developments in fields such as medicine and engineering reflected larger concerns, and what shaped the world we inhabit.

Fernand Braudel and his colleagues envisioned entire laboratories of historians in which scholars working together would be able to produce *histoire totale:* total history. Historians today seek more humble goals for our collective enterprise. But as the richly textured essays in these volumes reveal, scholarly collaboration has in fact brought us much closer to that dream. These volumes do not and cannot include every aspect of American history. However, every page reveals something interesting or valuable about how American society functioned. Together, these books suggest the crucial necessity of stepping back to view the grand complexities of the past rather than pursuing narrower prospects and lesser goals.

Peter C. Mancall

Series Editor

Introduction

Nothing seems more suited to exciting and nourishing curiosity than the aspect of the United States. Fortunes, ideas, and laws are constantly changing there. . . . Eventually, however, the sight of this much agitated society appears monotonous, and after having contemplated this very changeable spectacle for some time, the observer becomes bored. . . . The aspect of American society is agitated because men and things change constantly, and it is monotonous because all the changes are alike (de Tocqueville 2000, 268).

Many Americans in the Jacksonian period would likely have disagreed with this observation of Alexis de Tocqueville. Monotonous was not a word that Americans would have recognized as applying to their society during these years. The Jacksonian era was one of the most significant times of transformation in American history. Often hailed as the "Age of Egalitarianism," the period brought positive changes for many Americans, who found themselves with the opportunity to expand their political, social, economic, and gender roles. At the same time, many of those same individuals experienced significant opposition to these changes, and some even discovered that their place in American society regressed.

In recent years, historians have proposed that the substantial changes that occurred during the Jacksonian period were due in large part to the Market Revolution. According to one historian, the Market Revolution occurred in the early 1800s when "a largely subsistence economy of small farms and tiny workshops, satisfying mostly local needs through barter and exchange, gave place to an economy in which farmers and manufacturers produced food and goods for the cash rewards of an often distant marketplace" (Stokes and Conway 1996, p. 1). This economic change was very complex and had important implications for the social life of Americans.

One of the major precipitating factors for the Market Revolution was the increasing amount of land under American control. In 1803, Thomas Jefferson was able to purchase the Louisiana Territory from France, a purchase that roughly doubled the size of the nation. During and after the War of 1812, Andrew Jackson forced Native Americans to cede millions of acres to the United States, then compelled Spain to sell Florida when he invaded that territory in 1818. American expansion slowed until the 1840s, when it once again exploded with the annexation of Texas, the settlement of the U.S.-Canadian border in Oregon, and the acquisition of most of what is now the American Southwest, including California, after the Mexican-American War. (The rest of the Southwest was added during the 1850s with the Gadsden Purchase.)

The expansion of the United States was fortuitous, as the American population was growing rapidly as well. In 1750, the population of the thirteen British colonies was 1,170,800. By 1800, that number had risen to 5,308,483, and it roughly doubled itself every twenty years until 1860, when the population stood at 31,443,321 (U.S. Census). The expanding population needed somewhere to go, and the territory acquired gave them that opportunity.

Traversing the United States became more problematic as the nation grew, of course; therefore, transportation improvements were imperative to helping the population move westward. Building better roads, both inter- and intrastate, was one important step that Americans took. Developing a more extensive water transportation network also became a necessity. Americans began building canals in an attempt to provide better and faster access to inland production sites and markets. Steamboats made the movement of both goods and people up and down rivers easier. The development of railroads had probably the most dramatic impact. Trains could move even larger numbers of products and people at a speed twice that of stagecoaches and four times that of water transportation. American businessmen understood how important they were; in 1840, rail mileage was 3,328, and by 1860, it had reached 30,636 miles (Taylor 1951, pp. 79–80).

The transportation revolution also helped facilitate emerging industries and growing urban centers. The United States joined the first Industrial Revolution in the 1790s, although not until after the War of 1812 did it really begin to take hold. Textile manufacturing, centered in New England, was the centerpiece of the budding factory system. Iron production also became important, particularly as railroad building began in earnest. The standardization and mass production of interchangeable parts made possible a number of products, including the McCormick reaper and the Singer sewing machine. By 1860, industrial products produced in the United States were for the first time worth more in value than agricultural products.

Urbanization went hand-in-hand with industrialization, as concentrated populations centers were necessary to provide workers for factories. The five largest cities in both 1820 and 1860 were, in order of size, New York, Philadelphia, Baltimore, Boston, and New Orleans. The growth of these cities' populations was substantial. New York went from 123,700 in 1820 to 1,080,330 in 1860; Philadelphia, from 112,800 to 565,529; Baltimore, from 62,700 to 212,418; Boston, from 43,300 to 177,840; and New Orleans, from 27,200 to 168,675. A significant portion of this population growth resulted from immigration into the United States, particularly during the eleven years of 1847–57. During this period, the number of immigrants was never less than 200,000 and peaked at 427,833 in 1854. The total number of immigrants during those years was 3,328,665, while the annual average was 302,606 (U.S. Census).

All of these changes could not have taken place, at least not with as much success, without some government support. Between the American Revolution and the War of 1812, Americans were generally reluctant to allow the national government too much direct influence over economic development. (The First Bank of the United States, which held a congressional charter from 1791 to 1811, was a notable exception.) After the Treaty of Ghent was signed, however, those restrictions began to loosen, although they never gave complete freedom. Nevertheless, the American System, proposed by Henry Clay in the postwar euphoria, went a long way toward helping the market revolution progress. Clay's program called for the chartering of a new national bank, the passage by Congress of protective tariffs, and federally supported internal improvements, all of which gained approval during the 1810s. In *Gibbons v. Ogden* (1824), the United States Supreme Court endorsed the idea that the federal government, not the states, had the authority to govern interstate commerce.

Where urbanization and industrialization were largely centered in the northern states, circumstances in the South were significantly different. In that region, agriculture, particularly cotton, predominated in the decades between the War of 1812 and the Civil War. Other cash crops, including sugarcane, tobacco, rice, and hemp, were important to the antebellum economy, but none as much as cotton. To give some perspective, between 1790 and 1810, American cotton production increased from 3,000 bales annually to 178,000 bales. In 1860, it had increased to nearly 5 million bales. The demand for cotton from New England and foreign textiles manufacturers convinced southerners to pursue this market, forming an alliance between "the lords of the lash and the lords of the loom" (Donald 1960, p. 169).

As cash-crop production in the South increased, so did the need for slaves to work the fields; this led to a burgeoning internal slave trade in the antebellum period. (The trans-Atlantic slave trade had been outlawed in 1808, although some Africans were still imported illegally.) Slavery, which had been a significant part of Virginia's history, grew only 15 percent in that state between 1820 and 1860, but increased 209 percent in Louisiana and 1,231 percent in Mississippi during those same years. The substantial expansion in these states largely derived from the movement of slaves from the Upper South into the Deep South, although natural increase also helped the slave population expand from 697,897 in 1790 to 3,953,760 in 1860. About 55 percent of southern slaves worked with cotton; 10 percent grew tobacco; 10 percent produced sugar, rice, or hemp; 15 percent were domestic servants; and the remainder worked in trades and industries (U.S. Census).

Paradoxically, direct slave ownership decreased, as that form of property wealth came to be concentrated in the hands of a smaller number of southern elites. When counting families as slaveholders, approximately 25 percent (nearly 2 million) of white southerners were directly tied to slave ownership in 1860. The number of direct slave owners was much smaller, however. In 1830, 36 percent (1,314,272) of 3,650,758 white southerners owned slaves; in 1860, that number had declined to 4.7 percent (383,673) of 8,097,463. By 1860, almost half of the South's slaveholders owned fewer than five slaves. Only 12 percent (approximately 46,000) owned more than twenty. Around

1 percent (approximately 3,800) owned fifty or more slaves. Owners of over 100 slaves numbered 2,292. There were only fourteen with 500 or more slaves, and just one with more than 1,000. Interestingly, of the fourteen largest slave owners, nine were rice planters; the largest, Joshua Ward, was a South Carolina rice planter (Parish 1989, pp. 26–28; U.S. Census). These figures indicate that by 1860, the typical slaveholder owned few slaves, but the typical slave lived on a sizable plantation.

One can imagine, then, that slave life was not easy. Slaves had to wonder if their family would be broken up as one or more members were sold to slave traders in the internal slave trade. Also, working in the fields was grueling labor; working in a plantation house, while not as taxing physically, could be demanding in other ways. Slaves had to make sure that they were on their best behavior, sufficiently submissive, and obedient, or risk punishment. Female slaves had to live with the knowledge that rape was a realistic possibility. It was little wonder that running away, feigning sickness, and using other forms of active and passive resistance were also part of a slave's existence.

Just like the Market Revolution shaped slave families, so it also affected white households. The size of households in the Northeast, for example, decreased throughout the Jacksonian period. This happened for several reasons. One was that women chose to marry later, thus limiting the number of years of fertility within a marriage, which usually defined when a female could conceive without social disapproval. Married couples were also deliberately choosing to limit the number of children that they had. The reason for this change seemed to hinge, at least in part, on the decline in available resources in the Northeast. Those who chose to stay in that region presumably decided that dividing family resources among many children made less sense than dividing them among fewer children. Future generations theoretically would have had better opportunities in this scenario. On the western frontier, where land was cheaper and more abundant, household patterns tended to remain traditional in terms of size.

In addition to the Market Revolution, the democratization of politics also affected the social change that was taking place. Most people who are familiar with this era recognize that the Jacksonian period brought democracy to the forefront of American politics. The traditional view is that General Andrew Jackson, who had defeated the British at the Battle of New Orleans in January 1815, was swept into the presidency in 1828 on a wave of popular discontent with the restrictive and elitist political system then in place. Jackson, the argument goes, was a man of the people who had himself been a victim of the political elites when they had stolen the 1824 presidential election from him by way of a "corrupt bargain" between presidential aspirant Henry Clay and eventual victor John Quincy Adams. Jackson had won a plurality of both the electoral and popular votes in that fall's election, but because he had not won a constitutional majority, the election went to the United States House of Representatives. There, Clay, who had been Speaker of the House, used his political clout to sway state delegations to give their votes to Adams, which several did. Shortly after Adams was declared president-elect, he offered the secretary of state position to Clay, completing their presumed contract. Jackson and his supporters believed that this was enough evidence to claim that the presidency had been stolen not only from Jackson but also from the voters, who had clearly indicated their choice for the executive mansion. It was the outrage from this election result, then, that enabled Jackson to win against Adams in 1828 and opened up American politics to more people.

There is some truth to this account, of course. The 1820s were a transformative decade, as universal white manhood suffrage became the norm in many states, as state legislatures became more responsive to these voters, and as state constitutions also incorporated democratic changes. How much was due to Jackson is questionable; it is more likely that he benefited from, rather than precipitated, the expanding democratic practices. While white males like Jackson were finding their path in politics clearer, other groups were finding the road not as easy to maneuver, not just in politics but also in life.

Almost always a part of households in which white males held the power, white females found their lives changing in substantial ways. In the formative years of the American nation, women were charged with helping preserve and perpetuate the new republic by encouraging virtuous conduct among the members of their households, particularly children; historians have labeled this expectation "republican motherhood." By educating sons in virtue, mothers would ensure that they entered the public world well equipped to defend the nation's political ideology. As for daughters, mothers would inculcate virtue in them to ensure that they would be able to provide a strong moral compass for future husbands and children. In most instances, republican motherhood did not expect women to act publicly but, rather, privately, with public effect.

Some women, mostly from the upper classes, refused to accept these restrictions, however. They argued for more legal, educational, political, and even marital rights. Their success was limited by republican motherhood, but the advent of the Market Revolution in the 1810s and the apex of the Second Great Awakening in the 1830s opened opportunities for women to gain more control over their lives. The economic changes wrought by the Market Revolution moved some women, usually girls, out of the home and into factories, giving them a chance to earn their own wages and to exercise some independence from the male members of their households, especially their fathers. Many women also realized that having their husbands moving away from farm life to factory work gave them a chance to focus on more domestic duties that did not involve contributing to the heavy labor in the fields. Their lives could hardly be called leisurely, but it must have been some relief to take care of a household without the added expectation of working the crops.

Women also embraced the egalitarianism of the religious revivals that spread across the nation during the Jacksonian period. The weight given by Charles G. Finney and other evangelicals to spiritual equality and the free will of individuals encouraged women to reconsider their place in broader society. More significantly, evangelicals of the period emphasized the need for Christians to move beyond their own spiritual atonement and growth and look to use their spiritual virtue to improve the world around them. The focus on reform gave women in particular the opportunity to move beyond the home, both physically and in terms of their influence.

Women made up the backbone of the reform movements that sprang up during this period. Many of them were middle class, although the most recognizable figures remembered by history tended to come from wealthier backgrounds. Most of the female participants were from the northern states, where the larger, urban population centers were located and where some issues tended to cause more concern. Female reformers were concerned with ending slavery; improving education; helping those marginalized by society, including the poor and the incarcerated; combating the consequences of alcoholic consumption; winning property and marital rights for those who were married; and expanding their own political rights.

The climax of female reform, at least in regard to the rights of women, came in 1848 with the Seneca Falls Convention. Organized by Elizabeth Cady Stanton and Lucretia Mott, the meeting attempted to give direction to the growing women's rights movement. "We hold these truths to be self-evident: that all men and women are created equal," declared the convention's "Declaration of Sentiments." It listed a number of wrongs, both political and social, committed by men against women in their attempt to establish "an absolute tyranny" over American wives, mothers, and daughters. "In view of this entire disfranchisement of one-half the people of this country, their social and religious degradation—in view of the unjust laws above mentioned, and because women do feel themselves aggrieved, oppressed, and fraudulently deprived of their most sacred rights," the Declaration concluded, "we insist that they have immediate admission to all the rights and privileges which belong to them as citizens of the United States" ("Declaration of Sentiments").

The most prominent reform movement with which women were involved was abolitionism. Arguing against the institution of slavery was not a new idea in the Jacksonian period. During the eighteenth century, four currents of thought had emerged to challenge slavery. The first was the First Great Awakening and its emphasis on the contradiction between the Christian concept of equality and the enslavement of other human beings. The second was the Enlightenment, which undermined the hierarchical assumptions of slave society. The third was the development of laissez-faire economics as propounded by Adam Smith in his *Wealth of Nations*, who believed that slavery was an outdated mode of production. Last, the American and French Revolutions served as examples of liberty that could not help being contrasted with the absence of freedom for slaves.

Influenced by these four factors, the Pennsylvania Society for Promoting the Abolition of Slavery (PAS) served as the model for abolitionism in the early United States. The PAS, which was led by white males, was predominantly conservative and elite in membership. It advocated gradual, collective abolition and appealed to reason and law to justify the end of the institution. The PAS also placed preserving the Union above achieving racial equality. Abolitionists in the Early Republic were reluctant to challenge the property rights of masters and feared that immediate emancipation might lead to the abandonment of elderly slaves. This conservatism eventually gave rise to the colonization movement, which sought to emancipate slaves, then remove them to Africa as a way of protecting them, preserving white society, and preventing racial assimilation.

In the 1830s, abolitionism began to take a different course. Usually referred to as Garrisonian abolitionism, after William Lloyd Garrison, antebellum abolitionism seemed to draw its initial radicalism from David Walker's *Appeal to the Coloured Citizens of the World* (1829). Basing his argument on religion, history, and republican ideology, Walker chastised white Americans, especially those claiming to be Christians, for subjecting Africans and African Americans to bondage and called on his black brothers and sisters to free themselves from the ignorance that kept them in submission. His *Appeal* may have encouraged Nat Turner, a Virginia slave, to lead a rebellion in 1831; it certainly influenced Garrison, a white Massachusetts newspaperman. After working with another abolitionist newspaper editor in Baltimore, Garrison returned to Boston and in 1831 founded *The Liberator*, which became the most recognizable antislavery weekly of the Jacksonian period.

Garrison's views encapsulated the change that was taking place among abolitionists. The New England Anti-Slavery Society (NEAS), which he helped establish in 1832, and the American Anti-Slavery Society (AAS), founded in 1834, were the standard-bearers for antebellum abolitionism. In contrast to PAS, these two new antislavery societies argued for immediate and individual emancipation for slaves by appealing to emotion and focusing on the personal stories of slaves. Their membership was more inclusive, in terms of gender, race, and class. They also had racial equality as their ultimate goal. Over time, Garrison himself developed even more radical views, believing that slavery was so pernicious that United States society was corrupt almost beyond salvation and needed nearly complete reform. His staunch adherence to this and other controversial opinions led to the split of AAS in 1840. Garrison's opponents eventually formed the Liberty Party, which was the political forerunner of the Republican Party.

While Garrison was the most recognizable white abolitionist in the antebellum period, black abolitionists also participated in the movement to free slaves. (Ironically, they were often relegated to the background, except for prominent examples who had successfully overcome slavery, such as Frederick Douglass and Harriet Tubman.) Black females were a part of the female antislavery societies that grew up alongside of and within the larger abolitionist organizations. African Americans also formed associations whose members refused to buy products produced by slave labor. Black delegates met at conventions that produced resolutions calling for the rights of African Americans to vote, serve on juries, and obtain an education at integrated schools, to name just a few. Blacks found their public voice through newspapers such as Douglass's *North Star* and Samuel Cornish's *Freedom's Journal*.

The locus of black abolitionism was the local church. It was there that African Americans had the liberty to speak relatively freely about the injustices that they were suffering and to organize themselves in opposition both to slavery in the South and the prevailing racism of the North. The marriage between abolitionism and Christianity was logical, as both spoke to the freedom of the individual. Christian rhetoric and principles, in fact, were two of the most powerful weapons that abolitionists, both black and white, used in the war against slavery, although proslavery southerners also found them useful.

Another group that found its position in flux was Native Americans. The Jacksonian period saw the logical outcome of the United States' policy toward the various native peoples. Since its inception, the United States government had looked to move Native Americans off land that whites wanted; it was a course of action that found precedent in the colonial period. From the administrations of George Washington to John Quincy Adams, presidents had sought ways to convince Native Americans to give up their land. Sometimes, the land was purchased legally and fairly; more often, the land was taken in some coercive and unethical manner.

Andrew Jackson's administration continued in this vein, particularly in regard to the so-called Five Civilized Tribes in the Southeast: the Cherokee, Chickasaw, Choctaw, Creek, and Seminole. The Cherokees in particular suffered from the idea that native land belonged either to the United States or to individual states. By the time Jackson became president, the Cherokees had become one of the most assimilated native groups. They had a written constitution modeled on that of the United States, a written language, and a national newspaper. Many Cherokees had adopted the Christian faith, which had been transmitted to them by white American missionaries, and some of them even owned plantations and slaves. If any Native American group had tried to fit in with larger American society, it was the Cherokees.

Unfortunately for them, gold was discovered on tribal land in northern Georgia, and speculators began pressuring the state to move the Cherokees off of it. This discovery was followed shortly after by the Indian Removal Act of 1830, supported by Jackson and passed by Congress, which proposed the trade of native land east of the Mississippi River for land in the West. While presented as a voluntary proposal, everyone understood that the bill laid the groundwork for the forcible removal of Native Americans, including the Cherokees.

The Cherokees attempted to fight back using the United States Supreme Court. In two cases that appeared before that judicial body, *Cherokee Nation v. Georgia* (1831) and *Worcester v. Georgia* (1832), lawyers for the Cherokees argued that Georgia state laws had no jurisdiction over citizens of the Cherokee Nation. The Supreme Court ultimately ruled that the Cherokees were correct, but this did not stop Jackson from moving ahead with his plan to take their land. In a shrewd, but unethical, move, the Jackson administration negotiated a treaty with a small number of Cherokees who were not authorized to speak for the entire nation. The Treaty of New Echota (1835) agreed to an exchange of lands, a payment of $5 million to the Cherokees, assistance in moving to the new western land in present-day Oklahoma, and financial aid for one year upon arrival in the new territory.

Despite the obvious fraudulence of the treaty negotiations, the United States enforced its provisions. Some 2,000 Cherokees moved between 1836 and 1838, but many simply waited for their chief, John Ross, to find an alternative solution. None was forthcoming, however, and in the spring of

1838, United States soldiers began rounding up the Cherokees and placing them in confinement to wait for the forced journey west. Over the course of several months, mostly in the winter of 1838–1839, the Cherokees traveled what came to be known as the Trail of Tears; approximately one-quarter of the Cherokees died on the move west.

Even less assimilated than the Cherokees, the Seminoles in Florida faced a similar fate. In 1832, Seminole representatives were pressured into signing a treaty that would lead to their voluntary removal west by 1837. Complaints about the coercive nature of the negotiations were ignored; like the Cherokees, some Seminoles chose to move. Fearful that removal would be forced upon them and that their slaves would be taken away, some of the remaining Seminoles attacked a small force of American soldiers in December 1835. This precipitated the Second Seminole War. For seven years, the United States government waged a war that finally ended in the removal of those remaining Seminoles who had survived the military conflict.

Native Americans were not the only groups that found themselves forced to move westward. The Church of Jesus Christ of Latter-Day Saints (commonly referred to as the Mormons) also found themselves making the journey; like the Cherokees and the Seminoles, the Mormons did not make a voluntary decision. Joseph Smith Jr. founded the Mormons in Palmyra, New York, after he began experiencing visions in 1820. Smith alleged that these visions were messages from God telling him that he had been chosen to help restore authentic Christianity in the United States. They culminated in 1830 with the publication of *The Book of Mormon*, which chronicled (according to Smith) the coming to North America of members of the Lost Tribes of Israel and Jesus' appearance to them. Smith was able to accumulate followers who believed his story.

Despite these converts and the evangelical democratization of American Christianity during the Jacksonian period, Smith and his Mormon supporters found themselves persecuted. A large part of the opposition came from Smith's claim to have received divine revelation through visions and golden tablets that no one else was allowed to see. In 1831, he moved his family and congregation to Kirtland, Ohio, then to Independence, Missouri, finally settling in Nauvoo, Illinois. At each location, the Mormons encountered hostility, particularly after some of them began practicing plural marriage, or polygamy. Mormon exclusivity and political power also generated conflict, as did Smith's self-nomination for the presidency of the United States in 1844.

The tension between Mormons and other residents in surrounding areas eventually resulted in Smith's death. While Smith, his brother Hyrum, and several other Mormon leaders were in jail in Carthage, Illinois, for conspiring to spread Mormonism to Mexico, a mob hauled them out of the jail and killed the two Smiths. The Mormons split, with some remaining in the United States under the leadership of Joseph Smith III and the rest traveling with Brigham Young to present-day Utah, which at the time was still Mexican territory. Following the Mexican-American War, the United States turned the area into the Utah Territory and made Young its governor. In 1857–1858, a short military conflict broke out between the United States and the Mormons after President James Buchanan removed Young from his position as territorial governor over concerns about the Mormon practice of plural marriage.

The rapidity and enormity of social change in the United States and the negative effects that it had on some Americans produced national self-reflection. The most pronounced and influential critique that emerged from examining the nation's course of progress came in the form of Transcendentalism, an intellectual movement focused on individualism, nature, and social justice. Transcendentalism took its inspiration from European Romanticism, which rejected the Enlightenment idea of reason as society's guiding principle. Transcendentalism found its strongest adherents in New England and included Ralph Waldo Emerson, Henry David Thoreau, Margaret Fuller, Walt Whitman, Nathaniel Hawthorne, and Herman Melville. They communicated their message through public speeches, novels, poetry, and their own short-lived journal, the *Dial*.

Emerson was the leading spokesperson for the Transcendentalist movement. A former Unitarian minister, he abandoned the organized religion of his youth in favor of pursuing a life of individual perfection. Emerson believed that Americans were not living up to their potential because they clung to traditions of the past. To better their quality of life, they needed to rediscover their connection with nature, which would reinvigorate their spiritual lives. He also argued that the industrialization and urbanization of the United States was detrimental to Americans, leaving them enslaved to greed and exploitation. Emerson's philosophy, in turn, influenced Thoreau, whose *Walden, or Life in the Woods* (1854) became an essential text for understanding Transcendentalism. Thoreau also wrote "On Civil Disobedience," which asked, "Unjust laws exist: shall we be content to obey them, or shall we endeavor to amend them, and obey them until we have succeeded, or shall we transgress them at once?" In his own case, the answer was to break the law, as he protested a Massachusetts poll tax to demonstrate his opposition to the Mexican-American War.

Emerson's ideas also had an effect on Margaret Fuller and Walt Whitman. Fuller was born into a well-off Massachusetts family and enjoyed a classical education. In the late 1830s, she began having conversations, or discussion groups, for women to talk about their place and purpose in American society. Fuller served as co-editor of the *Dial* with Emerson when it began publication in 1840; this position gave her a public arena in which to express her belief that men and women were equal and that women simply needed freedom to allow their abilities to flourish. She eventually became the *New York Tribune*'s literary critic. Whitman was also a journalist and editor. His collection of poems, *Leaves of Grass* (first published in 1855), included one piece entitled, "Song of Myself." It began, "I celebrate myself, and sing myself. And what I assume you shall assume, For every atom belonging to me as good belongs to you." The theme emphasized both individuality and communality, suggesting that for Whitman, as for many Transcendentalists, their movement was not about narcissism but improvement of both the self and society. Ironically, the Civil War provided both the societal improvement that the Transcendentalists longed for and a proliferation of many of the circumstances about which they were critical.

The decades from 1830 to 1860 served as the bridge between the founding and early growth of the American republic and its rending asunder by the secession of several southern states and the civil warfare that followed. While the politic battles of the period have provided perhaps the most visible explanation of why that great cataclysm occurred, Americans would be remiss if they neglected to understand that the nation's social transformation also played a vital role in the maturation of the United States.

Mark R. Cheathem

Assistant Professor of History
Southern New Hampshire University

References and Further Reading

Boller, Paul. *American Transcendentalism, 1830–1860: An Intellectual Inquiry.* New York: Putnam, 1974.

Bushman, Richard. *Joseph Smith, Rough Stone Rolling: A Cultural Biography of Mormonism's Founder.* New York: Knopf, 2005.

Donald, David. *Charles Sumner and the Coming of the Civil War.* New York: Knopf, 1960.

DuBois, Ellen C. *Feminism and Suffrage: The Emergence of an Independent Women's Movement in America, 1848–1869.* New York: Cornell University Press, 1978.

Horton, James O., and Lois E. Horton. *In Hope of Liberty: Culture, Community, and Protest among Northern Free Blacks, 1700–1860.* New York: Oxford University Press, 1997.

Larkin, Jack. *The Reshaping of Everyday Life, 1790–1840.* New York: Harper and Row, 1988.

Newman, Richard S. *The Transformation of American Abolitionism: Fighting Slavery in the Early Republic.* Chapel Hill: University of North Carolina Press, 2002.

Rothman, Adam. *Slave Country: American Expansion and the Origins of the Deep South.* Cambridge: Harvard University Press, 2005.

Salerno, Beth. *Sister Societies: Women's Antislavery Societies in Antebellum America.* DeKalb: Northern Illinois University Press, 2005.

Satz, Ronald N. *American Indian Policy in the Jacksonian Era.* Lincoln: University of Nebraska Press, 1975.

Stokes, Melvyn, and Stephen Conway, eds. *The Market Revolution in America: Social, Political, and Religious Expressions, 1800–1880.* Charlottesville: University Press of Virginia, 1996.

Taylor, George Rogers. *The Transportation Revolution, 1815–1860.* New York: Holt, Rinehart, and Winston, 1951.

Tocqueville, Alexis de. *Democracy in America.* Trans. Stephen D. Grant. Indianapolis: Hackett, 2000.

Walters, Ronald G. *American Reformers, 1815–1860.* New York: Hill and Wang, 1978.

Watson, Harry L. *Liberty and Power: The Politics of Jacksonian America.* New York: Hill and Wang, 1990.

Wilentz, Sean. *Chants Democratic: New York City and the Rise of the American Working Class, 1788–1850.* New York: Oxford University Press, 1984.

About the Editor and Contributors

Mark R. Cheathem is an assistant professor of history at Southern New Hampshire University. He is the author of *Old Hickory's Nephew: The Political and Private Struggles of Andrew Jackson Donelson* (LSU Press, 2007). He is currently writing a biography of Andrew Jackson that examines his southern identity.

Mary Beth Fraser Connolly is lecturer of history at Purdue University North Central and the historian for the Sisters of Mercy Chicago Regional Community. She received her doctorate from The Catholic University of America in Washington, D.C.

Michael J. Connolly is assistant professor of history at Purdue University North Central. He received his doctorate from the Catholic University of America in Washington, D.C., and is the author of *Capitalism, Politics, and Railroads in Jacksonian New England* (Missouri, 2003).

Steven Deyle is an associate professor of history at the University of Houston. His specialty is nineteenth-century social and political history. He is the author of *Carry Me Back: The Domestic Slave Trade in American Life* (Oxford University Press, 2005), as well as several other articles dealing with slavery and its role in American society.

Michael P. Morris is an assistant professor of history at Dalton College in Georgia. He is a 1993 graduate of the history PhD program at Auburn University. He is the author of one book on the Southeastern Indians plus numerous journal and review articles. He is currently at work on a second book on Native American women through University of Tennessee Press.

Gail S. Murray is an associate professor and chair of the Department of History at Rhodes College, Memphis, Tennessee. She is the author of *American Children's Literature and the Construction of Childhood*, which is part of the Twayne's History of American Childhood Series, edited by N. Ray Hiner and Joseph Hawes (1998). Her current work centers on maternal rhetoric and biracial organizing among Memphis women in the civil rights era. She edited and contributed an article to *Throwing Off the Cloak of Privilege: White Southern Women Activists in the Civil Rights Era* (University Press of Florida, 2004).

Elaine Naylor is an associate professor of history at Mount Allison University in New Brunswick, Canada. Areas of interest include the American frontier, ethnic and gender relations, and economic development. She is currently working on a book about frontier Puget Sound.

David J. Voelker (PhD, University of North Carolina at Chapel Hill, 2003) teaches history at the University of Wisconsin–Green Bay. He is working on a book about Orestes Brownson and the problem of authority in nineteenth-century America. He takes great interest in the complex relationships among democracy, religion, and capitalism in U.S. history.

Matthew S. Warshauer is the author of *Andrew Jackson and the Politics of Martial Law: Nationalism, Civil Liberties and Partisanship* (University of Tennessee Press), and the forthcoming biography, *Andrew Jackson in Context: First Men, America's Presidents* (Nova Science Publishers). He is an associate professor of history at Central Connecticut State University.

Educated at Princeton University and the University of Pennsylvania, **Kirsten E. Wood** is associate professor of history at Florida International University. Her 1997 article on the Eaton Affair won the James Madison Prize from the Society for History in the Federal Government. Her *Masterful Women: Slaveholding Widows from the American Revolution through the Civil War* (University of North Carolina Press, 2004) won the Southern Historical Association's Francis B. Simkins Prize. She is currently studying early U.S. taverns.

Chronology

1829 David Walker's *Appeal to the Coloured Citizens of the World* was published.

The Eaton affair began in Jackson's administration. Ostensibly a social dispute over the marriage of Jackson's secretary of war, John H. Eaton, and Margaret O'Neale Timberlake, it eventually split Jackson's advisers, helped alienate John C. Calhoun from Andrew Jackson, and paved the way for Martin Van Buren to become Jackson's vice president.

Gold was discovered on Cherokee land in northern Georgia, leading to white demands for the territory.

James Smithson bequeathed £100,000 to establish the Smithsonian Institution.

New York's Workingmen's Party was founded, in part, by Robert Dale Owen, Thomas Skidmore, and Fanny Wright. It advocated free public education and rights for workers.

Samuel Guthrie discovered chloroform.

1830 Congress passed the Indian Removal Act, which authorized the voluntary removal of Native Americans to land west of the Mississippi River in exchange for their land in the East.

Joseph Smith founded the Church of Jesus Christ of Latter-Day Saints (Mormons) and had the *Book of Mormon* published.

One of the most influential women's magazines, *Lady's Book* (later known as *Godey's Lady's Book*) first appeared in print.

Peter Cooper built the first locomotive in the United States.

The total United States population was approximately 12,866,000; 2,009,043 were slaves.

The Washington *Globe*, under the editorship of Francis P. Blair, began publication in Washington, D.C., as the official newspaper voice of the Jacksonian Democrats.

1831   Alexis de Tocqueville arrived in the United States to begin his inspection of the American penitentiary system.

Charles G. Finney conducted a revival in Rochester, New York, as part of the Second Great Awakening.

Congress revised the nation's copyright laws, extending the original length from fourteen to twenty-eight years and keeping the fourteen-year renewal period.

Former president James Monroe died on July 4.

Nat Turner's Rebellion took place in Virginia; nearly sixty whites were killed. Perhaps 100 blacks were killed during the rebellion and the manhunt that followed. Twenty blacks, including Nat Turner, were executed after being tried and convicted.

The United States Supreme Court handed down its ruling in *Cherokee Nation v. Georgia*. Justices determined that the Cherokee Nation was a "domestic dependent nation."

William Lloyd Garrison began publishing *The Liberator*, an abolitionist newspaper.

1832   President Andrew Jackson won reelection.

The New England Anti-Slavery Society was founded by William Lloyd Garrison.

Samuel F. B. Morse invented the telegraph.

The United States Supreme Court handed down its ruling in *Worcester v. Georgia*, declaring that the laws of the state of Georgia had "no force" within the Cherokee Nation.

1833   After merging with the New England Anti-Slavery Society, the American Anti-Slavery Society was formed by Theodore Weld and Arthur and Lewis Tappan.

Lucretia Mott organized the Philadelphia Female Anti-Slavery Society.

The New York *Sun*, the first successful "penny" daily newspaper, began publication.

Oberlin College in Ohio became the first coeducational college in the United States when it began accepting women.

The United States Supreme Court ruled in *Barron v. Baltimore* that the Bill of Rights protected citizens from the federal government, but not state governments.

1834   Cyrus McCormick patented the mechanical reaper.

Debates at the Lane Seminary in Cincinnati, Ohio, centered on slavery and the colonization movement.

The first volume of George Bancroft's *History of the United States* was published; it eventually comprised eleven volumes.

President Andrew Jackson ordered federal troops to quell discontent among Irish railroad workers in Maryland.

1835   Augustus Baldwin Longstreet's *Georgia Scenes, Characters, and Incidents* was published.

Charles G. Finney's *Lectures on Revivals of Religion* was published.

A Charleston, South Carolina, mob seized abolitionist tracts from the post office and burned them.

The *Cherokee Phoenix* newspaper ended publication.

The first volume of Alexis de Tocqueville's *Democracy in America* appeared. The second volume would be published in 1840.

Labor strikes were declared illegal by a New York Court in *People v. Fisher*.

The national debt was paid off.

Richard Lawrence unsuccessfully attempted to assassinate President Andrew Jackson.

Samuel Colt patented the revolver.

The Treaty of New Echota, signed between the United States government and a minority faction of the Cherokee leadership, exchanged all Cherokee land east of the Mississippi River for $5 million, land west of the Mississippi River, and the cost of making the transition.

1836   The American Temperance Union held its first national convention.

Arkansas was admitted as a state.

The charter of the Second Bank of the United States expired.

Congress established the Bureau of Indian Affairs.

Congress passed the Patent Act, which created a separate Patent Office and revised standards for protecting inventions.

Former president James Madison died at his Virginia home, Montpelier.

Iowa Territory was organized.

Land sales generated over $40 million in excess revenue for the national government. In an attempt to reduce the surplus, the Jackson administration issued the Specie Circular, which mandated that in most cases, specie would be the only acceptable method of payment for public lands.

Martin Van Buren became the eighth president of the United States.

Mary Lyon founded Mount Holyoke Female Seminary (now Mount Holyoke College), the first permanent women's college.

Ralph Waldo Emerson's *Nature* appeared in print.

The Republic of Texas was established.

Wisconsin Territory was organized.

1837   Chicago incorporated as a city.

Elijah P. Lovejoy, an antislavery newspaper editor in Alton, Illinois, was killed after being attacked by a mob.

The House of Representatives passed the so-called "gag rule," which automatically tabled antislavery and abolitionist petitions, memorials, and other material that made their way to the chamber's floor.

John Deere introduced the steel plow to the United States.

Michigan was admitted to the Union as a state.

The Native American Association, a nativist organization, formed in Washington, D.C.

Spawned in part by both domestic and international circumstances, the Panic of 1837 began. It lasted for seventy-two months.

The individual states received $28 million of the government surplus.

The *United States Magazine and Democratic Review* began publication.

The United States Supreme Court ruled in *Charles River Bridge v. Warren Bridge* that community interest in economic development outweighed private claims ambiguously presented in a state-granted charter.

1838   John Greenleaf Whittier's *Poems Written during the Progress of the Abolition Question* was published.

Samuel F. B. Morse invented the code that bears his name.

The Cherokees endured the Trail of Tears, in which approximately 4,000 of 16,000 emigrants died.

1839   The *Amistad*, a Spanish ship transporting Africans with the intention of selling them as slaves, was captured off Long Island, New York. The Africans on board had seized control of the ship, but they were imprisoned in New London, Connecticut, where they were put on trial.

The Antirent War began in upstate New York. This series of disturbances, which did not end until 1846, resulted from attempts to collect back rent from agrarian tenants.

Charles Goodyear discovered the process of vulcanizing rubber.

The Liberty party was founded in New York; its first presidential nominee was James G. Birney, a Kentucky native and former slaveholder.

Lowell Offering, which contained pieces written by the female Lowell mill workers (the "Lowell girls"), first appeared.

Theodore Weld and his wife, Angelina Grimké, published *American Slavery as It Is*, an account of slavery based on southern newspapers and black and abolitionist testimony.

The Transcendentalist periodical the *Dial*, edited by Margaret Fuller, began publication.

1840   The Independent Treasury system was established.

The "Log Cabin" campaign of William Henry Harrison and John Tyler brought the Whig party victory over incumbent Democratic president Martin Van Buren. The Whig campaign was marked by its depiction of Harrison as a frontiersman and hero of the War of 1812. Harrison supporters employed Jacksonian strategy by using public rallies, raucous songs, and other democratic means to attract voters.

Theodore Weld, Arthur and Lewis Tappan, and Angelina and Sarah Grimké broke from the Garrisonian abolitionists and formed the American and Foreign Anti-Slavery Society. This group focused on using moral suasion and political involvement to bring about an end to slavery.

The total United States population was approximately 17,069,000; 2,487,355 were slaves.

1841   The Independent Treasury system was abandoned.

The New York *Tribune*, founded by Horace Greeley, began publication.

President William Henry Harrison died of pneumonia after only one month in office. His death has often been attributed to his exposure to cold and inclement weather during his inauguration. Vice President John Tyler assumed office.

Transcendentalists set up the Brook Farm Association, a cooperative living experiment, in Massachusetts.

The United States Supreme Court ruled that the Africans on the *Amistad* should go free. John Quincy Adams had argued for their release.

1842   Phineas T. (P. T.) Barnum opened his American Museum in New York City.

Rhode Island experienced the Dorr Rebellion, a split in the state that resulted in competing state governments. The dispute arose over the extension of voting rights to all white males instead of just property owners. Thomas W. Dorr's group, which supported universal white manhood suffrage, lost the dispute, but soon after, the state adopted more liberal voting rights.

Slaves on the *Creole*, an American slave ship, revolted and took the ship to British Nassau. British authorities refused to return the slaves to the United States and freed all slaves on board except those actually involved in the mutiny.

The United States Supreme Court ruled in *Prigg v. Pennsylvania* that federal law superseded state law. At issue was the conflict between the federal fugitive slave law and a state "personal liberty" law meant to protect fugitive slaves.

William E. Clarke administered ether during a dental procedure, introducing modern anesthesia.

1843 The nativist and anti-Catholic American Republican Party was founded in New York. Its members were concerned about the growing immigrant and Catholic influence in the United States. The major issues that galvanized its supporters included the use of public funds to support Catholic parochial schools; Catholic opposition to the use of the King James Version of the Bible in public schools; and restricting voting and office holding by Catholics and immigrants.

Baptists in the United States split over the issue of slavery, with southern members forming the Southern Baptist Convention.

"Old Dan Tucker," a song probably penned by Daniel D. Emmett, appeared.

The Virginia Minstrels gave the nation's first full-length, public minstrel show in Boston.

William Miller predicted that the Second Coming of Jesus Christ would occur soon.

1844 Alfred Vail, in Baltimore, sent Samuel F. B. Morse, who was in Washington, D.C., the first telegraph message.

American Journal of Psychiatry was first published.

The Association of Medical Superintendents of American Institutions for the Insane (now the American Psychiatric Association) was founded.

Joseph Smith, founder of the Mormons, was lynched outside of a Carthage, Illinois, jail.

Methodists in the United States split over the issue of slavery, with southern members establishing a separate organization.

Secretary of State Abel P. Upshur and several others died when a defective gun on board the steamboat U.S.S. *Princeton* exploded. John C. Calhoun took Upshur's position in President John Tyler's cabinet.

Tennessean James K. Polk defeated Henry Clay to become the eleventh president of the United States.

1845   Congress passed an act naming the Tuesday following the first Monday in November the official election day for future presidential elections.

Edgar Allan Poe's *The Raven and Other Poems* was published.

Florida was admitted as a state.

Former President Andrew Jackson died at his home, the Hermitage.

Frederick Douglass's *Narrative of the Life of Frederick Douglass, an American Slave, Written by Himself* was published.

Henry David Thoreau began living at Walden Pond.

Nativists held their first national convention in Philadelphia and formed the Native American Party.

The Naval School (later the United States Naval Academy) opened in Annapolis, Maryland.

The Republic of Texas was annexed to the United States and admitted as a state.

The term "Manifest Destiny" (God had predestined white Americans to control North America from the Atlantic to Pacific Oceans) appeared in the columns of the *United States Magazine and Democratic Review*. Its coining was attributed to editor John L. O'Sullivan, although recent scholarship suggests that it may have been the product of Jane McManus Storm Cazneau, a female staff writer with the magazine.

William Miller and his followers founded the Adventist Church.

1846   The Adventist Church split, with the Seventh-Day Adventists leaving Miller's original church.

The *Californian*, the first California newspaper, began publication.

The *Commercial Review of the South and the West* (later known as *De Bow's Review*) began publication.

Congress passed an act establishing the Smithsonian Institution.

The Donner party, a group of settlers moving to California, became trapped in the Sierra Nevada mountains. Some survivors resorted to cannibalism to live.

Elias Howe invented the sewing machine.

The first Pacific Coast newspaper, the *Oregon Spectator*, was established.

The Independent Treasury system was reestablished.

Iowa was admitted as a state.

Richard M. Hoe invented the rotary printing press.

1847   The American Medical Association was founded.

Brigham Young and other Mormons settled near the Great Salt Lake in present-day Utah.

Frederick Douglass established the newspaper, the *North Star*.

Horace Bushnell's *Christian Nurture*, which embodied theological liberalism and its emphasis on mysticism, free will, and Christian nurture, was published.

The Synod of Free Presbyterian Churches, a group of New School Presbyterians opposed to slavery, was established.

1848   Brigham Young proclaimed that the practice of polygamy was divinely sanctioned.

Former president John Quincy Adams died after collapsing on the floor of the House of Representatives.

James W. Marshall discovered gold on the claim of Johann Augustus Sutter, which was near present-day Sacramento. News of the discovery led to the California Gold Rush; by the end of 1849, California's white population had reportedly grown from 4,000 Americans to more than 100,000.

Lucretia Mott and Elizabeth Cady Stanton, among others, organized the Seneca Falls Convention. The attending delegates passed several resolutions supporting women's rights, including a call for female suffrage.

Mexican War hero Zachary Taylor became the twelfth president of the United States.

Stephen C. Foster's song, "Oh! Susanna," appeared.

Oregon Territory was organized.

Wisconsin was admitted as a state.

1849   The Astor Place Riot flared up, ultimately killing twenty-two people. It was sparked by a rivalry between two actors and inflamed by nativist elements.

The House Department (later called the Department of the Interior) was established with a cabinet-level appointment. It contained the Census Office, the Bureau of Indian Affairs, and the General Land Office.

Elizabeth Blackwell became the first female medical graduate, receiving her MD degree from the Medical School in Geneva, New York.

Former president James K. Polk died just over three months after leaving office.

Henry David Thoreau's essay, "Civil Disobedience," appeared in print.

Minnesota Territory was organized.

The Mormon state of Deseret was established.

Nationally respected Baltimore newspaper *Niles' Weekly Register* ended publication.

The Order of the Star Spangled Banner was founded in New York City. A nativist secret society, it joined with other nativist and anti-Catholic organizations to form the American Party, commonly referred to as the Know-Nothing Party. It ran the ticket of Millard Fillmore and Andrew Jackson Donelson during the 1856 presidential election.

Walter Hunt invented the modern safety pin.

1850   California was admitted as a state.

Harper's New Monthly Magazine (later known as *Harper's Magazine*) began publication.

John C. Calhoun died.

Nathaniel Hawthorne's *The Scarlet Letter* was published.

President Zachary Taylor died. He fell ill after drinking iced water and milk and eating chilled cherries, cucumbers, or perhaps cabbage on July 4. The cause of his death was gastroenteritis (severe inflammation of the stomach lining and intestines). Vice President Millard Fillmore assumed the presidency.

New Mexico Territory was organized.

Stephen C. Foster's song, "De Camptown Races," appeared.

The total United States population was approximately 23,191,000; 3,204,313 were slaves.

Utah Territory was organized.

1851   Herman Melville's *Moby-Dick* was published.

The House of Seven Gables, by Nathaniel Hawthorne, appeared in print.

The Illinois Central Railroad was chartered. It was the first land-grant railroad.

Narciso López attempted a second filibustering expedition against Cuba, which failed and cost him his life.

Stephen C. Foster's song, "Old Folks at Home" (often referred to as "Swanee River"), appeared.

1852   The American Pharmaceutical Association was founded.

The Christiana affair, involving fugitive slaves who fought off their master's attempts to take them back into slavery, occurred in Christiana, Pennsylvania.

Elisha G. Otis invented the passenger elevator.

Franklin Pierce of New Hampshire became the fourteenth president of the United States.

Harriet Beecher Stowe's *Uncle Tom's Cabin* was published. Its depiction of a cruel southern slave system bolstered the growing antislavery movement in the North.

Henry Clay, the "Great Compromiser," died.

The multiauthor work, *The Pro-Slavery Argument*, presented essays arguing positively for slavery on the basis of historical, religious, cultural, economic, and racial arguments.

1853　Stephen C. Foster's song, "My Old Kentucky Home," appeared.

Washington Territory was organized.

1854　Abraham Lincoln gave a speech at Peoria, Illinois, that was his first public condemnation of slavery.

Commodore Matthew C. Perry reopened trade with Japan.

Eli Thayer founded the Massachusetts Emigrant Aid Society (later called the New England Emigrant Aid Company). Its purpose was to encourage anti-slavery adherents to move to Kansas in an attempt to make slavery there illegal.

Foreign immigration into the United States reached its pre–Civil War peak of 427,833 individuals.

George Fitzhugh, a southern apologist, had published *Sociology for the South; or, the Failure of Free Society*. Its argument that southern slavery was a superior labor system when compared to northern factory work gave southerners more evidence of their region's rightness.

Henry David Thoreau's *Walden* was published.

Kansas and Nebraska Territories were organized.

The United States government, through its ministers Pierre Soulé, John Y. Mason, and James Buchanan, issued the Ostend Manifesto. This diplomatic message to the Spanish government declared that the United States would attempt to seize Cuba from Spain if the latter country refused to sell it.

Virginia slave Anthony Burns, who had run away from his master, was captured in Boston. His return to slavery infuriated abolitionists and led to increasing opposition to the federal Fugitive Slave Law.

1855　American filibuster William Walker seized control of the Nicaraguan government; he became the country's president the following year.

The first volume of Washington Irving's *Life of Washington* was published; the work was completed in 1859.

Frank Leslie's Illustrated Newspaper (later known as *Leslie's Weekly*) began publication.

Frederick Douglass published his second autobiography, *My Bondage and My Freedom*.

Henry Wadsworth Longfellow's *Song of Hiawatha* appeared in print.

Walt Whitman's *Leaves of Grass* appeared in its first edition.

1856   Civil war between pro- and antislavery supporters broke out in Kansas. Incidents such as the sack of Lawrence and the Pottawatomie massacre (committed by John Brown and his sons) led to the territory being labeled "Bleeding Kansas."

James Buchanan became the sixteenth president of the United States.

Preston Brooks assaulted Charles Sumner on the floor of the United States Senate after the latter criticized the South's support of the violence in Kansas.

1857   *Atlantic Monthly*, first edited by James Russell Lowell, began publication.

George Fitzhugh's *Cannibals All! Or, Slaves Without Masters* was published.

Hinton Rowan Helper's *The Impending Crisis of the South: How to Meet It* was published.

J. S. Pierpoint's song, "Jingle Bells," appeared; it became a Christmas holiday staple.

The "Mormon War" between Utah Mormons and the United States began; it ended the next year.

Speculation in railroad securities and real estate precipitated the Panic of 1857. It lasted for eighteen months.

The United States Supreme Court ruled in *Dred Scott v. Sandford* that Scott, a Missouri slave, was not a citizen of the United States; that residency in a free state did not give slaves standing to sue for their release; and that the Missouri Compromise was unconstitutional.

The United Synod of the South, made up of a schism group of New School Presbyterians, was founded.

1858   Abraham Lincoln gave his "A House Divided" speech on the floor of the Illinois Republican state convention.

Abraham Lincoln and Stephen Douglas engaged in a series of debates during the Illinois senatorial campaign. Lincoln won the popular vote, but the state legislature chose Douglas for the Senate seat.

Minnesota was admitted as a state.

William H. Seward gave his "Irrepressible Conflict" speech in Rochester, New York.

1859   Daniel D. Emmett wrote "Dixie's Land" (usually just called "Dixie"), which later became the Confederate States' unofficial anthem.

Harper's Weekly, a weekly newsmagazine, began publication.

John Brown, a radical abolitionist, led a small group of men in a raid of the federal arsenal at Harpers Ferry, Virginia. His plan to instigate a slave rebellion failed when the men who survived a standoff with United States Marines, including Brown, were captured and put on trial. Brown was convicted of treason and criminal conspiracy and was hanged. He became a martyr for northern abolitionists and a rallying figure for proslavery southerners.

A meeting of the Southern Commercial Convention in Vicksburg, Mississippi, passed resolutions demanding that the federal government support the foreign slave trade.

Oregon was admitted as a state.

1860   Congress passed the Pacific Telegraph Act, which allowed the United States to establish a telegraph line from Missouri to California.

New York City became the first American city with a recorded population of over 1 million residents.

Oliver F. Winchester invented the repeating rifle.

The Pony Express was established.

The total United States population was approximately 31,443,000; 3,953,760 were slaves.

Upon hearing of Abraham Lincoln's election as sixteenth president, South Carolina seceded.

African American Revolutionaries 1

Mark R. Cheathem

S peaking to an assembly in Rochester, New York, on July 5, 1852, Frederick Douglass reminded the nearly 600 people gathered there of the revolutionary character of the United States' origins. Those American colonists who defied Great Britain "were accounted in their day, plotters of mischief, agitators and rebels, dangerous men." Now, as they looked back in celebration of American independence, Douglass reminded his audience that those once considered "rebels" were now deemed "great men . . . great enough to give fame to a great age. . . . They were statesmen, patriots and heroes" (Douglass 2003, pp. 150, 152).

Little did Douglass know that, one day, many Americans would look back and see him, David Walker, and Nat Turner in the same vein as they viewed George Washington, Samuel Adams, Patrick Henry, and other "Founders." These three individuals were at the forefront of one of the most significant social movements of the Jacksonian period: abolitionism. Each was a revolutionary in his own way. Walker wrote in support of action to free African Americans from enslavement and bring them into equality with white Americans. Turner spoke, not with words, but with actions, leading a bloody revolt in the South Carolina countryside. Douglass spoke extensively as an advocate for African Americans. Unlike the others, however, his tempered, often pragmatic, approach allowed him access to political circles off-limits to other blacks and those encouraging violence. Their actions and words helped bring about social and political upheaval that changed American society in significant ways.

David Walker

Often ignored in American history, David Walker was, in many ways, one of the founders of the antebellum abolitionist movement. Like many southern

African Americans, the details of his childhood are largely lost to history. He was probably born in 1796 in Wilmington, North Carolina; his mother was likely a free black and his father a slave. If he spent many years in or around Wilmington, Walker was no doubt influenced by the Methodism of the area, which had a distinct African American character at that time. At some point, probably in the early 1820s, he headed north, eventually winding up in Boston, Massachusetts, in 1825.

Walker found himself on the rise socially in Boston. The city had a thriving black community, and he made sure to avail himself of its advantages. He married, joined an African Masonic lodge, and became a member of the May Street Church, a black Methodist congregation. Walker's association with the lodge and the church also introduced him to *Freedom's Journal*, the first black newspaper in the United States, and he became one of its principal agents in Boston. Additionally, he helped found the Massachusetts General Colored Association, an organization that looked to unite African Americans in opposition to slavery and in favor of improving the quality of life for blacks.

Walker's involvement in these social organizations stirred within him a fervor that found its fullest expression in September 1829, when his pamphlet, *Appeal to the Coloured Citizens of the World*, appeared in print. Subsequently published in three editions, Walker's work was, in the words of one historian, "one of the most neglected yet most important political and social documents of the nineteenth century" (Walker 2000, p. xxv). Calling the "coloured people of the United States . . . the most degraded, wretched, and abject set of beings that ever lived since the world began," Walker channeled the frustration of his people into a call for action (Walker 2000, p. 3). Partly a denunciation of the institution of slavery and the racism that accompanied it, partly an endorsement of black violence and resistance, the *Appeal* was a rhetorical masterpiece.

The *Appeal*'s preamble indicated the grounds upon which Walker would fight his written war against the southern slave system. He primarily based his arguments in three areas: religion, history, and republican ideology. White Americans, in his estimation, wanted "to keep us in abject ignorance and wretchedness" because they were "of the firm conviction that Heaven has designed us and our children to be slaves and *beasts of burdens* to them and their children." If that were true, he argued, then "would he be to us a God of justice?" Not surprisingly, much of Walker's historical argument had biblical origins, although he also cited Plutarch, Josephus, and other prominent historical figures. One of his purposes, as he saw it, was to encourage in African Americans "a spirit of inquiry and investigation respecting our miseries and wretchedness in this *Republican Land of Liberty!*" (Walker 2000, pp. 3–8).

The bulk of the *Appeal* comprised four articles. Article I, entitled "Our Wretchedness in Consequence of Slavery," presented Walker's comparison of the plight of African Americans with those of other oppressed groups in history. He emphasized his belief that American blacks had suffered more insult and cruelty than even the Hebrews, God's chosen people. At least they had been enslaved "under *heathen Pharaoh*," Walker argued; his people had been enslaved and were being treated cruelly by the "*enlightened Christians of*

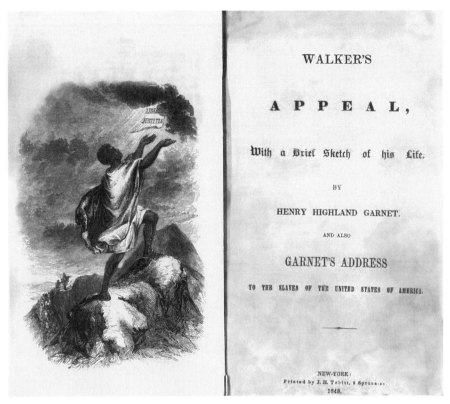

David Walker's *Appeal to the Coloured Citizens of the World* was one of the most significant literary influences on the American abolitionist movement. (*Library of Congress*)

America." He compared the mistreatment of African Americans to other sub-jugated groups, specifically the helots in ancient Sparta, concluding that even their position had been better than that of African Americans (Walker 2000, pp. 9–20).

Article II, "Our Wretchedness in Consequence of Ignorance," indicted, although with qualifications, African American complicity in the situation of slaves and freemen. Walker decried the "groveling servile and abject submission to the lash of tyrants" that existed among African Americans, as well as the "ignorance . . . [that] gnaws into our very vitals." Slaves in particular found themselves the victims of these two flaws, as they beat, spread malicious gossip about, and deceived each other, "all to pacify the passions of unrelenting tyrants." Walker made it clear that these weaknesses, as offensive as they were to his sensibilities, were the result of the slave system (Walker 2000, pp. 21–36).

The last two articles focused on the perceived evils of Christianity and the colonization movement in perpetuating African American submission and ignorance. "Our Wretchedness in Consequence of the Preachers of the Religion of Jesus Christ" lambasted the hypocrisy of American Christianity. Its white adherents would rather send missionaries across the world to convert foreign "heathen" than show mercy to their slaves at home, Walker wrote accusingly. Instead, they would rather *"beat a coloured person nearly to death, if they catch him on his knees, supplicating the throne of grace."* He was especially searing in his criticism of the Catholic Church, which he had previously called "the scourge of the nations," and of the "wretch" Bartolomé de Las Casas. Walker blamed the Franciscan friar who had accompanied Christopher Columbus on his last voyage to the Americas for helping to encourage the importation of African slaves to the so-called New World. There was little to encourage blacks to embrace this type of Christianity, in his opinion (Walker 2000, pp. 23, 37–45).

"Our Wretchedness in Consequence of the Colonizing Plan" concluded the *Appeal* with a lengthy and often disjointed condemnation of the colonization movement. Walker believed that the colonization movement was no more than a ploy by slaveholders, including men such as Henry Clay, to continue the oppression of African Americans by having them return to Africa "to dig up gold and silver" for them. It was also an effort on their part to deprive African Americans of the sweat of their brow; however, Walker would have none of it. "America is more our country, than it is the whites," he argued. "We have enriched it with our *blood and tears*. The greatest riches in all America have arisen from our blood and tears" (Walker 2000, pp. 47–82).

What courses of action did Walker advocate for African Americans, then, in fighting against their enslavement and oppression? First, they needed to gain education and religion. "You have to prove to the Americans and the world, that we are MEN, and not *brutes*," he encouraged. "I pray that the Lord may undeceive my ignorant brethren, and permit them to throw away pretensions, and seek after the substance of learning." In addition to improving their education, African Americans also needed to embrace religion, in particular, the true Christianity that valued them as part of God's creation. "I believe it is the will of the Lord that our greatest happiness shall consist in working for the salvation of our whole body," Walker told his readers. "You must go to work and prepare the way of the Lord." It was his "solemn belief" that if the world were ever to be converted to Christianity, it would be "under [the] God of the *Blacks*" (Walker 2000, pp. 20, 32–35).

Finally, Walker emphasized the need for resistance. When the day of liberation came, slaves could be assured that "the God of justice and of armies" would give them victory over "those enemies who have stolen our *rights*." The Divine would raise up a black Hannibal in a holy crusade to deliver them from their "deplorable and wretched condition under the Christians of America." Yet, Walker's call for resistance, while implying that violence might one day be necessary, was tempered in its radicalism. In his view, the victory over American slavery and racism would come only when African Americans were no longer enslaved by ignorance and when God deemed it appropriate (Walker 2000, pp. 14, 22).

Still, the *Appeal* was intended to awaken American blacks. Its immediate influence seemed more imagined than real. Some whites blamed Walker for inciting uprisings in North Carolina and Virginia. It certainly seems probable that blacks in those states had heard of, if not read, the *Appeal*. Its long-term influence on abolition, however, is unquestionable. Maria Stewart, Frederick Douglass, Henry Highland Garnet, William Lloyd Garrison—all four prominent abolitionists (and many others) acknowledged the effect of Walker's pamphlet in galvanizing opposition to slavery. Historian Eric Foner has suggested that the *Appeal* helped to make immediate abolition the primary goal of the movement. Unfortunately for Walker, he died in 1830 before he could see the culmination of his influence.

Nat Turner

Walker's polemic may have reached Southampton County, Virginia, in 1831. It was there that Nat Turner would lead the best-known American slave revolt. Born in 1800, Turner found himself a slave often changing masters, having at least five (four legal, one informal) in his lifetime. From an early age, as Turner recounted later, others considered him special. He supposedly was able to read without being taught and could relate events that had taken place before his birth. Turner struggled with his uniqueness, eventually praying that God would verify to him that he "was ordained for some great purpose in the hands of the Almighty" (Turner 1996, p. 46). The confirmation came in his early twenties, and Turner began to speak to his fellow slaves of his supernatural visions, which he believed told him of a significant event in which he would play an important role.

Turner recalled that God continued to speak to him, even telling him to return to his master after a successful escape. This seeming submission to the plantation system caused other slaves to doubt Turner's authority. It was difficult for him to understand, but a vision affirmed the need for the sacrifice: "I saw white spirits and black spirits engaged in battle, and the sun was darkened—the thunder rolled in the Heavens, and blood flowed in streams—and I heard a voice saying, 'Such is your luck, such as you are called to see, and let it come rough or smooth, you must surely bare [sic] it'" (Turner 1996, p. 46). For the next six years, he isolated himself from other slaves. This self-imposed spiritual exile led to more visions. One occurred in 1828, during which the Holy Spirit informed Turner that he was to "fight against the Serpent, for the time was fast approaching when the first should be last and the last should be first" (Turner 1996, pp. 47–48). Three years later, in February 1831, the sign for which he had been waiting appeared: a solar eclipse. At that moment, Turner remembered, "the seal was removed from my lips, and I communicated the great work laid out for me to do, to four in whom I had the greatest confidence" (Turner 1996, pp. 48).

The men decided on July 4, 1831, as their day to act. Turner's illness that day postponed the day of reckoning, but when a similar sign appeared in mid-August, they took action. On Sunday, August 21, Turner and his inner circle met for dinner and made final preparations. Early the next morning, they killed their first whites. The initial victims were members of the Travis family on Turner's own plantation. Joseph Travis, who was his informal master, and his wife, Sally, lost their lives first. Putnam Moore, Turner's twelve-year-old legal owner, and Travis's apprentice were next. The rebels missed the Travis's infant son, but later doubled back and smashed his head against a fireplace.

Nat Turner's Rebellion in 1831 resonated throughout the South for decades. (*Library of Congress*)

From there, the rebels, probably numbering less than twenty, moved from farm to farm. They killed most, but not all, they found. At some farms, noticeable resistance led Turner's men to bypass the residence, while inhabitants at others were spared intentionally and by oversight. Surprisingly, Turner personally killed only one individual, a young white woman named Margaret Whitehead. Her death came slowly, as Turner recalled: "after repeated blows with a sword, I killed her by a blow on the head, with a fence rail" (Turner 1996, p. 50). As the morning sun rose, the number of victims grew to almost two dozen, and the number of rebels roughly doubled. Turner seemingly lacked a plan beyond wreaking havoc among whites in the countryside. There was some indication that the group intended to seize Jerusalem, the county seat, but its members never made it that far.

By mid-morning on August 22, word had spread that a slave rebellion was under way. White patrols organized and rode out to meet the rebels. A pitched battle between the two forces took place near a bridge that crossed the Nottoway River and would have led the rebels directly to Jerusalem. Turner's men were chased away and began a meandering route that took them away from Jerusalem. By the time the rebels rested that night, their numbers, which had crested near forty, had been cut by more than half. Over the next two days, the rebellion evaporated as white resistance increased.

By the end of the month, at least 100 blacks, far more than had participated in the rebellion, had been killed in retaliation for the fifty-eight whites killed on that fateful Monday. The rebels' deaths were often just as violent as those of their victims. Some were decapitated and had their heads placed on pikes at crossroads. Others were disemboweled and disfigured before and after death. The sixty-plus blacks who made it to trial faced mixed fates. Eighteen were hanged, another fourteen were exiled from Virginia, and the rest were freed.

Nat Turner himself escaped capture and death by hiding in the area; he was not discovered and brought in until October 30. Over the next several days, he was interviewed about his role in leading the rebellion. Turner agreed to speak with a local attorney named Thomas R. Gray and to allow him to write down Turner's life story. The account that Gray recorded served to convict Turner, who was hanged on November 11. After Richmond publishers refused to print the manuscript, Gray took it to Washington, where he acquired a copyright, then on to Baltimore, where a printer published it. *The Confessions of Nat Turner*, as it was entitled, achieved a wide circulation, initially selling perhaps as many as 50,000 copies in three printings.

The influence of Turner's rebellion and published confession were significant in shaping white attitudes toward blacks and, consequently, the growing abolitionist movement. Reeling from the violence carried out by both blacks and whites, Virginians debated the place of slavery in their state. Thomas Jefferson Randolph, his namesake's grandson, introduced legislation calling for the gradual emancipation of the state's slaves. The legislature eventually refused to endorse Randolph's proposal, thus solidifying the institution's place in Virginia. Turner's rebellion also reminded white southerners that their slaves, and even their region's free blacks, might be conspiring to mimic the actions of "General Nat" and his followers.

The 1831 uprising also held import for the abolitionist movement. William Lloyd Garrison, editor of *The Liberator* newspaper and an emerging abolitionist leader, did not condone the rebellion. He did, however, observe that Turner "deserves a portion of the applause which has been so prodigally heaped upon [George] Washington, [Simon] Bolivar, and other *heroes*, for the same rebellious though more successful conduct" (Greenberg 2003, pp. 151–153). Robert Dale Owen warned white southerners that "a knowledge of the world's history, and man's nature should teach them that there is a point beyond which oppression cannot be endured, and they ought to anticipate the horrors of the oppressor when that day shall come" (Greenberg 2003, pp. 151–153). Turner's rebellion seemingly made clear to white abolitionists in particular that violent revolt, while not the method that they would have chosen, might be the only way to shake slaveholders free from their commitment to the institution of slavery.

Frederick Douglass

Violence was not the most common form of resistance undertaken by those intent on eradicating slavery, however. Increasingly, abolitionists in the Jacksonian period turned to rhetoric to attempt to persuade white Americans to open their eyes to the evils of slavery. One of the most effective individuals to use pen and voice to fight the institution was a former Maryland slave who found himself an international symbol against the arguments used in support of slavery: Frederick Douglass.

Frederick Augustus Washington Bailey was born in Maryland in 1818. (Frederick would not choose the name Douglass until 1838, when he and his wife escaped to the North.) His racial heritage was mixed; he had a black slave mother, an unidentified white father, and at least one Native American ancestor. His first master, Aaron Anthony, died when Douglass was eight,

Frederick Douglass was widely viewed as the most prominent spokesperson for abolitionism in the antebellum period. (*National Archives*)

and he was sent to the home of Anthony's relative, Thomas Auld. Douglass later remembered that he had "seldom met with one so entirely destitute of every element of character capable of inspiring respect" as his second master. "I thought him incapable of a noble action. The leading trait in his character was intense selfishness" (McFeely 1991, p. 41). His disappointment in Auld seemed to stem from his unwillingness, even after having converted to Christianity, to free Douglass or at least treat him and his other slaves better.

Living in the Auld household did have one major benefit for Douglass, though. As a young slave boy, Douglass learned how to read, and it was Thomas Auld's sister-in-law, Sophia, who taught him. His first reading material was, not surprisingly, the Bible, which was on the bookshelf of so many southern households. Sophia's husband, Hugh (who was Thomas Auld's brother), was not happy with his wife's efforts. "If you teach that nigger . . . how to read the bible, there will be no keeping him," Douglass recalled him saying (McFeely 1991, p. 30). His ability to read served him well when he discovered, as a teenager, *The Columbian Orator*, a textbook commonly used by American schoolchildren. Filled with lessons intended to encourage republican behavior, it helped instill in him a love for democracy and liberty and taught him that effective oratory came from repeated practice.

Around the same time that Douglass bought his copy of *The Columbian Orator*, he also experienced a religious conversion. He later recalled: "The air seemed filled with bright, descending messengers from the sky. . . . I was not without the suggestion, at the moment, that it might be the harbinger of the coming of the Son of Man; and, in my then state of mind, I was prepared to hail Him as my friend and deliverer" (McFeely 1991, pp. 41–42). A meteor shower had brought to Douglass a sense of the supernatural, which he interpreted within a Christian framework. Although he became a minister in the African Methodist Episcopal Zion Church in 1839, Douglass eventually soured on the hypocrisy that he observed among white churchgoers. Still, Christian themes of equality and justice would pervade his spoken and written words until his death.

Another formative period for Douglass occurred during the months that he spent in 1834 under the control of a farmer by the name of Edward Covey. Covey was a hard and cruel man, according to Douglass, which was exactly what Douglass's master, Thomas Auld, wanted from him. Auld believed that his sixteen-year-old slave needed to be broken, needed to learn to bend to a master's will. Covey often beat his slaves, including Douglass, and worked them hard in the fields. Six months into his time of enslavement to Covey, however, things changed. Tired of Covey's mistreatment of him, Douglass fought back in a fight that lasted, by his account, "nearly two hours." Following the brawl, Covey never beat him again. It was, as Douglass famously recounted in his *Narrative*, "an epoch in my humble history," one that showed "how a slave was made a man" (Douglass 2003, p. 84).

The next significant year of change was 1838. Douglass escaped his life of slavery in September of that year, traveling to New York City. There, he received help from a local black abolitionist society. Douglass's fiancée, Anna Murray, a free black woman in Baltimore, joined him in New York, and they married. Soon after, the newly married couple moved to New Bedford, Massachusetts. Douglass found in that port town ties to the abolitionist movement that would make him famous.

Between 1839 and 1841, Douglass acquainted himself with the prevailing rhetoric and concerns of abolitionism. He read William Lloyd Garrison's abolitionist newspaper, *The Liberator*, extensively, absorbing the language and arguments presented there. In 1839, he gave his first public abolitionist speech, which concentrated on his opposition to African colonization. But Douglass's breakthrough came in 1841, when he spoke before the Massachusetts Anti-Slavery Society. Impressed by his oratorical skills, the Society leadership, headed by Garrison, enlisted Douglass to begin traveling as a speaker for the abolitionist cause. He agreed to do so, and for the rest of his life Douglass had a public audience. Garrison considered those who heard Douglass speak "fortunate . . . [to] have been melted to tears by his pathos, or roused to virtuous indignation by his stirring eloquence against the enslavers of men" (Douglass 2003, p. 31).

The 1840s also witnessed the publication of Douglass's famous *Narrative of the Life of Frederick Douglass, an American Slave, Written by Himself*. Written

Through his claim that the Constitution was proslavery, William Lloyd Garrison helped to make the abolitionist movement more radical. (*National Archives*)

over several months in 1844–1845, the book appeared first in Boston in May 1845. Noted abolitionist Wendell Phillips encouraged Douglass to share his knowledge of the "Valley of the Shadow of Death" of southern slavery and to "tell us whether, after all, the half-free colored man of Massachusetts is worse off than the pampered slave of the rice swamps!" (Douglass 2003, p. 39) The book was an instant success, selling 5,000 copies in its first four months in print. Seeing the success that Douglass was achieving as a speaker and an author, his supporters encouraged him to begin a speaking tour of Great Britain. From August 1845 until the spring of 1847, he spoke to receptive audiences in England, Scotland, and Ireland. The tour made Douglass the most recognized black advocate for the end of slavery and bolstered sales of his *Narrative*, which became an international best seller.

Upon returning to the United States, Douglass moved Anna and their four children to Rochester, New York, where he began publication of his own newspaper, the *North Star*. This period marked a time of transition for Douglass, as he became increasingly independent of white abolitionists, particularly Garrison. Garrison had determined to take an uncompromising stand against slavery, which led him to avoid any association with white slaveholders. He wanted nothing to do with politicians and their parties, organized religion, or even the United States government itself. All of them, in his estimation, were complicit in the sin of slavery. Douglass, on the other hand, was more realistic. He believed that political institutions and churches, as hypocritical as their members often were, could be used to limit and eventually eradicate slavery; avoiding them out of a sense of idealism was simply unthinkable for him.

Throughout the 1850s, Douglass found himself at the center of the debate over slavery. He maintained ties with the Liberty, Free-Soil, and Republican parties, all of which emphasized their opposition to the South's peculiar institution. He also became involved in supporting violent opposition to slavery. In 1851, he helped runaway slaves involved in the Christiana conflagration. More famously, Douglass allowed John Brown to live in his home prior to the latter's raid of Harper's Ferry in 1859. While he seemed unaware of the radical abolitionist's ultimate intentions, Douglass found himself under suspicion for his association with Brown. Preferring to be cautious, he went into self-imposed exile in England for a few months, returning to his home in 1860.

The advent of the Civil War brought Douglass newfound influence. He argued early on that the United States Army should enlist black soldiers in the fight against the Confederate States government. He lent his voice to the public discussion of the war as he had for years, through speeches and

African American soldiers, such as the 4th U.S. Colored Infantry, were instrumental in the Union Army's success against the Confederacy. (*Library of Congress*)

newspaper editorials. He urged President Abraham Lincoln to do what no president had seriously considered before: emancipate the slaves. "Jefferson Davis is a powerful man," Douglass told one audience on July 4, 1862, "but Jefferson Davis has no such power to blast the hope and break down the strong heart of this nation, as that possessed and exercised by Abraham Lincoln" (McFeely 1991, p. 214). Not long after, with the Union victory at Antietam, Lincoln announced that emancipation was coming; it was not as a direct result of Douglass's speech, but the president could not have neglected to hear the anguish and urgency of the orator's call. On the night of December 31 of that year, Douglass waited with other abolitionists, both black and white, for the news that the Emancipation Proclamation would indeed take effect the following day. When a telegraph confirmed their hopes, those within Boston's Tremont Temple, including Douglass, erupted in exultation.

Once emancipation came, Douglass became more involved in the war effort. He focused particularly on ensuring that the Union army used black soldiers to fight for the promise of freedom and equality that a successful Union victory portended. Douglass personally traveled across the North and recruited men to join the Fifty-fourth Massachusetts, which became the most famous black regiment of the war. He also fought to raise black soldiers' pay to an equitable level with that of white soldiers and to secure fairness in promotion of rank for blacks. Additionally, he blasted the Confederacy's treatment of black prisoners and criticized Lincoln for not doing more to protect them.

Douglass wanted to see the war result not only in emancipation, but also in suffrage for former slaves. In a speech to a group of New York women in February 1864, he emphasized what he perceived was "the mission of this war": "liberty for all, chains for none; the black man a soldier in war; a laborer in peace; a voter at the South as well as at the North." A little over a year later, he wrote fellow abolitionist Lydia Maria Child, "I can see little advantage in emancipation without" African Americans also having the right to vote. Not long after, Douglass told an audience, "Without the elective franchise the Negro will still be practically a slave" (McFeely 1991, pp. 231, 246). After the war ended and Vice President Andrew Johnson of Tennessee succeeded the assassinated Lincoln in the White House, Douglass endorsed the plans that the so-called Radical Republicans had for a reconstructed South. He argued strenuously for black suffrage and was pleased by the passage of the Fifteenth Amendment, which gave black men the right to vote.

After Reconstruction ended in 1877, Douglass continued to speak for the rights of African Americans. The horrific explosion of lynching cases, usually directed toward African American males for allegedly raping white women, drew a severe reaction from the aging advocate for racial equality. In 1892, his essay, "Lynch Law in the South," appeared in the *North American Review*. Douglass wrote, "The crime imputed to the negro is one most easily imputed and most difficult to disprove, and yet it is the one the negro is least likely to commit." He discerned that the real problem was class conflict mingled with racial prejudice. The African American, he surmised, received "no resistance when on a downward course. It is only when he rises in wealth, intelligence,

Harriet Tubman

Like David Walker, Nat Turner, and Frederick Douglass, Harriet Tubman was also a revolutionary, although in different ways. Born Araminta Ross sometime around 1820, she grew up in Maryland as the daughter of enslaved parents. (Like Frederick Douglass, Araminta took a new name when she escaped slavery as an adult.) She suffered harsh treatment as a girl; one injury, to her head, left her with permanent damage.

In 1844, Araminta married John Tubman, a free black man in the area. In 1849, she decided to set out for the North and freedom on her own, which was quite a feat for a lone slave woman to accomplish. She eventually made it to Philadelphia; the following year, however, she returned to Maryland to free members of her family. She made a subsequent trip to help her husband find freedom, but John had remarried.

In making these trips, Tubman discovered that she could become an instrument of liberation for slaves outside of her family. As part of the Underground Railroad, a network designed to help slaves escape bondage, she reportedly made at least nineteen trips to the South before 1860 and freed nearly 300 slaves. (That number was actually much higher, as she also helped slaves during the Civil War.) Not surprisingly, the trips were marked with danger, which Tubman was often able to avoid through thoughtful planning and quick thinking. Her work as a "conductor" on the Underground Railroad earned her the name "Moses" of the Underground Railroad and brought her into contact with the prominent abolitionists of the day, including Frederick Douglass and Gerrit Smith.

During the Civil War, Tubman continued to help slaves escape; she also worked as a nurse,

Harriet Tubman was instrumental in the success of the Underground Railroad. (*Library of Congress*)

cook, and spy. Like other African Americans, she exulted in the news of the Emancipation Proclamation. Once the war was over, Tubman suffered one of her worst injustices as a free woman. On a train ride back to New York from Virginia at the end of the war, she was assaulted by a train conductor and several male passengers who wanted her to vacate her seat. She survived, but with considerable injuries.

Tubman spent the rest of her life in Auburn, New York, where she remarried. She used her celebrity to help unfortunate local blacks and became involved in the women's rights movement. She died in 1913.

and manly character that he brings upon himself the heavy hand of persecution" (McFeely 1991, p. 361).

Douglass died in 1895, leaving other African Americans such as Booker T. Washington, W. E. B. Du Bois, and Ida B. Wells-Barnett to continue fighting Jim Crow–era racism. What he, Walker, and Turner had effected, however, was a significant change in the lives of all black Americans. It would be foolish to ignore all of the problems that African Americans still faced and the struggle that would continue, in some ways, even until today. Yet, their accomplishments were revolutionary. They inspired free and enslaved blacks to seek change, to demand it, and then to take advantage of the transformation that came socially, politically, and economically. Emancipation and suffrage were no less a revolution for African Americans than the British colonists' fight against Great Britain in the eighteenth century had been for white America.

References and Further Reading

Clinton, Catherine. *Harriet Tubman: The Road to Freedom*. New York: Little, Brown, 2004.

Douglass, Frederick. *Narrative of the Life of Frederick Douglass, an American Slave, Written by Himself*. Ed. David W. Blight. 2d. ed. New York: Bedford/St. Martin's, 2003.

Greenberg, Kenneth S., ed. *Nat Turner: A Slave Rebellion in History and Memory*. Oxford: Oxford University Press, 2003.

Hinks, Peter P. *To Awaken My Afflicted Brethren: David Walker and the Problem of Antebellum Slave Resistance*. University Park: The Pennsylvania State University Press, 1997.

McFeely, William S. *Frederick Douglass*. New York: W.W. Norton, 1991.

Turner, Nat. *The Confessions of Nat Turner and Related Documents*. Ed. Kenneth S. Greenberg. New York: Bedford/St. Martin's, 1996.

Walker, David. *David Walker's Appeal to the Coloured Citizens of the World*. Ed. Peter P. Hinks. University Park: Pennsylvania State University Press, 2000.

Presidential Politics and Social Scandal | 2

Matthew S. Warshauer

S exual scandal is no stranger to Washington, D.C. In the late 1990s, President William Jefferson Clinton shocked America when he initially denied and then admitted to having engaged in a sexual act with then White House intern Monica Lewinsky. The scandal caused an impeachment hearing in Congress because President Clinton had perjured himself under oath when first denying the allegations of sexual misconduct. He was acquitted in the Senate, but his actions ignited moral outrage in the nation and subsequently influenced the attempt of his vice president, Al Gore, to win the presidency in 2000. Moreover, President Clinton's folly, among other problems, had a lasting impact on the overall health of the Democratic Party.

One might initially think that scandals such as this do not happen within the halls of power in the strongest nation in the world, or, at the very least, that they do not become known and affect entire political parties. Yet, they have. Historians, for example, have come to learn many years after the fact that President John F. Kennedy had a relationship with movie star Marilyn Monroe, among other women, while he served in the executive office. Since these affairs became known many years later, they had no impact on Kennedy's party at the time, though the knowledge of them has cast some shade over his character and legacy.

To be sure, sexual scandal is not limited solely to the twentieth century. Even in the early years, during the founding decades of the republic, sex, power, and intrigue swirled together and captured the attention of Americans. One such episode was what some historians have labeled "the Petticoat Affair." It did not specifically involve the actions of a president in a sexually compromising act, but it did pull President Andrew Jackson, the nation's seventh chief executive, into a battle over social mores, duty to friends, his own marriage to his wife, Rachel, and the problems that surrounded it. These issues stemmed from Jackson's defense of his friend and secretary of war,

John H. Eaton, and his marriage to Margaret Timberlake, which touched off a political firestorm that rocked the president's first administration and created a troubling atmosphere within his official presidential cabinet. One result for the "Eaton Malaria," argue some historians, was Jackson's creation of what became known as the "Kitchen Cabinet," a group of informal political advisers who took the place of Jackson's regular cabinet.

The fact that the president ultimately requested the resignations of his entire cabinet has fueled more speculation that Jackson's White House was paralyzed by the Petticoat Affair. The conclusion has been that the power of social etiquette and Jackson's inability to "make" his cabinet officers conform to his will and treat Margaret Eaton with courtesy doomed his first administration, necessitated the existence of a Kitchen Cabinet that in many ways allowed political intriguers to dominate the president, and also exploded some of the inner workings of Jackson's fledgling Democratic Party—all this over social decorum.

Yet the reality of the Petticoat Affair's impact and the nature of the Kitchen Cabinet was most certainly different from what recent historians have surmised. In the two most extensive articles on the Kitchen Cabinet, historians Richard Longaker and Richard Latner agree that Andrew Jackson's official cabinet, though certainly not peaceful, was not paralyzed by the Petticoat Affair and that they actually met on a regular basis when policy issues demanded their attention. Moreover, both historians dispel the notion that Jackson replaced his regular cabinet with the Kitchen Cabinet. Rather, they argue, the president utilized the rather amorphous membership of the Kitchen Cabinet as an extended network of unofficial advisers and confidants. Indeed, Latner argued that the advisory system Jackson engaged had more to do with his style of leadership than with the need to create a secondary cabinet because the first one had failed. Latner asserted, "Rather than compare the kitchen cabinet with the regular cabinet, it would be more useful to conceptualize it as an early prototype of the President's White House staff, a group of personal aides providing the President with a variety of services. The staff includes policy advisors, lobbyists, liaison people, publicity experts, speech writers, and friends" (Latner 1978, p. 378). Finally, both Longaker and Latner agree that the social, turned political, problem over John and Margaret Eaton was actually one among many problems that caused a serious political rift within Jackson's official White House family. Differences over South Carolina's attempt to nullify the nation's tariff laws, Jackson's attack on the constitutionality of the Bank of the United States, and his ongoing dispute with Vice President John Calhoun over Jackson's 1818 invasion of Florida all influenced the political currents within Jackson's administration.

Still, the Petticoat Affair, in its own day and ours, captures attention particularly because it mixes together sex, intrigue, social decorum, and political power. Newspapers in Jackson's day followed the scandal as closely as any of our modern tabloid newspapers and other media outlets would today. Consider the coverage of President Clinton's tryst with Monica Lewinsky. The American press made such play out of it that European news agencies began calling it "Zippergate," with obvious references to the Watergate scandal that forced President Richard Nixon to resign. Though there is no doubt that political jockeying for power within President Jackson's administration caused tensions, there is also no denying that the Petticoat Affair fueled and expanded upon those problems and ultimately melded them into a complex web of proper social etiquette and political backstabbing. This essay, then, is the story of the Petticoat Affair and its relation to the rise of Jackson's Kitchen Cabinet.

The Petticoat Affair

When Andrew Jackson, the Hero of the Battle of New Orleans, finally reached the White House in 1828, it was after a long road filled with political battles. Jackson believed that he had been robbed of the presidency in 1824 in what he and his supporters called the Corrupt Bargain. Jackson had won the popular vote and the most electoral votes, but not enough of the latter to actually be declared president. Instead, the top three vote recipients, Jackson, John Quincy Adams, and William Crawford, were voted on in the House of Representatives where Henry Clay, who had also vied for the presidency in 1824, worked his significant political magic to assure that Adams won the House vote. Clay was subsequently offered and accepted the position of secretary of state, the traditional stepping-stone to the executive office, and cries of corruption thundered from Jackson and his supporters. One of those supporters, John H. Eaton, had been by Jackson's side from early on. Eaton had served as a military aide to General Jackson when he fought the Creek Indians in the South, and when he won the famous Battle of New Orleans and became an overnight national hero. Eaton wrote the first biography of Jackson in 1817 and was among the first to consider him for the presidency and work toward that end. Eaton authored the anonymous "Letters of Wyoming," in which he championed Jackson's candidacy, and stood by the general throughout the many political trials along the way.

It was no surprise that Jackson would therefore reward his friend and loyal ally with a position, secretary of war, within the newly forming presidential cabinet. That Eaton was qualified for the position was never questioned. He had served in the military and was an able politician in his own right. The problem was Eaton's new wife, Margaret. The other cabinet wives had serious problems with Margaret's social standing and, more particularly, with the rather questionable path to her second marriage. Margaret had met Eaton when he and Jackson roomed at William O'Neale's boarding house in Washington City. Margaret was O'Neale's daughter and had grown up amid the politics of the day, meeting the nation's leading men and hearing them debate America's future. She was known as beautiful, flirtatious, and, perhaps, too forward. At the time of her acquaintance with Eaton, Margaret was married to John Timberlake, formerly a Navy purser. Eaton befriended the Timberlakes and when John was forced to return to sea because of financial woes, he entrusted Margaret's care to Eaton, even giving him power of attorney for Timberlake's affairs. Eaton and Margaret were seen together often, and the result was wagging tongues. People spied a scandal. A married woman seen frequently in the company of a man who was not her husband was socially unacceptable at this time in the republic.

One of Jackson's longtime Tennessee friends, John H. Eaton was appointed Old Hickory's secretary of war. (*U.S. Senate Historical Office*)

The simmering scandal only worsened when news of Timberlake's death arrived. The official cause was listed as pulmonary disease, but it soon became known that he had cut his own throat with a knife. As one historian explained, "Timberlake had committed suicide, the story spread, because, in a drunken and depressed stupor, he could no longer face his wife's infidelity with John Henry Eaton" (Marszalek 1997, p. 44). The building gossip would soon be unleashed in a full-scale political storm that embroiled the new president and his entire cabinet.

Andrew Jackson's connection to the problems encountered by Margaret and John Eaton were both personal and professional. On one level, Jackson, always devoted to friends, stood by Eaton because he had done the same for Jackson on so many previous occasions. Yet, on another level, the matter was more deeply personal for the president. Jackson's wife had died suddenly of a heart attack just days prior to his trip to Washington to be sworn in as the next chief executive, and the new president blamed his political foes

John Eaton's wife, Margaret, would prove a divisive figure in Jackson's first presidential term. (*The Hermitage: Home of President Andrew Jackson, Nashville, Tennessee*)

for her untimely death. Rachel Jackson was lambasted in the press as an adulteress and Jackson as a wife stealer in an attempt to sully Jackson's reputation during the 1828 campaign. Years earlier, in 1790, Rachel had separated for the last time after several splits and reconciliations with her husband, Lewis Robards. By this time, Rachel and Jackson had met and fallen in love. When Robards announced his intent to divorce Rachel and subsequently filed a petition with the Virginia Assembly, as it was the only body that could grant a divorce at that time, Jackson subsequently whisked Rachel off to Natchez in Spanish Territory and allegedly married her in 1791. The marriage was alleged because historians have questioned the validity of the timeline presented by Jackson and his campaign managers. Historian Robert Remini asserted that Jackson and Rachel most likely did not formally marry in Natchez and that this later fabrication was the result of needing to make everything seem proper in preparation for the 1828 presidential contest. In any regard, Jackson and Rachel officially married in 1794 when news arrived that Robards had not actually received a divorce until 1793.

For Andrew and Rachel Jackson, the damage was already done, and the ensuing scandal popped up periodically when someone wanted to prod Jackson or challenge his honor. Such events led to at least two duels, one of them

Rachel Jackson's death left the president emotionally drained and sensitive to accusations of impropriety made against the Eatons. (*The Hermitage: Home of President Andrew Jackson, Nashville, Tennessee*)

fatal for Jackson's opponent. Thus, Jackson's sympathy for Margaret Timberlake and John Eaton arose from his personal knowledge of social and political scandal. It should come as no surprise that the president ultimately counseled Eaton to shut everyone up by marrying Margaret, believing that this would rob intriguers of something about which to gossip. Jackson could not have been more wrong.

Margaret and John Eaton married on January 1, 1829, and in doing so launched a sexual and political scandal that caused problems in Jackson's first administration and, among other issues, seriously impacted any possibility for harmony within his presidential cabinet. The problem was that Margaret had married too quickly following the death of John Timberlake. As historian John Marszalek explained, "To think of marrying so quickly after the death of a husband violated one of the more serious proscriptions of genteel American society. A widow of gentility was to alter her life significantly for one to two years after her husband's death to indicate proper respect and acceptable grieving for him. . . . Society demanded a public expression of sorrow, and if a woman did not grieve according to the established rules, it revealed for all to see her lack of gentility and character" (Marszalek 1997, pp. 46–47). In the eyes of many, Margaret Eaton was a disgraceful woman.

This fact became eminently clear in the early days of President Jackson's new administration. Rigid social custom demanded certain protocols for visiting government officials and for returning those visits. The Eatons abided by such custom by calling at the home of Vice President John Calhoun, where his wife, Floride, received them. The visit was brief, and the next step in the social dance was for Mrs. Calhoun to return the call. She did not. "Floride Calhoun," wrote Marszalek, "the highest ranking woman related to the Jackson administration, had decided to snub Margaret Eaton" (Marszalek 1997, p. 54). Mrs. Calhoun's actions were a call to the administration wives, namely those related to the president's cabinet, to bar Margaret from their social circle.

Selecting cabinet officers was and continues to be an important function for any president. Cabinet positions are close to the seat of power, and observers look to these appointments as both an indication of the administration's potential direction and a way to determine who may be a future president. Consider that all of the previous presidents, except George Washington and John Adams, had served in cabinet positions and utilized those appointments as avenues to the presidency. Many believed that Jackson was too old and his health too fragile for him to serve more than one term in office; hence, aspiring politicians bided their time, hoping to be in enough of the political spotlight to make their bid for the nation's highest office following Jackson's departure. This was certainly true of Vice President Calhoun, who had withdrawn from the 1824 contest and opted to run for the vice presidency instead. He decided on the same course of action in 1828, strategizing that he would be in a good position when Jackson retired. Yet Martin Van Buren, the president's choice for secretary of state, had similar aspirations, and the political desires of these two men added to the fuel of the scandal that would soon engulf Jackson's presidential family. The other cabinet members entertained no clear presidential ambitions. Eaton served as secretary of war; Samuel Ingham was secretary of the treasury; John Berrien was the attorney general; John Branch was secretary of the navy; and William Barry served as postmaster general. He was also the only member of the cabinet whose family did not openly ostracize Margaret Eaton.

From the outset of the cabinet's formation, rumors and gossip swirled about the Eatons. One critic wrote of Eaton that "the great objection to this gentleman is his wife, whom, it is said, is *not* as *she* should be" (Marszalek 1997, p. 64). Jackson learned early on of the potential problems that he faced with the choice of Eaton as secretary of war. Colonel Nathan Towson visited Jackson shortly after the proposed cabinet became known, counseling that the president consider an alternative to Eaton. Jackson assured Towson of Eaton's talents and friendship, and inquired why there should be an objection. "There is none, I believe, personally, to *him*," explained Towson, "but there are great objections made to his wife" (Parton 1860, vol. 3, p. 161). Jackson nevertheless remained firm in his support of Eaton.

The first real onslaught came on the night of Jackson's inauguration. At the ball and dinner following Jackson's swearing in, Margaret was totally ignored by Floride Calhoun and the cabinet wives, including Jackson's own niece, Emily Donelson, who served as the president's first lady of the White

Jackson mistakenly focused on John C. Calhoun as the leader of the anti-Eaton faction. (*Library of Congress*)

House. From that point on, Margaret met with disdain and avoidance by the cabinet wives. For several months, rumors continued to swirl, with Jackson attempting to get to the bottom of the various allegations regarding Margaret's unwomanly conduct. Jackson continually championed Margaret's virtue and defended her against those who spread rumors. It was on September 10, 1829, that things came to a head with the cabinet. The president called into a meeting his secretaries Andrew Jackson Donelson and William B. Lewis, all of his cabinet members except Eaton, and the Reverends John N. Campbell and Ezra Styles Ely, who had been involved in spreading some of the allegations against Margaret and with whom Jackson had been arguing for some time. At the meeting, Jackson expected to settle the matter once and for all by demanding that the two ministers exonerate Margaret of wrongdoing. When confronted by the president, Reverend Ely was unable to do as the president expected, and Jackson thundered in reply, "She is as chaste as a virgin!" (Marszalek 1997, p. 102).

The meeting had no effect on Margaret Eaton's reputation, though it did worsen things in Jackson's cabinet. For Campbell's part in the meeting and his earlier criticisms of Margaret, he was challenged to a duel by Eaton. Campbell refused to take part, insisting that a court of law was the proper place to settle the dispute. Neither the duel nor the court action ever ensued. Jackson, to show his contempt for Campbell, left the minister's Washington

Martin Van Buren staunchly defended the Eatons, thus solidifying himself as Jackson's ally and political successor. (*Library of Congress*)

church, and Campbell ultimately escaped the storm by relocating to tend a congregation in Albany, New York. Nor was this the only fallout from the continuing affair. Jackson's cabinet was split, with Vice President John Calhoun, Secretary of the Treasury Samuel Ingham, Attorney General John Berrien, and Secretary of the Navy John Branch all opposing Margaret Eaton. On the other side stood Secretary of State Martin Van Buren, Secretary of War Eaton, of course, and Postmaster General William Barry. Van Buren had a particularly enviable position, for he had no wife or daughter and thus no female influence that could pressure or compel him to avoid associating in public with Margaret Eaton. More important, Van Buren achieved significant political points with the president by championing Mrs. Eaton and showing her social respect. Calhoun, alternately, was lowered in Jackson's esteem. This politicking by two formidable men, both of whom coveted the presidency, made what had begun as a social scandal something different. It was now about political power and the future of the presidency. As Daniel Webster, the well-known senator from Massachusetts, noted, "It is odd enough, but too evident to be doubted, that the consequences of this dispute in the social and fashionable world is producing political effects, and may very probably determine who shall be successor to the present chief magistrate" (Webster 1903, vol. 17, p. 483).

The Kitchen Cabinet

When Jackson began to rely on men outside his regular cabinet, like Francis Preston Blair and Amos Kendall, rumors circulated about the existence of a "Kitchen Cabinet." As Robert Remini described it, "Supposedly, there existed— according to those who invented and employed the term—a group of aides outside the official cabinet with special talents at political manipulation who advised Jackson on the running of the government, the distribution of the patronage, and the operation of the Democratic Party. Since they were not his official advisers, like cabinet officers—the official cabinet was sometimes called the 'parlor' cabinet—they were imagined as slipping into Jackson's study by way of the back stairs through the kitchen" (Remini 1981, p. 326). Remini, Richard Longaker, and Richard Latner all agree that one of the first times the term appeared was in private correspondence, a December 1831 letter in which the president of the Bank of the United States, Nicholas Biddle, worried that "the kitchen . . . predominate[s] over the Parlor" (Latner 1978, p. 374). It did not take long for the notion of a Kitchen Cabinet that held sway over Jackson's views to make its way into the mainstream press, especially after Senator George Poindexter of Mississippi published an article in the Washington-based *Telegraph* on March 27, 1832, in which he lashed out against Francis Preston Blair and Amos Kendall, charging that they are "familiarly known by the appellation 'Kitchen Cabinet'" (Remini 1981, p. 327). What is eminently clear is that Poindexter was in the Calhoun camp of the growing political divide and that his piece in the *Telegraph*, which was published by Duff Green, another Calhoun adherent, was followed by numerous editorials in which the idea of a Kitchen Cabinet flourished. Longaker and Latner are adamant that the concept of a Kitchen Cabinet "was largely the work of alienated Jacksonians, particularly of Calhounites like Green" who insisted that the president was under the malign influence of political intriguers. These Calhoun men were particularly concerned that the influence was opposition to the vice president and that the source of this movement was actually Secretary of State Van Buren.

A fitting question is whether Jackson's alleged Kitchen Cabinet was really a formal structure that met in place of his supposedly defunct official cabinet. This query was best indicated in the very title of Richard Longaker's article, "Was Jackson's Kitchen Cabinet a Cabinet?" The simple answer is no. Longaker refers to the idea as a "persistent minor legend of the American presidency" (Longaker 1957, p. 94). In reality, the Kitchen Cabinet was a constantly shifting group of friends and confidants whom Jackson trusted and from whom he sought counsel. Latner agrees, calling Jackson's group of counselors an advisory system.

Longaker counted some twelve men who, at various times, made up the Kitchen Cabinet membership and noted that the difficulty in compiling a list stems from the very makeup, or lack of makeup, of the group. Jackson most certainly never met the various members in one or a series of meetings to determine policy. These advisers were certainly not an alternative to the traditional cabinet because it failed to function properly as a result of the Petticoat Affair. Rather, the president met with different advisers at different times over different policy matters. These men included both his official cabinet members and his unofficial advisers. William B. Lewis of Tennessee, for example, was one of Jackson's most important confidants early in the administration and even lived in the White House, but as Jackson continued as president, Lewis's influence waned and he ultimately moved out of the presidential residence. A similar pattern existed with Duff Green, who was a consistent unofficial adviser to Jackson until the Eaton problem and other issues with John Calhoun caused problems in the administration. Other men who ebbed and flowed as part of Jackson's unofficial advisory group included Senator Thomas Hart Benton, Senator Hugh Lawson White, future president and fellow Tennessean James K. Polk, Isaac Hill of New Hampshire, and the president's nephew and personal secretary, Andrew Jackson Donelson. Francis Preston Blair and Amos Kendall moved into Jackson's inner circle prior to the complete rupture with the Calhoun wing of the administration and soared in influence once that break occurred. Blair's newspaper, the *Democratic Globe*, became the official mouthpiece of the administration when Duff Green's *Telegraph* was thrust aside after the political split. Kendall was made an auditor in the Treasury Department so that he could earn a living in Washington and thus stay close to Jackson. Both men remained Jackson's confidants throughout the remainder of his life.

Jackson as Administrator

To a large extent, Jackson operated as president in a distinctly military way. His greatest triumphs, his national appeal, and hence his road to the White House were paved with his successful, albeit controversial, acts as a military commander. Indeed, some opponents, most notably Henry Clay of Kentucky, warned that elevating a "military chieftain" to the presidency was a mistake. Yet Jackson did attain the executive office and he did utilize his advisers, both official and unofficial, as counselors and sounding boards on policy matters. He was the general/president in charge and used those around him for their particular talents. Blair was often a counselor and excelled at promoting Jackson's views in the press. Kendall was a master writer and crafted the president's ideas into finely honed legal and constitutional prose.

Jackson's official cabinet members also had their talents and, even in the midst of the Petticoat Affair, the president met with them on a variety of policy matters. Longaker insisted that it is "an unwarranted simplification to contend that his cabinet did not meet," and provided "definitive evidence that on at least sixteen occasions Jackson called the cabinet together to consider some specific question in which public policy was involved" and met with individual cabinet members on numerous other occasions (Longaker 1957, pp. 95–96). Moreover, there were a number of times when the president called his cabinet together after he had already determined a policy, such as in the Petticoat Affair and the Bank War, to hear their thoughts on the decision he had already made. As Thomas Hart Benton observed years later, "He did as he had often done in councils of war—called the council together to hear a decision. He summoned his cabinet—laid the case before

Andrew Jackson

"She is as chaste as a virgin!" So thundered Andrew Jackson in his battle over Margaret Eaton's character. Such bellowing statements from Jackson have caused many in his own day and ours to surmise that he was constantly out of control. One anti-Jackson campaign pamphlet from the period announced: "his conduct puts us in mind of the exasperated rhinoceros, wreaking his fury on every object that presents itself." Historians James C. Curtis and Andrew Burstein certainly believe that Jackson was psychologically impaired to the extent that he fumed and exploded at any conceived opposition to his views. Yet other historians doubt that Jackson was as out of control as these historians argue. Robert Remini, for example, believes that Jackson's anger was something that he could turn on and off for political effect, and

refers to the time that a group of business men went to the White House to implore that Jackson support the Bank of the United States. Martin Van Buren, who was present at the time, explained later that Jackson flew into a tirade on the Bank and ordered the men to go elsewhere, for there was no money in the White House. As soon as the men departed, Jackson allegedly returned to a calm demeanor and laughed about the men's reactions to his tirade.

The truth about Jackson certainly lay somewhere between these two extremes. Jackson was not the howling madman that Curtis and Burstein would have readers believe. Nor was he the always-in-control, calculating politician portrayed by Remini. Andrew Jackson was a man of passions. He could fume and explode. Yet the more important question is whether he

them—heard the majority of adverse opinions—and directed the order to issue" (Benton 1854–1856, vol. 1, p. 678).

This view of Jackson as the president in charge runs headlong against some historians' views of Jackson as a vacillating leader who lacked control in both his personal and political life. Historians such as James C. Curtis (*Andrew Jackson and the Search for Vindication*) and Andrew Burstein (*The Passions of Andrew Jackson*) contend that Jackson was a virtual madman who lashed out at perceived enemies and certainly made no strides in molding the presidency into a more modern entity. Nor did he, they argue, have a vision for the nation. The fact of the matter is that Jackson often prepared the first drafts of presidential messages and frequently discussed important policy matters in letters, both of which indicate his thinking and activity as president.

Longaker noted that in preparing the Nullification Proclamation concerning South Carolina's attempt to cancel the nation's tariff laws, Jackson was adamant that his beliefs be properly represented in the draft written by then Secretary of State Edward Livingston. William B. Lewis later explained that Jackson had "remarked that Mr. Livingston had not correctly understood his notes—there were portions of the draft, he added, which were not in accordance with his views, and must be altered" (Longaker 1957, 105). Jackson himself noted on another occasion, "In regard . . . to these complaints and others of a similar character founded on a pretended distrust of influences near or around me, I can only say that they spring from the same false view of my character. I should loathe myself did any act of mine afford the slightest colour for the insinuation that I follow blindly the judgement of

had the ability to reflect and, more important, to plan. This is a critical point because Burstein argues that Jackson had no vision for America; hence, he was not a planner, not a thinker.

In this author's view, such an assertion is absurd. One need only look to Jackson's early life when he made the very distinct decision to rise beyond the socioeconomic circumstances into which he had been born. His goal was to become of the aristocratic class and his ambitions knew no bounds. He focused on becoming a lawyer, did so, and then entered Tennessee politics as a force to be reckoned with. Essentially, whatever goals he set his sights on, he achieved.

Jackson's military skills are also often overlooked, being equated to luck or good fortune. Yet his abilities as a commander, his ability to plan and execute a strategy, were critical to his success as a general. Indeed, he was the only general in the entire War of 1812 to achieve great victories. As president, he approached political battles in much the same way, organizing his troops and following the battle through to completion.

Jackson was at times vain and demanding, and expected obedience to his will. Moreover, his policies were at times shortsighted. Yet to argue that his only focus in life was personal vindication over inner demons and that he entertained no long-term vision for America is off the mark. His successes, both military and political, are too numerous for this to be true. Jackson was either a seasoned, calculating politician, or the luckiest president in American history.

any friend in the discharge of my proper duties as a public or private individual" (Bassett 1926–1935, vol. 4, 372).

Two of Jackson's closest informal advisers, Blair and Kendall, confirm such a notion about Jackson making his own decisions. Blair insisted, "Whenever anything involves what he conceives the *permanent interest* of the country, his patriotism becomes an all-absorbing feeling, and neither *kitchen* nor *parlor* cabinets can move him" (Latner 1978, p. 384). Amos Kendall made the same assertion, explaining, "They talk of a Kitchen Cabinet, etc. . . . . There are a few of us who have always agreed with the President in relation to the Bank and other essential points of policy, and therefore they charge use with having an influence over him! Fools! They can not beat the President out of his long-cherished opinions, and his firmness they charge to our influence!" (Latner 1978, p. 384).

Split in the Cabinet

Despite Jackson's military command style, he was wholly unable to contain the growing chasm which had begun among his formal cabinet from his first day in office. The Petticoat Affair was an entering wedge that presaged the future lack of harmony and eventual disintegration of the cabinet. As a matter that involved sexual scandal and intrigue, the social and political fault lines related to John and Margaret Eaton's marriage captured the attention of Washingtonians and citizens throughout the nation. Yet the affair was in many ways a two-sided dilemma; it was a social problem that caused a political problem, and a political problem that furthered the social problem. In other words, many members of Jackson's official White House family entered the administration with a jealous eye toward those who would have Jackson's ear and who might ride his significant coattails to the presidency following the old man's retirement. Both John Calhoun and Martin Van Buren strove for supremacy and, in the words of Duff Green, they both jockeyed for "the controlling influence in the cabinet" (Latner 1978, p. 370). Richard Latner noted that one of Calhoun's particular fears was that Eaton was using his influence with Jackson to further Van Buren's presidential hopes. Additionally, argued Latner, Eaton's leanings toward Van Buren boded poorly for Calhounite desires regarding tariff reform. South Carolinians had, in fact, slowed down their move toward open nullification of the tariff laws in the hope that Calhoun would be able to work some magic with the newly elected Jackson.

In many ways, as Richard Longaker pointed out, Jackson's original cabinet was a smattering of disparate John Quincy Adams and Henry Clay foes, most of whom were appointed to the cabinet because of sectional demands and political debts owed as a result of the campaign of 1828. Previous to Jackson's administration, Calhoun and Van Buren had certainly never been great political allies. Their opposition to Adams and Clay brought them both to Jackson's camp. One must also remember that this period represented the earliest organization of the newly formed Democratic Party. It was hardly the well-oiled machine that it ultimately became.

In such an atmosphere of political maneuvering, there is little wonder that tensions were high and that a power struggle ensued. This, of course, is not to negate the fact that Jackson most certainly made the Eaton problem more severe by attempting to force a solution on his cabinet members and their families in a matter that involved social etiquette. The wives were not a part of the general's troops, and he could not, as he liked to do, issue an order and expect to have it followed. Nor could the husbands issue any such directive, even if they were inclined to do so; many of them were not. Thus Jackson blew the smoldering embers of the controversy into a fire by entering the realm of social decorum and propriety. His actions on the matter most certainly stemmed from his loyalty to Eaton, a comrade who had been with the general since his early days, as well as the circumstances of the president's own marriage to Rachel and her premature death prior to inauguration.

It is difficult to deny that Jackson's stubbornness on the Eaton matter polarized the cabinet even further than perhaps it might have become had he stayed out of the matter. Even in admitting this, however, there remains no evidence to prove that the Petticoat Affair completely paralyzed the president's cabinet. Jackson still utilized members of the group for counsel on a variety of policy matters. Moreover, the battle over the Eatons was certainly not the only political matter within the cabinet. As previously mentioned, there were serious differences of opinion over tariff policy and the South Carolina stand on nullification, as well as differences over Jackson's concerns regarding the constitutionality of the Bank of the United States. The Seminole Affair also created tension that was both political and personal in nature and which ultimately was the final straw in moving the president and vice president to a breaking point. Thus in many ways the Seminole Affair was equally as fractious as the Petticoat Affair and therefore deserves some brief attention.

The Seminole Affair

The arguments over the Seminole Affair actually stemmed from incidents some ten years earlier when John Calhoun was secretary of war and at the time General Jackson's superior. In 1818 Jackson had been ordered to the Georgia/Spanish Florida border to defend American settlers from Seminole Indian raids. Though he was ordered to avoid conflict with Spanish authorities and not to pursue the Seminoles should they take cover in a Spanish town, Jackson did so anyway and in the process captured, tried, and executed two British citizens. The incident touched off an international dispute and President Monroe's cabinet met to discuss options for dealing with the matter. Jackson had always been of the opinion that Calhoun had supported the general's bold action against the Indians. When Jackson learned otherwise early in his first administration—most likely through a letter sent by William Crawford, former secretary of the treasury under Monroe and politically aligned with Martin Van Buren—he fumed over the matter and attempted to gain clarity from Calhoun. When Calhoun ultimately published their correspondence on the matter to defend his position, the split between the two men was irreparable.

The Eaton controversy renewed interest in the Seminole affair, which ultimately drove Jackson and Calhoun apart. (*North Wind Picture Archives*)

The tensions over the Seminole Affair, then, were rising at exactly the same time that the Petticoat Affair had become an entrenched point of dispute. As such, it is impossible for historians to cleanly separate the two issues, or others, such as nullification. Hence, one cannot assert that Jackson's unofficial cabinet, his Kitchen Cabinet, grew purely as a result of the battle over John and Margaret Eaton. The two matters became intertwined. Indeed, prior to the publication of the Seminole correspondence, Calhoun approached John Eaton and asked that he consult with Jackson on the subject. As Robert Remini explained it, "Eaton did nothing. Since the Vice President was presumed to be the instigator of the plot to ostracize Peggy [Margaret], Eaton let Calhoun think that Jackson approved the pamphlet and its publication. It was sweet revenge" (Remini 1981, p. 306). The political scheming within Jackson's administration was indeed high.

The dissolution of Andrew Jackson's presidential cabinet followed just a couple of months after the publication of the Seminole correspondence in 1830. Jackson had been unable to regain harmony in his cabinet due in part to the Petticoat Affair, and the Seminole business had worsened matters. The initial impetus for the resignation of the cabinet officers came from Martin Van Buren, who felt it best for his own political fortunes to get out of the cabinet. Calhoun's followers had implicated Van Buren as the arch conspirator who was attempting to damage Calhoun in the eyes of the president. Van Buren, in turn, viewed it as his best course of action to resign. When he finally convinced Jackson, a conversation with John Eaton ensued and he too decided to resign. It was then easy for Jackson to request the resignations of his other cabinet officers: Ingham, Branch, and Berrien.

Yet, the intriguing did not end there. Van Buren had suggested that Jackson appoint him foreign minister to England following the resignation, a post that Jackson dutifully approved for the former secretary of state. Van Buren even packed his bags and departed for Great Britain prior to the Senate confirmation vote on his new position. This was when John Calhoun exacted his revenge. As vice president, Calhoun cast the deciding vote in the Senate should a tie exist. This was precisely what occurred, and when Calhoun killed Van Buren's confirmation, he gleefully boasted of the vote's effect on Van Buren: "It will kill him, sir, kill him dead. He will never kick sir, never kick" (Remini 1981, p. 349). The reality, however, was more accurately described by Benton, who, after the vote turned to a colleague and announced, "You have broken a minister, and elected a Vice-President" (Remini 1981, p. 349). The senator was, of course, correct. Van Buren became Jackson's vice president and followed him as chief executive following Jackson's retirement in 1836. For Calhoun's part, he resigned his position as vice president late in Jackson's first administration due specifically to political difficulties over nullification within his home state of South Carolina.

Petticoats and Political Ambition

There is no question that the Petticoat Affair, in which John Eaton's marriage to Margaret Timberlake O'Neale became a social scandal, had a detrimental

Opponents took great delight in highlighting the disruption that the Eaton affair was having on Jackson's presidency. (*Bettmann/Corbis*)

effect on Andrew Jackson's presidency. Jackson did not handle the matter delicately, believing that he could essentially force obedience among his cabinet underlings. The president quickly learned that in matters of social etiquette and genteel propriety, he had no sway among Washington's elite. He certainly had no sway with the cabinet secretaries' wives. Yet the Petticoat Affair was merely one matter amid a host of political issues that divided the men in Jackson's administration. The larger problem was the political ambition of Jackson's leading advisers. John Calhoun and Martin Van Buren both coveted the executive office and each spied the other jealously, hoping to gain greater influence with the president. The cabinet officers were aligned with one faction or the other and this power struggle infused Jackson's administration with an immediate competitiveness and lurking distrust. There is no doubt that the Petticoat Affair involved real matters of social decorum and propriety. Yet, it is equally true that Margaret Eaton was abused for political reasons that had nothing to do with her forward nature and questionably timed marriage to John Eaton.

The creation of Jackson's so-called Kitchen Cabinet has, for many historians, revolved around the problems instilled by the sexual scandal over the Eatons. They have argued that the president's cabinet was paralyzed and ultimately disintegrated due to the pressure of the affair and the disharmony that it caused. This is simply not the case. The Petticoat Affair did cause problems for Jackson and his cabinet secretaries, but as Richard Longaker and Richard Latner have forcefully proven—and no historian has engaged in better studies of the matter—the Kitchen Cabinet was not an alternative to the official cabinet. Rather, it was a supplementary advisory system of trusted friends and political allies who counseled the president on a wide variety of issues related to administrative policy.

Whether Jackson envisioned a more professional core of White House advisers and thus ushered in a more modern notion of the presidency, as Latner argues, can be debated. What is more likely is that Jackson had always operated by gaining the counsel of those whom he trusted. His cabinet was filled with political men who had political aspirations, and Jackson had come to the presidency with a distinct distrust of such men and a mission to reform the government following the Corrupt Bargain of 1825. He therefore most certainly viewed the need for confidants as even greater than at any other time in his life. Hence the existence of what historians continue to call the Kitchen Cabinet. Whereas it is always valid and fun to study sexual scandal, we must remember that political machinations are never far below the surface, and there are inevitably ulterior motives at play.

References and Further Reading

Bassett, John Spencer. *Correspondence of Andrew Jackson.* Washington, DC: Carnegie Institution of Washington, 1926–1935.

Benton, Thomas Hart. *Thirty Years' View.* New York: D. Appleton, 1854–1856.

Cole, Donald B. *The Presidency of Andrew Jackson.* Lawrence: University Press of Kansas, 1993.

Latner, Richard. "The Kitchen Cabinet and Andrew Jackson's Advisory System." *Journal of American History* 65, no. 2 (September 1978): 367–388.

Longaker, Richard. "Was Jackson's Kitchen Cabinet a Cabinet?" *Mississippi Valley Historical Review* 44, no. 1 (June 1957): 94–108.

Marszalek, John F. *The Petticoat Affair: Manners, Mutiny, and Sex in Andrew Jackson's White House.* New York: Free Press, 1997.

Parton, James. *Life of Andrew Jackson.* New York: Mason Brothers, 1860.

Remini, Robert V. *Andrew Jackson and the Course of American Freedom.* New York: Harper and Row, 1981.

Webster, Daniel. *Writings and Speeches of Daniel Webster.* Boston: Little, Brown, 1903.

Children and Culture | 3

Gail S. Murray

In the late summer of 1840, the country's two political parties faced off in the nation's first grassroots presidential campaign. Replete with slogans, songs, cartoons, and rallies, the Whigs sought to upend the Democrats' domination of the White House with vigorous campaigning in all twenty-six states. The nation's children, however, barely registered such events. Young Lucy Larcom considered "'Lection Day" one of the year's major holidays in New England, with special dinners and cakes on offer. The world of antebellum children was circumscribed by locale, wealth, education, race, and gender—not politics. While twelve-year-old Andrew Taylor Still spent that summer farming with his father and hunting squirrels and rabbits with his three dogs in rural Tennessee, sixteen-year-old Lucy Larcom was working in a Lowell, Massachusetts, textile factory to help support her mother and seven siblings. A few years later, Charlotte Forten's childhood diary reflects a precocious young free black woman whose days were spent practicing music, discussing local civic events, strolling along the river, and studying with a private tutor. In Ohio, young William H. McGuffey attended a subscription school six miles from his home, and by age fourteen he had become a certified teacher himself. Further south, Frederick Douglass was chafing under the bonds of slavery as he was moved unwillingly from plantation to city, furthering his desire to escape to freedom.

Early nineteenth-century childhood experiences were as broad as the boundaries of the new nation and as varied as its peoples. Children did not progress from discreet and uniformly understood categories such as kindergartner, school boy, adolescent, part-time worker, college student, and adult. Instead, the vagaries of location, class, gender, education, financial status, and luck interacted to create a great variety of childhood experiences. Loss of parents, fluctuating finances, or westward treks presented new anxieties and opportunities for young people. Children did not follow predictable paths, for the uncertainties of life far outweighed well-laid plans, even for

Lucy Larcom

"We were taught to work almost as if it were a religion; to keep at work, expecting nothing else," wrote Lucy Larcom about her childhood in Lowell, Massachusetts (Larcom 1889, p. 9).

Born in 1824, Lucy grew up in a large family with nine siblings. Her father had been a sea captain but retired to run a small shop. By age three, Lucy was attending school with her older sisters. The class met in the kitchen of "Aunt Hannah," and all children studied in one room, with the smallest lying in the corner for afternoon naps. From memorizing the alphabet to reading one- and two-syllable words, Lucy soon progressed to reading sentences from the Bible.

Lucy and her brothers and sisters spent plenty of time outdoors playing games and enjoying nature, but never on weekends. Saturday afternoons were reserved for cleaning the house and doing all the cooking and baking needed for Sunday dinner. The children even took their baths on Saturday so that the entire Sabbath might be given over to worship and

Lucy Larcom's *A New England Girlhood* remains an important source for understanding nineteenth-century childhood. (Cirker, Hayward and Blanche Cirker, eds., *Dictionary of American Portraits*, 1967)

the wealthy. As children reached their teens, many found far more opportunities for mobility, paid labor away from the home, and advanced education than had the generations before the Revolution. Understandings of "childhood" as a discreet social category underwent significant alteration during the tumultuous Jacksonian period, resulting in the gradual development of a "children's culture" characterized by notions of "girlhood" and "boyhood." In addition, children's literature, child-specific consumer goods such as juvenile periodicals and toys, emphasis on more intensive maternal supervision, and greater vocational options also emerged.

This delineation of childhood is perhaps best seen in family portraiture. Whereas paintings of colonial children reveal stiff, elongated figures with somber expressions, dressed in facsimiles of adult clothing, antebellum family portraits emphasize children's individuality and the close-knit family circle. Colonial Americans might have understood childhood as something to be survived, a time of preparation both physically and religiously for the assumption of adult roles. However, the nineteenth century embraced a more

rest. To occupy herself during the long Sunday sermons, Lucy memorized the words to hymns.

Mr. Larcom suddenly died when Lucy was barely ten, leaving her mother to raise eight children. The older ones immediately found work, including her eighteen-year-old brother, who joined the crew of a merchant ship only to be captured by pirates. He barely escaped with his life and returned to Massachusetts to pursue a safer occupation. To support the family, Mrs. Larcom moved the family to Lowell, Massachusetts, where she ran a boarding-house for female mill workers. Lucy and her sister spent that preceding summer hand-hemming dozens of bed sheets for the new enterprise.

As someone who loved poetry and drawing, Lucy dreamed of attending a proper school. She found, however, that one teacher and one monitor (an older pupil) were hardly sufficient to provide much real instruction to the dozens of children in the class. Within the year, Lucy and her sister left school to work in the mills for the $1 a week they could bring home. Thus, at age twelve, Lucy found herself replacing bobbins on the spinning machines and attending school only during the three-month spring session. Staying in the noisy, dusty mill throughout the beautiful summer was almost unbearable, but the work was not all drudgery. She could visit with other girls and learn from them about life in faraway villages. She took pride in helping support her family.

Lucy's one break from work was when she moved in with an older sister's family to help with two young children. This common practice proved to be the chief way that girls learned how to perform all the household tasks expected of women, like making clothes, laundering, ironing, mending, child care, gardening, cooking, baking, and nursing the sick. Later, Lucy returned to the mills until her early twenties when she moved to Illinois to teach grammar school and attend one of the new women's "seminaries" or high schools.

modern notion of childhood. Drawing deeply on philosopher John Locke's educational theory that children were born with neither moral instincts nor original sin (his famous "blank slate" analogy), antebellum educators stressed the malleability and fragility of the child's psyche. Parents, especially mothers, were expected to instill moral values via stories and examples, creating in children an internal gyroscope that would steady and deepen their moral character in an increasingly mobile, diverse, impersonal world. Such intensive parenting became possible partly because family size declined from the eighteenth-century average of eight to ten children per family to an average of five children per family by 1850. In addition, a thriving market economy freed women from some domestic chores and comanagement of self-sufficient farms. Women found more items for purchase, whether eggs and butter from another villager, infant gowns and toys from a village shop, or a subscription to one of the new women's magazines.

Children also came more directly under their mother's influence in the Jacksonian era because of more sharply defined gender expectations. As men

This engraving shows the domestic scene of the Jacksonian Age. (*Library of Congress*)

cultivated careers away from the home, wives became the administrators of all things domestic: household design, standards of cleanliness, clothing purchases, religious and moral guides, and models of decorum. Catharine Beecher's *Treatise on Domestic Economy* (1841) became the middle-class guide to all aspects of proper domestic life.

Much of what has been written about childhood (and parenting) in antebellum America centers on what is called "prescriptive literature": materials that tell people how to behave, such as sermons, advice books, and didactic children's stories. These materials assume that all family systems operate in the same way and all parents want their children to embrace a standard set of values and behaviors. As such, they signify how adults constructed the ethos of childhood, how they thought children ought to be and do, but they tell us little about how real children actually lived and thought. Only by examining autobiographies, letter collections, and the few existing childhood memoirs can we know how closely parents and children followed such proscriptive advice. Perhaps the flood of parental advice literature is no surprise, given the social, political, and economic "revolutions" of the Jacksonian era.

The majority of children in antebellum America grew up in rural areas and lived at home until their late teens or early twenties. Their labor contributed significantly to the household economy. They began daily household chores at ages as young as three or four, and boys began paid labor or worked daily on the family farm by age twelve. Towns and villages provided tuition-based grammar schools, while rural children often walked to subscription schools during the nonagricultural seasons. Most states did not provide free public schools, and only Massachusetts and New York required school attendance prior to the Civil War. Children's daily lives were shaped by their work routines, a small circle of schoolmates and acquaintances, and their families. By the 1830s, however, an increasing number of young women and men left home in their late teens to seek work in factories or shops. As the opening paragraph illustrates, children growing up in Jacksonian America experienced a variety of work, school, home, religious, and play activities. This chapter now begins with the greatest obstacle facing the child born in the 1830s: survival. It will then turn to the ways that major antebellum social movements—school reform, evangelicalism, "child-saving," and the growing market economy—affected the lives of white native-born children. The next section explores the particular burdens of immigrant and slave children. Finally, the essay turns to a discussion of the "ideal child" found in prescriptive parenting manuals and children's literature and ends with assessing the material culture that was developing for middle-class child consumers.

Child Health

As it had in the colonial period, infant mortality remained a grave concern for antebellum parents. In the 1820s, for example, about 11 percent of Boston deaths occurred in babies under the age of one. The U.S. census of 1850 (the first to take account of mortality and admittedly fraught with collection errors) suggests that 17 percent of all deaths occurred in children under the age of one. Regional differences were minimal in terms of infant mortality, although rural areas generally had somewhat higher infant survival rates. Babies who died suffered from gastrointestinal illnesses, diarrhea, nursing difficulties, and common infections. Home accidents also took a large toll: babies suffocated in bed with their parents, nurses, or other children. Toddlers fell into open fireplaces or streams or wells, and farm animals trampled small children. In all regions, children frequently died from common communicable diseases. Family members drew on a wealth of oral tradition, herbal remedies, and a few published advice manuals to nurse their children through many illnesses. Where doctors were available and could be afforded, most subscribed to the "vascular theory" first popularized by Dr. Benjamin Rush in the eighteenth century. Believing that disease built up bad vapors that traveled through the body in the blood stream, doctors treated children by leeching, cupping, purging, and blistering the skin to release the "pressures" in the body. Probably as many children died from the effects of these treatments on already weakened immune systems as died from the disease itself. The drug laudanum was commonly prescribed for pains and fevers, although too heavy a dose could cause death. Charles King discovered that one mother whose child was burned from a powder flash treated her with thirty drops of laudanum and put sweet oil on her. She revived after thirty days.

Dr. William Dewees authored the first American text on childhood diseases in 1826. He was a professor of midwifery and thus observed firsthand many of the health struggles of young infants. He advocated breast feeding and observed that children needed different treatments from those used for adults. Little is known about birth defects and mental impairment among antebellum children. Cleft palates and cleft lips were common. Though parents might succeed in improvising feeding techniques for children with such handicapping conditions, life expectancy was much shorter than is true today.

Many antebellum writers painstakingly recorded their children's struggles with illness and even death, noting the child's deteriorating conditions, the futility of the purging and bleeding, and the waning of health. After his young daughter's death, Henry Wadsworth Longfellow expressed an "unappeasable longing to see her . . . which I can hardly control" (King 1993, p. 42). North Carolinian Caroline Mordecai Plunkett lost two children within three days, and her third child died thereafter at age nine months. A father writing in 1828 described the fifth child funeral in his family.

Among African American families, losses of infants and children were even greater. In constructing black infant mortality for the decades of the 1840s and 1850s, scholar Charles King found that twice as many African American as white babies died. For slaves, estimates of mortality of children under six range as high as 50 percent. Newborns suffered because their mothers had insufficient diets and were forced to continue strenuous work routines right up until delivery. Ironically, the poor nutrition of slave mothers meant their babies were often underweight, making delivery somewhat easier on the mother. Enslaved infants suffered from communicable diseases, worms, unsanitary conditions, and insufficient nutrition. Plantation diaries suggest that at least some slave infant deaths occurred at the hand of a mother who could not bear to raise a child in bondage.

Common Schools

Children who survived the first few years of life did not necessarily enroll in the local public school, for no uniform school program existed. The "common school reform movement" dedicated to free and mandatory public schooling took decades to achieve. In colonial America, education had been the responsibility of the family, and most children learned basic literacy at home or in the kitchen of a neighboring woman. By the mid-eighteenth century, private tutors and private academies provided European-style, classical education for the children of the affluent. Towns in New England and the middle colonies often contained various private or subscription grammar schools. Children in rural families, particularly in the southern colonies, learned what they could at home or were taught by a hired tutor.

After the American Revolution, many influential voices argued for the necessity of a well-educated citizenry now that men would govern themselves in the new republic. Thomas Jefferson drafted a proposal for universal (white) education for Virginia, which the legislature consistently declined to adopt. In Philadelphia, Dr. Benjamin Rush founded a Female Academy, arguing that young women, as future mothers, must receive a good education if they were to provide the moral context for future leaders. However, the gap between the "public good," evidenced by literate, informed voters, and the reluctance of citizens to tax all for the benefit of only some families was not successfully broached until the reform movements of the Jacksonian period. When reformers surveyed the hodge-podge of charity schools, private academies, Sunday Schools, and seasonal rural schools, they sought allies across the country to establish voluntary associations to promote better access to public education. Horace Mann and his sister, Elizabeth Mann Peabody, among many others, advocated longer school terms, division of students into classes, standards for teacher training, greater numbers enrolled, American (not British) textbooks, and a standard age for beginning school. (Parents commonly sent three- and four-year-olds to school with older siblings as a form of day care.) Reformers argued that schools were the best vehicles for teaching democracy to all while also inculcating such civic virtues as obedience, punctuality, politeness, and honesty. Reformers petitioned states to levy taxes to support a coherent system, keep attendance records, compel attendance up to a given age, and establish teacher colleges. However, most legislators resisted allocating state funds for what they considered local issues.

As towns and cities grew and the growing market economy provided more jobs that demanded accounting and literacy skills, reformers had an easier time securing longer school terms and establishing teacher training colleges. Class sizes in common schools could range from fifty to eighty pupils, so teachers relied on older students (monitors) to proctor and discipline the younger ones. Rural schools also varied widely in size, with all ages taught in one or two rooms. Because the school term was dictated by agricultural needs, some students, particularly males, needed many years to attain a basic grammar school education. Learning was mostly rote memorization followed by recitation. The entire community turned out for the end-of-the-year performances: spelling bees, declamations, and debates. In small towns across the nation, the public schools brought communities together by serving as community centers, social halls, and polling places.

Regardless of the number of African American families in the area, common schools were almost exclusively white. While white Quakers established some integrated schools, popular opinion led to almost complete segregation by the early 1800s. Abolitionist societies established a few African American schools. Because free blacks looked on education as a prerequisite for social and economic advancement, black churches and benevolent societies often established their own schools.

The need for a standard American reading text (as opposed to the common British texts) led two Cincinnati publishers to contract the services of William Holmes McGuffey, a former school teacher turned college professor. *McGuffey's First Eclectic Reader* (1836) taught beginning students basic reading skills while also injecting a solid dose of moral guidance and civic virtue into the stories. McGuffey streamlined the reading process as well, moving from the alphabet to short words and simple sentences, thus bypassing the arduous syllabic memorization that had typified the British instructional system. Through a series of increasingly difficult works, McGuffey's First through Fourth readers provided a basic grammar school education, while the Fifth and Sixth readers took young adults through a college preparatory curriculum. Revised twice during the century, these texts became the most commonly read books of the nineteenth century, second only to the Bible.

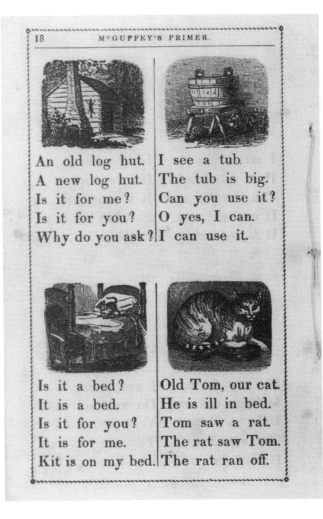

McGuffey's readers served as both educational and moral guides for school-age children. (*Library of Congress*)

As immigration swelled in the 1840s and 1850s, McGuffey's readers and the common schools in which they were used provided a communal body of moral stories, political speeches, and aphorisms designed to "Americanize" a wildly diverse population. Nonwhite characters appeared rarely and stereotypically. Told from a child's point of view, McGuffey's stories underscored the romantic innocence and goodness of children that permeated nineteenth-century culture. McGuffey also promoted national pride by featuring American authors like John Greenleaf Whittier, Washington Irving, Horace Greeley, and Daniel Webster. The private academies continued to provide a classical education for their elite clientele, but the common school curriculum based on McGuffey prepared young men for civic responsibility as well as for participation in the lively market economy and urban business.

Because of the common schools' emphasis on character development, school boards gradually came to hire more women as teachers, believing that women provided children more nurture and encouragement than did their male counterparts, thus opening up a new vocation for young unmarried women. Emma Willard's Troy Female Seminary in New York (1820) and Mary Lyon's Mount Holyoke Seminary (1837) offered diverse educational opportunities for middle-class girls. Catharine Beecher, a graduate of Willard's school, went on to establish the equally prestigious Hartford Female Seminary. Lucy Larcom attended Monticello Seminary in Illinois while she served as a teacher in the attached preparatory school. Female academies sought to provide a curriculum that would fit young women for their roles as wives, mothers, and teachers of young children.

Sunday Schools

The Protestant evangelicalism that swept down the eastern seaboard and followed circuit riders beyond the Appalachians in the early part of the nineteenth century redefined American culture. It also introduced a new social and educational opportunity for children: the Sunday School. Adopted from the English evangelical idea that working children could be taught to read on Sundays, the American Sunday Schools began in the 1790s. Early materials used simple biblical stories and conversion narratives to teach basic literacy and Christian beliefs. By the antebellum period, Sunday Schools had moved from urban settings to towns and rural churches. They became vehicles for the moral socialization of thousands of middle-class Protestant children. As in other aspects of the evangelical movement, women became the driving force, serving as Sunday School teachers while men almost always held the position of superintendent. Gender-divided classes met for Bible study and prayer on Sundays, but the entire Sunday School often gathered for social evenings, picnics, and other activities.

Although denominationalism remained strong in the Jacksonian era, mainline Protestants—Presbyterians, Congregationalists, Episcopalians—joined forces to establish the American Sunday School Union in 1824. Some 700 separate Sunday Schools came under its umbrella. (Methodists created their own Sunday School organization.) Organizers believed they could play an important role in shaping the youth of America by providing Bible study materials, moralizing children's fiction, and planting new Sunday Schools. In the early years, their publications concentrated on basic literacy, but by the 1840s, most of their publications centered on children's books and magazines. Eschewing specific doctrine, the Sunday School Union materials emphasized generic evangelicalism by teaching correct moral conduct and biblical literacy, and by urging repentance and conversion. They contracted with scores of authors to produce morally explicit tales that often featured a moral dilemma that the child protagonist solved or a deathbed conversion that stood as an example to the reader. To ensure wide readability, the books were affordably priced and could be purchased as a set for as little as $2.00. The *Youth's Friend and Scholar's Magazine* was available by subscription and arrived monthly in the mail, featuring stories, poems, and Bible verses. The American Sunday School Union thus had a major role in establishing a particular cultural content for the children's book market that gained momentum in the 1830s.

Work

Influential as evangelical religion and common school reform were on the life experiences of young people, antebellum children were first and foremost laborers. The majority of American families engaged in some form of agriculture throughout the period, suffusing children's lives with hard physical labor on a daily basis. Boys and girls alike began household chores by the age of five or six and often had full responsibility for certain aspects of the farm or household by age twelve. Boys plowed, planted, harvested, repaired implements, tended animals, built fences, and hauled products to market. Girls worked in the fields during harvesting, but during the rest of the year they also milked cows and gathered eggs; made butter, cheese, and sausage; and pickled vegetables. They worked in the vegetable garden, cooked, baked, hauled water, laundered, mended clothing, and tended siblings. Farm children attended school when they could, usually a three- to four-month winter term and a three-month summer term, although weather and illness could result in sporadic attendance. Once boys in particular had completed the third or fourth McGuffey reader, they often took paying jobs in the offseason rather than continue in school.

Except for the very wealthy, urban youngsters belonged to the world of work as well. Whereas many had trained as apprentices during the eighteenth and early nineteenth centuries, by the antebellum era industrialization and piecemeal production ended the distinction between skilled craftsman and laborer in many fields. Only butchers and shipbuilders took many apprentices. Instead, children worked various unskilled or semiskilled jobs. Both boys and girls could earn wages in the textile mills. In cities, boys served as runners and errand boys for urban businesses, unloaded wagons, sold food from carts, and hawked newspapers on the streets. By the 1850s, urban reformers like Charles Loring Brace began a lifelong effort to "rescue" urban boys from the "evil influences" of the city. Whole families might work in small apartments rolling cigars or making silk flowers for women's hats. Girls and women made lace and did fine embroidery for the growing commercial fashion industry, especially millinery. With developments in technology during the Civil War, boys began picking slate from the anthracite coal. These "breaker boys" sat for long hours near cold, drafty coal shoots with handkerchiefs covering their mouths to keep out the coal dust. They suffered continually bleeding fingers as the rough minerals tore at their unprotected hands. When families headed west onto the plains, children took up many pioneering tasks, including breaking up the thick sod with axes and butcher knives and hunting for edible roots and berries.

Few accounts exist that convey how children felt about their work. Earliest photographs (1850s) suggest drudgery and danger, yet children could also turn their tasks into games and pass the time by chatting with their comrades. Lucy Larcom entered the Lowell textile mills in the 1840s intent on helping her widowed mother support the family. In her memoir published near the end of her life, she noted, perhaps nostalgically, that there was a lot of play mixed in with her work, "frolicking around among the spinning-frames, teasing and talking to the older girls, or entertaining ourselves with

Children working in industrial settings was not uncommon. (*Library of Congress*)

games and stories in a corner" (Larcom 1889, p. 154). After paying for her board, she earned a dollar a week, more than she would have made as a seamstress or a teacher. Depending on family situations, most children's wages went to support the household, but in some cases, children kept back a few cents with which to buy candy or see a traveling show. Because the majority of children worked for their families, they saw no wages at all.

Children in Trouble/Orphans

Of course, not all children had families or relatives to care for them. Beginning in the revolutionary era, orphans became a major social concern in American cities. The city of Charleston established an orphanage in 1790 that cared for young children and apprenticed them out for wages as early as age ten. It was not uncommon for widows or widowers to indenture their children to an orphanage so that the parent could work full time for wages. Neighbors, clergy, and family members sometimes sent application letters to orphanages, urging them to take in a neglected child. Some letters stressed the dire poverty of a widow and her children; others sought the "moral improvement" that they believed the orphanage would provide. In such cases, the orphanage board would investigate the circumstances, and then ask the responsible party to sign a formal, legal indenture form. The parent thus relinquished his or her rights to the child for a specified period of time, usually until the child reached age eighteen. Some institutions accepted infants, while others remanded the infants back to the Overseers of the Poor, who had to hire a private nurse for the infant. Historian Priscilla Clement found that parents in Philadelphia sometimes used the orphanage as a temporary care facility until their financial situation improved, at which time they reclaimed their children. This practice so angered public officials that they began to require repayment for the care of children who were removed from their institution by a relative.

Whether cities, churches, or private benevolent societies established the orphanages, an appointed board of directors set the admission policies, arranged apprenticeships, and established house rules. They employed a matron and usually a cook to run the day-to-day operations and to keep a tight lid on expenditures. The children themselves took charge of housekeeping chores, including laundry, housecleaning, gardening, and dishwashing. Older children assisted younger ones in dressing and grooming. Most institutions required their charges to wear uniforms, making them readily identifiable as wards of the state when they traversed the streets going to church or school. Discipline was strict and corporal punishment common. Matrons worked hard to explicitly instill the virtues of obedience, punctuality, honesty, gratitude, and thrift in their charges.

Some Catholic and private benevolent societies set up institutions exclusively for free black children, such as the Philadelphia Association for the Care of Colored Children. For the most part, however, free African American children were reared within the African American community and were put to work as soon as practical. African American mutual aid societies assisted widows or widowers in supporting their children. Very poor black families were more vulnerable to having the courts remove their children from the home than were poor white families, and the courts usually bound out such children for domestic service to a white family.

Children born out of wedlock were another matter altogether. State paternity laws illustrated the courts' unflagging dedication to identifying the father of the child so that he, and not the state, could be held accountable for his child's upkeep. If such search efforts failed, most courts would force the mother to turn the child over to an orphanage or to the Overseers of the Poor to be apprenticed out and thus removed from the "evil influence" of the wayward mother.

Antebellum city officials also exerted control over children who visibly roamed the streets, neither working nor attending school. Authorities labeled their very presence "suspicious" and believed they were, or would soon be, involved in petty crime. Such children and teens were commonly sent to jail along with adult criminals. Members of the Society for the Prevention of Pauperism (SPP) in New York City argued that such children needed only honest work and a moral education to become productive citizens. They established the first house of refuge for child offenders in 1825 and drew their clientele from city jails, police referrals, struggling relatives, or their own patrolling of urban streets. Officials remanded children to a house of refuge less for criminal activity than for status offenses—acts like begging, idleness, or for being abandoned or "incorrigible." Children remained in the custody of the SPP until the age of majority. The New York House of Refuge took in over 500 children in its first four years. Ideally designed as a "home away from home," with skill-building work and moral guidance provided, the expenses involved in such "reprogramming" led institutions to contract out the children's labor for wages. The daily routine mimicked the antebellum orphanage in many ways, with children outfitted in uniforms or wearing badges. Corporal punishment for infractions of the rules was common and daily chores were mandatory. These institutions might provide basic literacy training, but they made no efforts to furnish real schooling. Houses of refuge proliferated to seventeen cities during the Jacksonian period. Although officials targeted boys far more often than girls, many cities built separate female facilities. One parent challenged the constitutionality of such incarceration and lost. Mrs. Crouse, unable to handle her daughter Mary Anne, implored the Philadelphia House of Refuge to take responsibility for her. Mary Anne's father sued the city for abrogating his parental rights in assuming her care. In *ex parte Crouse* (1838), the court found in favor of the House of Refuge, declaring that "it would be an extreme act of cruelty to release" the girl from the institution because the parents were "unequal to the task of education" of their child.

By the end of the antebellum period, the number of children labeled as potentially criminal or destitute far out-ran the spaces available in the houses of refuge. A new institution, the reform school, began to replace the urban houses of refuge. These institutions were built in rural areas, away from the "dangers" of urban life. They too met with limited success as they broke familial bonds; placed youngsters in impersonal, highly regulated institutions; struggled with indifferent employees; and operated on low budgets. Yet another solution for vagrant or troubled teens and/or impoverished children was Charles Brace's urban rescue. Brace was a twenty-seven-year-old Methodist minister when he founded the Children's Aid Society (CAS) in New York City in 1853. Its goal was to remove orphaned, indigent, and troubled children from the city and send them to live and work in rural households. One of the society's slogans was "The best of all Asylums for the outcast child is the farmer's home." The CAS rationalized the severing of parental rights by claiming that the fresh air and farm training available would save the child from urban temptations and a probable life of crime. Its main impact, however, came in the years following the Civil War up to the 1930s when thousands of youngsters rode "orphan trains" to the Midwest and the plains, some to happier lives but many to serve as unpaid laborers to grudging foster parents. Many ran away and looked for lost relatives or simply made their way on their own.

Slave Childhoods

Like almost all rural children, enslaved children could expect to begin household chores and farm tasks by age six at least. But there the similarity to white antebellum children ended. Regardless of skin tone, a passerby could identify the enslaved child by his or her muslin shift (no underwear) and lack of shoes. Oversight of babies and toddlers lay in the hands of an older slave woman, for mothers returned to the field or domestic chores for the slaveholding family soon after childbirth. On farms with a small slave population, babes accompanied their mothers to the field. Most youngsters saw little of their birth parents, as slave labor usually lasted from dawn to dusk, six days a week. Even urban slave children spent most of their day doing tasks for the owners, separate from parental oversight. Children's diets consisted of bread soaked in milk, cornmeal mush with molasses, or corn bread with greens and other vegetables. By the age of ten, most slave children found themselves at work full time.

Few jobs performed by slaves required reading or writing skills. Although Lafayette Price learned to read so that he "could tend to business," such opportunity rarely occurred. Occasionally white children taught some letters or words to their black playmates. Frederick Douglass related in his autobiography how he delighted in tricking the white boys of Baltimore into defining and spelling new words for him. Although the Great Awakening at the turn of the century resulted in some slave owners establishing Sunday Schools and teaching Scripture, by the 1830s such Christianizing of slaves was already on the wane.

Perhaps one of the most egregious aspects of bondage was the loss of parental authority over their children that slave parents experienced. When given conflicting advice or instruction by a parent and a white person, slave children quickly learned whom they must obey. As much as an enslaved parent might have desired obedience from his or her children, the parent had to teach them to obey white people first and foremost. Enslaved parents tried various subterfuges, like distraction, lying, or creating a disturbance, to protect children from punishment or excessive labor. Slave children had to learn to camouflage their own feelings and constantly curry favor with the slave-owning family. As they approached puberty, children faced sexual exploitation or sale. The most productive teenage boys were often sold to someone moving to the old Southwest (Mississippi, Alabama, Louisiana, and Texas). With the expansion of the cotton kingdom, planters chose the healthiest and strongest young slaves to accompany them to new settlements, drain the swamps, and clear the land. Teenage girls also became part of the lucrative intrastate slave trade. According to the Swedish traveler Fredericka Bremer, light-skinned, attractive slave girls often found themselves sold as "fancies"—girls who served white masters as mistresses. The market for young slaves was so well established that many teenagers who were sold away never saw their parents again.

In addition to enslaved children, thousands of other children in America could not claim citizenship even though they were born within the country. Whether living in settled Cherokee farming communities in Georgia or as transient members of one of the Plains Indian families whose villages moved according to season, Native American children could depend on little formal education. Most of them shared almost none of the dominant culture's values or socialization, and few recorded their childhood memories for historians' use. One such exception is the letter written by a young Cherokee girl, Nancy Reece, to the Reverend Fayette Shepherd in 1828 as some Cherokees fought white land grabs and Indian removal to the Oklahoma territory. She described the very "Americanized" curriculum of her mission school where students studied the usual Anglo subjects, participated in Sunday School classes taught by missionaries, and learned "useful trades." Even as a child, she understood the disruption to family and community that forced removal would bring and tried to argue for the protection of her people.

Advice Literature

Just as there is no agreement today among child development experts on the best way to train and discipline children, neither was there such agreement in the Jacksonian era. Rather, parenting advice fell along a spectrum that ranged from a strict disciplinarianism tied to evangelical Protestantism to a rational child guidance that acknowledged developmentally appropriate behaviors and skills. Mothers in particular sought guidance on how to instill moral values and provide effective discipline for their charges. The 1830s saw a proliferation of child-rearing manuals. Unlike eighteenth-century manners books, these later guides addressed a generation of parents anxious about the fitness of the next generation to accept civic responsibility and govern the young republic.

Many parents, particularly in New England, continued to practice the strict discipline they and their parents before them had experienced. Calvinism taught that children were by nature sinful and disobedient. The parents' most critical task was to break the child's will in order that the child be obedient to authority, whether that authority be parent, teacher, employer, or God. The *American Baptist Magazine* in 1831 carried a letter from "a plain man" (later identified as the Reverend Francis Wayland), who described how he had finally broken the willfulness of his fifteen-month-old son. The child had cried when handed over from his nurse to his father, so Wayland put him in his room alone until such time as the boy would respond affectionately toward his father. After repeated attempts to get the boy to take a piece of bread from him without crying, the father left the child to cry it out. The process took over a day and a half, during which time the child had nothing to eat and only a little water to drink. Eventually, the child responded affirmatively to Wayland, who wrote that ever after, the boy was "mild and obedient . . . kind and affectionate." For many evangelicals and mainline Calvinists, such breaking-of-the-will practices remained alive in the Jacksonian Era.

However, other parents adopted the more nurturing methods advocated by the popular parenting books of the 1830s: Lydia Maria Child's *The Mother's Book* (1831), Jacob S. C. Abbott's *The Mother at Home* (1833), and the Reverend Theodore Dwight's *The Father's Book: or, Suggestions for the Government and Instruction of Young Children* (2nd edition, 1835). These "child experts," among many others, embraced John Locke's belief in the malleability of the young child and sought the deep and lasting moral guidance that only parents could provide. Antebellum mothers supposedly had more time to devote to child nurture, since many domestic items could be purchased in the market economy rather than made at home. Family size began a slow decline in the eighteenth century as well, resulting in fewer children per family for the antebellum mother to nurture. Although parental authority certainly remained paramount, these manuals encouraged parents to govern children by appealing to their "affections," with the gentlest methods most likely to produce the best results. The newer, enlightened attitudes toward child rearing can be summed up in Lyman Cobb's work, "The Evil Tendencies of Corporal Punishment," published in 1847. All of these guides represent idealized prescriptions for rearing a child. The reality was undoubtedly as mixed and varied as children's personalities themselves.

Antebellum Child Culture

As the world of childhood expanded from the household in the colonial era to the worlds of family, school, and town in the antebellum period, a specific "child's culture" gradually developed during the nineteenth century. Evidence can be found in the material culture of the day: more child-specific furniture, specially crafted toys, and books and magazines just for children. With greater opportunities for schooling and nonagricultural employment, with westward expansion and greater religious pluralism, American culture "invented childhood" in the early nineteenth century. By 1830, girls in particular faced more options than at any previous time. Common schools and girls' academies multiplied educational options, jobs opened in New England textile factories, and reform activities drew many young women into an expanding female public sphere. Some domestic chores like spinning and sewing moved outside the home, freeing girls for other activities. Ironically, more rigid gender categories emerged at the same time, making "girlhood" a new signifier of cultural identity. Lucy Larcom wrote her memoirs with great nostalgia for her village school, leisurely reading, playing with her brothers, and working in the textile mill. Many families expected girls to forgo rigorous outdoor play in favor of more genteel pastimes. A thriving market economy embracing cash crops for farmers, new modes of transportation, and increasing numbers of manufactured goods made store-bought dolls readily available for Jacksonian girls. By the 1850s, girls' play mimicked the prescribed domestic sphere by including elaborately dressed dolls and fancy china tea sets.

"Boyhood" might best be defined in opposition to girlhood. Boys were encouraged to be physically active, to use errands and farming to explore the natural environment, and to adhere to a strict moral code while remaining loyal to friends and family. Boys were permitted more physical and moral leeway than girls, and much of their play took place outdoors as they set about running errands and doing farm chores. Toys and games prescribed for boys included marbles, stickball, jump rope, blind man's bluff, swimming, and ice skating.

Another marker of child culture was clothing and fashion. Children of both sexes wore long gowns during infancy and even after they learned to walk. Many nineteenth-century portraits show young boys in dresses. Not

Boys in the Jacksonian Age often engaged in traditional masculine activities. (*Library of Congress*)

until a boy was ready to attend school or assume farm chores did he begin to wear trousers, a tradition called "breeching." Beginning in the 1840s, military-style replicas of sailor suits became popular for the more affluent boys. Girls, of course, simply continued to wear dresses with long skirts or skirts, blouses, and aprons in imitation of their mothers.

Nothing reveals the child-centered focus that began to develop in the antebellum era more than the proliferation of juvenile periodicals and books. This emerging periodicals market brought mass-produced, affordable children's magazines into thousands of homes. They carried entertaining stories that nonetheless stressed proper manners, politeness, cleanliness, moral virtue, kindness to inferiors, and the nurture of animals, friends, and siblings. Popular author Lydia Maria Child edited one of the most widely circulated periodicals, *Juvenile Miscellany,* from the early 1820s until her forced resignation (over abolitionist stories) in 1835. Dozens of other popular periodicals carried poems, letters from readers, and didactic stories by such as-yet-to-be-famous writers as Louisa May Alcott, Jacob S. C. Abbott, and Harriet Beecher Stowe. Their stories helped to socialize youngsters into their appropriate gender roles and model domestic harmony and piety. In the last decade of the antebellum era, girls' domestic fiction featured "model" youngsters being orphaned, suffering debilitating illness, or being sent to live with unsympathetic relatives while never losing their good humor, kindness, or patience. The reader's own adolescent struggles thus paled when compared to the sufferings of the fictional protagonist. Susan Warner's best-selling *Wide, Wide World* (1850) found a large readership among girls and women alike, as it idealized and sentimentalized middle America's domestic ideal.

A surprising number of book titles for children came not from commercial publishers but from the presses of the American Sunday School Union. This organization contracted with scores of authors to produce morally explicit tales with formulaic plots. Affordable and available in collections, the

28   THE NEW-ENGLAND BOY'S SONG.

Over the river, and through the wood—
When grandmother sees us come,
She will say, Oh dear,
The children are here,
Bring a pie for every one.

Over the river, and through the wood—
Now grandmother's cap I spy!
Hurra for the fun!
Is the pudding done?
Hurra for the pumpkin pie!

Children's literature flourished during the years before the Civil War. (*Library of Congress*)

books often comprised the entire "children's library" of small towns. The stories avoided denominational commentary and focused instead on underscoring broad cultural values and gender roles. The immensely popular *The Dairyman's Daughter*, for example, used the untimely death of the title character to bring about a moral reawakening in others and sold over a half-million copies in the United States and Britain.

One evangelical, moral theme adopted by the secular press was temperance. Children's magazines carried messages about the dire consequences of alcohol: financial ruin, family strife, physical debility, and spiritual loss. One author wrote that the road to perdition began with "confections (plums, raisins, and candy), proceeding to cordials, and winding up at the grog shop." Temperance leaders across the country formed children's clubs known as "The Cold Water Army." They marched in parades under the temperance banner, signed pledges never to drink, and published their own magazine. In the Jacksonian era, Sunday Schools, school textbooks, and parental advice manuals conspired to imbue children with a conscious set of gender role expectations, moral values, and expectations of success.

By the 1840s, many American printers brought out children's books to meet the growing middle-class demand. Like the stories in periodicals, these books were chiefly instructive, stressing such themes as the importance of work, obedience, honesty, and self-reliance. The newer, enlightened parenting methods held that children should develop a conscience to guide them into self-governing adolescence without the need for constant supervision. No better vehicle for such training existed than children's stories and books. Jacob S. C. Abbott, a New England professor of math and an educational theorist, began writing popular stories for boys in the 1830s. His first *Rollo* book led to a series of some fifteen books about Rollo's boyhood experiences, followed by a second series entitled *Rollo's Tour of Europe.* Although Rollo's exploits might land him in trouble, he learned from these experiences—and so did his readers. Contemporaries praised these works as the single most important influence on children in Jacksonian America. The popularity of these semi-didactic stories prepared the way for the independent, middle-class aspirations of Horatio Alger, whose books became best sellers in the post–Civil War era.

Conclusion

No single characterization can capture the varied lives of children living in Jacksonian America. The extent and quality of their education, their participation in wage labor, their leisure activities, and their participation in organized religion varied immensely, depending on their family's location, financial status, ethnicity, and opportunity. The luckier children had choices about their future, but many did not. By 1860, the introduction of public schools, mass merchandising of toys and books, and advances in technology all changed the ways many children spent their days. The modern construction of childhood was about to emerge.

References and Further Reading

Gorn, Elliot, ed. *The McGuffey Readers.* Boston: Bedford/St. Martin's, 1998.

Greven, Philip. *The Protestant Temperament: Patterns of Child Rearing, Religious Experience, and the Self in Early America.* Chicago: University of Chicago Press, 1977.

Hawes, Joseph M. *The Children's Rights Movement: A History of Advocacy and Protection.* Boston: Twayne, 1991.

King, Charles R. *Children's Health in America: A History.* New York: Twayne/McMillan, 1993.

Larcom, Lucy. *A New England Girlhood.* Boston: Houghton, Mifflin, 1889.

McCullough, David Wallace, ed. *American Childhoods: An Anthology.* Boston: Little, Brown, 1987.

Mintz, Steven. *Huck's Raft: A History of American Childhood.* Cambridge: Belknap Press of Harvard University, 2004.

Murray, Gail S. *American Children's Literature and the Construction of Childhood.* New York: Twayne/McMillan, 1998.

Renier, Jacqueline. *From Virtue to Character.* New York: Twayne, 1996.

Schwartz, Marie Jenkins. *Born in Bondage: Growing Up Enslaved in the Antebellum South.* Cambridge: Harvard University Press, 2000.

The Jacksonian Frontier | 4

Elaine Naylor

Traditionally, Americans have thought of the frontier as a meeting ground between competing forces of community in the wilderness. The denizens of "civilization" may be envisioned as solitary frontiersmen, Daniel Boone- or Davy Crockett-like figures—clad in buckskin, flintlock at the ready with which to fight Indians or to hunt. Or, given the ubiquity of television reruns, the Ingalls family of the *Little House* series may spring to mind as the ultimate frontierspeople, determined to establish home, farm, and community in the wilderness The denizens of the wilderness are often stereotyped as Indian warriors. However, as understanding of the many complex societies of pre- and post-Columbian North America has been incorporated into the larger narrative of American history, such thinking about the frontier has shifted. No longer is the frontier perceived to be where the civilized and not-so-civilized struggled for supremacy. Rather, the frontier is where diverse peoples—non-European and European—came together, often in conflict, but always engaged in the creation of new societies. Thus, while Boone, Crockett, and the Ingalls may represent our most persistent and beloved stereotypes of frontier life, the identities and lived experience of frontier settlers are recognized to be far more varied. Certainly, there are some general characteristics that can be attributed to settlers. However, the diverse push/pull factors of migration, the various environments and economies of each different frontier region, and the broad range of both resident and immigrant cultures on any frontier, Jacksonian or otherwise, means that difference was as much a given as similarity. The primary goal of this essay, then, is to provide insight into Jacksonian frontier life with an emphasis on some of its diversity.

Acquisition of Western Lands

During the early nineteenth century, the American frontier lay west of the Appalachian Mountains and east of the Mississippi River, lands secured to the United States through the 1783 Peace of Paris and Rush-Bagot Treaty of 1817. The Louisiana Purchase made in 1803 pushed American sovereignty into the trans-Mississippi West, and the Adams-Onis Treaty of 1819 added Florida to the United States. The latter set Spanish/American boundaries in the West between Louisiana and Spanish Texas, then followed the Red and Arkansas Rivers to the Rockies, and the forty-second parallel to the Pacific. North of this boundary, Spain relinquished any claims to the Oregon Country that it shared with Russia, the United States, and Britain, but retained Texas, the Southwest, and California. In 1825, Russia finally withdrew its claims to Oregon, and in 1828, the United States and Great Britain agreed to joint occupancy. Thus, in 1830, American continental sovereignty was circumscribed by Mexico (independent of Spain from 1821) and Great Britain. However, the Jacksonian era was one of great territorial expansion; by 1853, the United States had reached its present-day continental configuration (excepting Alaska).

Even before the 1830s, however, Americans were leapfrogging across the continent, often moving beyond American borders as they spread American interests and settlement into Mexican territory and jointly controlled Oregon. As early as the 1790s, Americans built a Pacific Coast trade with Spanish California and Northwest Coast Indians. The 1820s saw traders traveling between St. Louis and Santa Fe, and in the same period, American interests in those towns developed a Rocky Mountain fur trade. In the early 1820s, Americans began to move into Texas, and by 1830, some 10,000 Americans resided there. In the 1830s, American immigration to Oregon began—at first missionaries who wanted to convert Indians—but by the 1840s, significant numbers of land-hungry Americans were on the move to the Oregon Country, settling primarily in the fertile Willamette Valley. At the same time, the inland valleys of California drew Americans.

By the mid-1840s, the growing American presence in Oregon both demanded and supported American expansionist goals to control at least part of Oregon; and in 1846, British and American diplomats negotiated a boundary along the forty-ninth parallel that divided Oregon between the two nations. In 1836, Texan Americans staged a successful revolt against Mexico, established the Lone Star Republic, and soon clamored for annexation to the United States; Texas became the twenty-eighth state in 1845. The 1848 Treaty of Guadalupe-Hidalgo, which marked the end of war between Mexico and the United States (1846–1848), and the 1853 Gadsden Purchase brought Jacksonian expansion to a conclusion. This period also saw the final removal of most Indian nations from the eastern United States to the trans-Mississippi West, a process that led to the creation of new Indian frontiers. From the standpoint of most Americans, Indian removal was important for securing Indian lands for Euro-American settlers in the trans-Appalachian west and the prairie lands along the Mississippi River.

Manifest Destiny, the idea that God had preordained the spread of the United States from the Atlantic Ocean to the Pacific Ocean, provided the popular and political rhetoric with which American expansion was promoted and justified. Many frontier settlers likely perceived themselves to be instruments of America's destiny; and, indeed, American settlement was essential

The idea of Manifest Destiny, that God had predestined the United States to conquer the North American continent, was central to the westward expansion of the nation. (*Library of Congress*)

to expansion. From the standpoint of most settlers, however, a more imme-diate reason to immigrate was the belief that the frontier would provide the economic opportunity lacking in more settled regions. Hundreds of thou-sands of Americans flooded into the West between 1830 and 1860, and when, during 1849 and 1850—the peak years of the California Gold Rush migration—some 300,000 people journeyed to California, their frenzy to strike it rich was only the most obvious and dramatic example of that Ameri-can connection between economic opportunity and the frontier.

The Western Settlers

Most westering Jacksonians traveled and settled in family groups. From rural backgrounds, their ideal was agrarian, and their goal was to acquire as much cheap land as they could so that they and their families could live as inde-pendent farmers and landholders. For settlers with northern backgrounds, the agrarian model was the family-operated farm; for southerners, it was the plantation. The decision to go west was made by the male head of the family; women rarely migrated independent of their families, and few initiated the move. Whether instigator or follower, however, it was hard to leave kith and kin, and people tended to immigrate with extended family and/or neighbors. Those who traveled together often stayed together once the journey was completed, helping each other to build homes, barns, churches, schools, and businesses. But even as settlers worked to create communities, further migration was not unlikely as individuals sought greater opportunity through moving again and again within the West. In every community, village, or town, then, there were those residents who stayed or persisted, but any community's population was also in flux.

Another significant immigrant group were miners, men who were mostly single or, at least, unaccompanied by their families. They hoped to strike it rich, and they were drawn to the West by mineral rushes in gold, silver, copper, or lead. More often, they ended up working for wages as laborers in large mines; as clerks, bartenders, loggers, sailors, and agricultural laborers; or as mill, construction, or transport workers. Early mining camps were very different from family-oriented farming villages and towns. If churches and schools were the center of farming communities, then saloons and brothels constituted much of community life in mining camps and in seaports and mill towns where the male population was also high. Even mining camps became increasingly respectable, though, as the number of resident families grew; over time, disreputable pursuits in any town or city were relegated to specific areas or prohibited. Just as most settlers hoped to find economic opportunity in the West, so they ultimately sought to re-create life as they knew it in the East, with well-built homes, prosperous farms, and flourishing businesses and industries, and with families and family life at the core of society.

Most Jacksonian settlers were Euro-Americans, and there were a few Mexican or Chinese immigrants. Another significant group were Indians who had been displaced from their homelands by Euro-Americans. Many such immigrated into what was called Indian Territory, a loosely defined area south and west of the Missouri River that included present-day Kansas, Nebraska, and Oklahoma. Many Native Americans, especially those whose traditional territories had been east of the Mississippi but north of the Ohio River (the Old Northwest), immigrated to Kansas. Between the late eighteenth century and the 1840s, some 10,000 people—Potawatomis, Delawares, Sauks and Foxes, Kickapoos, Shawnees, and others—immigrated to the west and settled in Kansas. Their earliest immigration was voluntary escape from American expansion. However, by the Jacksonian period, Indian settlement in Kansas had become involuntary, the result of a series of treaties negotiated between the federal government and various eastern tribes and bands—treaties that mandated settlement in Kansas.

Kansas, as part of the Louisiana Purchase, was visited by several American explorers, one of whom wrote that the Central Plains, of which Kansas is part, were not fit for agriculture. He called the region an American desert; the description stuck, and for many years, Americans traveled through Kansas and the Central Plains on their way to "better" places farther west. But Kansas was not a desert, nor was it unpeopled, even though most Euro-American settlers tended to think so before they arrived. There were hunting peoples in Kansas at least 12,000 years ago, and complex cultures developed there: hunters and gatherers who followed the buffalo; others who farmed, growing squash and beans and developing a variety of corn best suited to the growing conditions of Kansas; and tribes who combined both pursuits. Settled in Kansas when it became American were Wichitas, Pawnees, Osages, and Kaws or Kansas. The American Revolution, the intermittent warfare, including the War of 1812, that followed, and pressure on eastern tribes by the United States to cede land brought further peoples into Kansas seeking either new hunting grounds or homes.

Relocation and Acculturation of Native Americans

Some groups of eastern Indians initially settled in Missouri or Arkansas. In 1825, Osages and Kansas ceded not only lands there that were intended for American settlement, but also lands in eastern Kansas to be settled by Shawnees and Delawares, who then began piecemeal immigration to Kansas. However, there were many tribes and bands who refused to leave the Old Northwest even as pressures for Indian land increased and federal Indian policy shifted toward the goal of total removal of Indians from the trans-Appalachian West.

As federal Indian policies had developed, a constant goal had been to acquire Indian lands for American settlement. Early policy makers had also formulated a civilization program through which federal agents and Christian missionaries would Americanize Indians by teaching them to be Christian, independent, family farmers. Once Americanized, the theory went, Indians would not need their hunting territories, which would then be available for American expansion. Indians, melded into American society, would disappear as definable peoples. There were many factors that contributed to changes in this thinking, but most important, President Andrew Jackson, elected in 1828, favored removal of all Indians to the trans-Mississippi West, a position that brought him much voter support in the South and the Old Northwest, regions where the desire for Indian lands was a critical issue. The Indian Removal Act of 1830 mandated such removal. Jackson promised Indians that in exchange for their lands in the East he would set aside lands west of the Mississippi, guaranteed forever to those who settled on them. There was much resistance to the act, including the Black Hawk and Seminole Wars; but by 1850, most Indians had been removed from the eastern United States; by 1846 the Kickapoos, the Potawatomis, Sacs and Iowas, some Chippewas, and others had joined the Shawnees, Delawares, and additional tribes in eastern Kansas. (Most southern Indians were removed to present-day Oklahoma.)

Culturally speaking, who were the Kansas Indians? If the term calls forth an image of warriors wearing buffalo-hide leggings, riding out from a village of tepees to hunt buffalo or wage war with bows and arrows, the image—at least in reference to eastern Indians—is inaccurate. Indeed, differences between the indigenous peoples of the Central Plains and Indians from the East were so great that there was little likeness between the two groups. The Potawatomis, Delawares, Shawnees, Kickapoos, and others had been in close contact with Europeans for up to 150 years, and they were acculturated. The indigenous Plains peoples, meanwhile, were still largely traditional in culture. To say that eastern Indians were acculturated is not, however, to say that they were less "Indian" than the traditional Plains peoples. Eastern Indians had not been assimilated, or Americanized, and their self-identities were tribal and Indian. Yet their economies, politics, and cultural practices had absorbed over time some European attributes. Potawatomi acculturation, for instance, was reflective of their long history with the French, with whom they had been allies against the British and partners in the Indiana and Michigan fur trade from the 1670s to the 1760s. As cultural brokers, the colonial French had been merchants and entrepreneurs; and the Potawatomis, especially the many Métis among some bands, had built on generations of their own commercial experience in the fur trade to become successful entrepreneurs. They built log homes, rode fine horses, and dressed in a combination of European and traditional styles: women wearing skirts, blouses, shawls and leggings; men, ruffled shirts, frock coats, and leggings, both displaying impressive silver jewelry. Once removed to the West, many Potawatomis, female and male, reestablished themselves as entrepreneurs, especially capitalizing on the passage of American settlers through Potawatomi lands on their way to the far West. Potawatomis—who farmed, constructed gristmills and sawmills, and raised livestock—sold their produce, cornmeal, lumber, meat, and horses to travelers. Some operated ferries at river crossings or built toll bridges over streams and rivers; others supplied provisions to the military. Potawatomi women ran inns and restaurants. Some Potawatomi farms were successful enough to ship surplus crops east, and it was Potawatomis who used the first McCormick's Reaper in Kansas. Thus, some historians have argued that it was the Potawatomis and other acculturated eastern Indians who brought Euro-American ways to the Plains frontier decades before Euro-Americans settled there in any numbers.

Possession of firearms was another important aspect of acculturation. Largely settled along the Kansas border with Missouri, eastern Indians were closer to eastern trade centers than indigenous Indians, so they had greater access to firearms. Use of firearms, but also tactics of warfare acquired through acculturation, sometimes gave eastern Indians an edge in the very competitive world that was the Central Plains. The Delawares, for example, had become buffalo hunters when they migrated across the Mississippi, but only by continual fighting could they survive, their homes being near territory defended so well by Pawnees that reportedly strangers risked almost certain death hunting there. So intense was the warfare between Pawnees and Delawares that the federal government negotiated a treaty in 1833 by which the Pawnees ceded hunting territory for the use of the Delawares and other eastern Indians. Warfare was renewed between Pawnees and Delawares, however. Despite negotiating agreements of peace with tribes as many as 2,000 miles to the west, Delawares, in adapting to survival in Kansas, became experts at maintaining a competitive edge through violent exchanges not only with the Pawnees, but also with Kiowas, Sioux, Cheyenne, and others throughout the Great Plains. Shawnees, Sacs and Foxes, and Potawatomis also established themselves as formidable competitors with indigenous tribes. For instance, in the summer of 1853, a group of Pawnees and one of

Potawatomis and Sacs and Foxes were hunting buffalo. Pawnees were attacked by a large body of Cheyennes, Arapahoes, Kiowas, Kiowa-Apaches, and Brule Sioux. The Pawnees sought the aid of eastern Indians who were not only well armed but were also trained in tactics acquired in warfare as British allies in the War of 1812. Using British troop formations, the Potawatomis forced the aggressors to retreat. In a similar incident a year later, 200 Potawatomis and Sacs and Foxes defeated some 800 Cheyennes, Kiowas, Comanches, and Osages.

Forced to settle in Kansas, eastern Indians had to compete. Their acculturation provided valuable tools of survival, but they were not assimilated and had no desire to be. Yet the federal Indian agents and missionaries attached to specific tribes and bands were committed to the federal assimilationist program. They tried to inculcate Indian men, who were to give up warfare, in farming and livestock-raising, and Indian women in such domestic arts as spinning, weaving, and household management. Families were expected to live in nuclear households in log cabins on individual farmsteads. Collective activities were to give way to individual pursuits; for instance, family farming replacing traditional communal farming. Children would attend school and speak English; all would become Christian. Thus, while many eastern Indians were engaged in getting and keeping a foothold on the Central Plains so as to hunt, their agenda ran counter to that of the Indian agents and missionaries settled among them. However, even as hunting and warfare remained essential to the survival of many eastern Indians in Kansas, cooperation with the proponents of the civilization program became another means of survival.

Shawnees provide an example. Up until the end of the eighteenth century, despite incorporating some European trade goods into their culture, Shawnees had continued to follow a traditional lifestyle. They maintained semi-permanent villages but were also mobile, variously hunting, fishing, gathering, and farming—all while resisting American expansion. However, a few Shawnees—especially the band of Black Hoof—concluded that their survival might require adapting some American ways, and they welcomed missionaries who introduced the civilization program. As the social disruption caused by military defeats, territorial displacement, disease, and alcohol abuse spiraled in the early nineteenth century, increasing numbers of Shawnees came to believe with Black Hoof that their traditional way of life must give way to the American. Further, in Kansas, those who did try to follow semi-nomadic ways found that the growing competition for game between indigenous and eastern Indians made this lifestyle increasingly more precarious. Thus, more and more Shawnees acculturated, if only for their children's sake. There was a Shawnee willingness to collaborate with government agents and missionaries by becoming farmers, an occupation at which Shawnees were successful, and by asking that schools be established. As Black Hoof declared, education was an evil that must be endured so that Shawnee children would learn to survive in their rapidly changing world.

However, far fewer Shawnees converted to Christianity than embraced farming and schooling. Traditional spirituality was too essential to Shawnee

The Vermillion Kickapoo in Kansas

Although most Jacksonian settlers moved to the frontier because they hoped to find economic opportunity, Indian settlers hoped to find survival. For some, partial adaptation to American ways was one of such means. The Vermillion Kickapoos demonstrate how taking on aspects of Euro-American culture facilitated not only Indian survival but also the freedom to remain identifiably Kickapoo. The Vermillion, followers of a charismatic religious leader and chief named Kennekuk, migrated to Kansas in the years following the Indian Removal Act.

When Kennekuk was wild and young, he had left his tribe following his murder of a fellow Vermillion. After years of wandering, he was inspired to return to his people, bringing with him a religious message that energized and renewed the Vermillion. In time, Kennekuk gathered some 400 dedicated followers who believed his teachings came from the Great Spirit. Kennekuk's gospel was not Christian, although it had Christian elements; these, in combination with aspects of traditional Kickapoo spirituality, created a syncretistic, Native American faith. Kenekuk told his followers that the Great Spirit wanted them to live in peace with one another because everyone—red, white, or black—was a child of God. He said that everyone should love one another and not fight with each other. He also told his followers

identity to be jettisoned. Nevertheless, just as the decision to send children to school or to practice Euro-American-style farming was a pragmatic choice, conversion could also be an exercise in expediency. American interference in Shawnee lives may have led to a conviction that it was better to attach oneself to the American God, as professing to be Christian could also bring political rewards. Missionaries and federal agents were powerful people in Indian Territory, and they favored those Indians who were willing to become Christian as well as to acculturate. Conversion and/or acculturation could cement relationships between ambitious leaders and agents or missionaries. For others, taking up Christianity may have been one more step in the process of adjusting to the intense change of the period. Nevertheless, by the late 1840s, while all 931 Kansas Shawnees were farmers, only approximately one-quarter were Christians. Some variation of acculturation, cumulative and/or pragmatic, was thus important as a means of survival for eastern Indians, although becoming acculturated did not mean becoming less Indian.

Throughout most of the Jacksonian period, Kansas was at the edge of American territory; completion of continental expansion shifted it to the center of the nation. When Indian Kansas became Kansas Territory in May 1854, the question of whether Kansas should be a slave or free state catapulted the territory into that violent rehearsal of the Civil War known as Bleeding Kansas. Of more importance to Kansas Indians, however, was not the question of slaves; it was the resurgence of American desire for Indian lands. Beginning in the early 1850s, Shawnees, Delawares, Potawatomis, Kickapoos, and the other eastern Indians, as well as indigenous Kansas peoples, were pressured to cede their lands to Euro-American settlers. By 1875,

to abstain from drinking alcohol, and he persuaded the men to take up farming, which traditionally had been women's work among the Kickapoo.

Since warfare and hunting had been essential to Kickapoo masculinity, Kennekuk's religion was a radical departure from traditional Kickapoo life. Nevertheless, the Vermillion were well served by the maintenance of peaceful relations with others, abstinence from drinking, and dedication to Euro-American-style farming—in Kansas, they grew crops of corn, beans, and pumpkins; raised livestock and ponies; and harvested sufficient timber for their needs. They appeared to be assimilated, and their religion, because it had Christian elements, assuaged official concerns that the Vermillion convert to Christianity. Nevertheless, the religion's traditional elements supported the continuance of an Indian identity; it drew the Vermillions together and provided them with the group cohesion necessary to survive in Kansas. In 1854, when Kansas became a territory and was opened to American settlement, the same group cohesion that had ensured survival provided the Vermillion the strength to resist pressures from American officials and settlers to remove to what remained of Indian Territory in present-day Oklahoma—pressures they were able to resist.

of the 10,000 eastern Indians who had migrated to Kansas, less than 1,000 remained, the rest having removed to Oklahoma.

American Settlers in Texas

In 1820, Moses Austin, a bankrupt entrepreneur from Missouri looking to reestablish his family's fortunes, approached Spanish officials in San Antonio, Texas, with a proposal to bring American settlers to Texas. Up to this time, Spanish experience with Americans in Texas had been largely negative. American filibusters (private companies bent on seizing Texas territory) had plagued Texas in the 1810s. Other Americans who had crossed into east Texas beginning around 1815 were often poor subsistence farmers who were thought by the Spanish to possess little potential for the economic development of Texas. Austin promised to bring a "better" sort of settler to Texas, and his proposal was accepted. (Moses died of pneumonia, contracted on his journey back to Missouri, but his son Stephen replaced him as empresario, or promoter.)

Spanish officials were willing to accept Austin's proposal for several reasons. Long worried that the United States might try to annex Texas, they reasoned that if the non-Indian population of Texas grew through immigration, even if the immigrants were American, this might speed economic development, which in turn would block an American takeover. Also, the Spanish hoped that American settlers would act as a buffer between small, existing Mexican settlements and hostile Indian peoples living north of San Antonio. Thus, over a period of several years, Spanish and then Mexican

Stephen F. Austin was the principal leader of the United States' effort to colonize the northern Mexican frontier. (*North Wind Picture Archives*)

officials made land grants to Austin and other empresarios. Austin's first grant was for 200,000 acres of land along the lower Colorado and Brazos Rivers, thousands of which would be his. The rest of the land was to be settled by 300 families who would each receive either a labor (177 acres) of farmland or a league (4,428 acres) of grazing land. Austin received three further grants of land for 900 families, and by 1823, the Austin colony numbered some 1,500 settlers. At the same time, approximately 3,000 other Americans had settled in east Texas. Then, in 1825, the Mexican government passed the Colonization Act, which opened wide the doors of Texas to Americans. The act offered approximately 4,500 acres of land to any family for approximately $100 in fees paid over six years. By 1830, 10,000 Texians, or American Texans, and their 1,000 slaves greatly outnumbered 4,000 Tejanos, or Mexican Texans, although Indians were still the largest population group at 20,000. By 1836, the population count was 30,000 Anglo-Americans, 5,000 slaves, 4,000 Tejanos, and 20,000 Indians. American immigrants willingly left the United States in a quest for cheap land and economic opportunity. Indeed, the terms offered by the American government to its settlers were paltry in comparison to what could be obtained in Texas; public land purchased from the United States was $1.25 an acre, sold in lots of eighty acres or more, and the minimum selling price of $100 had to be paid in cash. Texas thus offered an opportunity that many thousands of Americans could not resist, even though immigrants were required to become citizens of Mexico and formally convert to Catholicism.

Following an established pattern in American settlement, in that immigration tended to flow along parallel geographic lines, settlers in Texas were largely southern in origin, those from the upper South settling in northeastern Texas and those from the lower South moving into southeastern Texas. Tensions based in part on their southern background developed early between the Texians and Mexicans, an important dividing point being slavery. There had been slaves in New Spain, but as an institution, it had economic significance only in Veracruz and had hardly existed in Texas. Further, abolition of slavery had been an essential ideal of the Mexican Revolution and reaffirmed in the Constitution of 1824. Texians seldom even questioned slavery. Indeed, many brought slaves with them to Texas, and through various means of legal subterfuge—freeing their slaves and then contracting with them to serve for ninety-nine years as indentured servants—Texians continued to own slaves despite Mexican prohibitions against slavery. Most early Texians were subsistence farmers who lived in log cabins, ranged hogs and cattle, and grew corn and greenstuff for their own consumption; they had no slaves. Cotton, however, was produced for export, and the nascent cotton economy almost guaranteed that slavery would continue in Texas, since it was perceived as essential for any family hoping to seize more than a modicum of the economic opportunity inherent in the large Texas landholdings. Few Tejanos grew cotton, nor did they own slaves, their economy having long been based on cattle ranching. Further, they were Catholics, and despite intermarriage between Tejano and Texian elites, both elite and ordinary Tejanos believed themselves superior to Texians, who fervently returned the sentiment. Thus, not only slavery but also cultural tensions divided Tejanos and Texians.

In 1830, divisions over slavery and a failed rebellion led to a ban on American immigration. The ban was so unsuccessful that it was raised in 1833. Its failure presaged the end of Mexican Texas, as political instability in Mexico City in the years following Mexican independence exacerbated strains already present in Texan society. When the decentralized Mexican federal government was replaced in 1835 with a very centralized one, many Texans feared it would severely limit Texan control over Texan affairs. On this issue, Texians and Tejanos could unite. Although often unsympathetic to one another, Texians and those Tejanos who wanted American-style economic development shared important goals. Both were opposed to anti-immigration laws, any ban on slavery, and a strong central government that would meddle in Texas affairs. Social and cultural differences had created difficulties between Texians and Tejanos, but more immediate economic and political concerns thrust Texas into revolution in 1835. Texan independence came in 1836, achieved by the unified efforts of both Texians and Tejanos.

The Lone Star Republic would have a shaky career. Financially and politically unstable, it sought annexation to the United States from the first, a goal accomplished in 1845. Despite its precarious state, the republic's population continued to increase dramatically; the acreage granted to settlers, while less than before the Revolution, remained high and attracted many. In

1847, an incomplete census found 102,961 settlers of Anglo/Celtic, German, or Mexican descent, 38,753 slaves, and 295 free blacks. Once stabilized by annexation and with its boundaries extended and secured by the Mexican War of 1846–1848, immigration leaped again as some 70,000 immigrants arrived between 1846 and 1851. By 1860, the total population, less Indians, was 604,215 (30 percent were slaves), three-quarters of whom were southern in origin.

At the time of the Revolution, most Texians and their slaves lived in east Texas—south of the Red River and east of the mouth of the Nuences River—while the majority of Tejanos and Mexican immigrants lived in south Texas—south and southwest from the San Antonio River to the Rio Grande River. As before the Revolution, east Texas settlers were farmers, and while the plantation remained their ideal, most owned no slaves. They sometimes grew cotton for market, but their family-based labor force permitted little beyond subsistence farming. However, those who did own slaves—approximately one-third—were able to focus on cotton production. A measure of their success is that during the 1850s, profits derived from cotton were reinvested in slaves and land so as to produce more cotton. By 1860, Texas was fifth in the nation in cotton production.

In south Texas, secured to the state by the Mexican War, cattle ranching predominated. It was in this region that relations between Texians and Tejanos degenerated in the years following the Revolution and the Mexican War. Trust between the two groups evaporated as Texian fear of Tejano support of Mexico exacerbated cultural tensions already present. Tejanos were pressured to get out of Texas, and those who stayed had increasingly to accept political and economic subordination to Texians. Both symbolic and representative of the trend by which even Mexican elites in south Texas were divested of their social and economic power was the rapidity with which land changed hands; for instance, more than 1 million acres were transacted between 1837 and 1842, almost all from Mexican to Texian.

In 1836, there was still a great deal of open land in east Texas, but Texians pushed the frontier west and northwest in succeeding years. Indian peoples in east Texas had presented little challenge to Texians. Diminished in numbers by disease and early conflicts with Texian settlers, most struggled merely to survive on the insufficient territory left to them; some had formed protective alliances with the Texians against hostile tribes, especially Comanches. With expansion north and west, however, Texian settlers encountered a much different situation, one in which Indians and Texians became locked in a pattern of intermittent violence. Similar to conditions on the Central Plains, survival on the Texas plains and prairies had long meant a fierce struggle between the inhabitants—Comanches, Apaches, Kiowas, Wichitas, Caddos, and others—over hunting territory. As the Texian frontier advanced, competition increased for hunting grounds, and also for land. Partially sedentary agricultural tribes were forced from their territories, and competition over hunting increased, exacerbated by the destructive effects of cattle diseases on the buffalo herds. Raiding for horses, goods, slaves, and children (to be adopted), which had long been an aspect of Southern Plains culture, increased in step with the Texian onslaught on the Indians' world. Perhaps the most famous raid occurred in May 1836, when some 500 warriors attacked the settlement of Parker's Fort, in what is now Limestone County, Texas. They killed five men and two women; several other women were severely wounded, and all were reportedly raped. Five captives were taken: Rachel Plummer and her baby James, Elizabeth Kellogg, and John and Cynthia Ann Parker, aged six and nine. Once away from the settlement, the raiding party stopped, tortured, and again raped the two women; the party then split up. Rachel, who was pregnant, remained a captive for eighteen months. During that time, her little boy was taken from her, and her newborn was tortured and killed. Elizabeth Kellog was sold from one band to another, but finally was returned to her family seven months after the raid. The boys, John Parker and James Plummer, were ransomed in 1842.

As violent as was the raid on Parker's Fort, it is important to juxtapose it with another raid, one that led to Cynthia Ann Parker's return to her family in 1860. Cynthia Ann grew into womanhood among Comanches. She married Peta Nocoma, a war chief, and together they had two sons and a daughter. In 1860, she was taken prisoner in a raid on an Indian camp; the attackers were a force of settlers, Texas Rangers, and cavalry who were in pursuit of a group of Comanches who had recently attacked an isolated homestead. After driving that family from their cabin, the Comanche raiding party had chased the pregnant wife, stripped, tortured, and raped her. The wife died four days later after giving birth to a stillborn child. The Texan party tracked the Comanche raiders to where they and their families were encamped, the women preparing winter stores of buffalo meat and berries. Surprising the band, the pursuers killed not only warriors, but the women of the band, who, knowing its importance to their families' survival, were trying to escape burdened with heavy stores of dried and partially dried foodstuffs. Even the Indians' dogs were slaughtered as they tried to defend their owners against the Texans. Cynthia Ann, identified as non-Indian because of her blue eyes, was taken prisoner and returned to family members. She died in 1870. During her remaining years, Cynthia Ann never ceased to mourn the loss of her sons, whom she was forced to leave behind, and her daughter, who died of pneumonia in 1864. Cynthia Ann's son, Quannah Parker, grew up to become a great Comanche leader in war and in defeat. After the Comanches were confined to a reservation in Oklahoma, Quannah was tireless in his efforts to help his people survive reservation life. Cynthia Ann's story illustrates how two-sided the violence was as Indians and Texians struggled, one people to remain on what was their homeland, the other to create new homes in the same territory.

Governmentally, this struggle was reflected in the failure of both the republic (and later the state) of Texas and federal officials to effect a peaceful solution to the conflicting goals of Indians and Texians. Even when some Indians successfully established themselves on agricultural lands that had been set aside for them, conflicts between raiders and settlers doomed the experiment, as all Indians were perceived to be hostile by most Texians. In the summer of 1859, reservation Indians were removed to what is now Oklahoma. Warfare on the frontier between warring Indians and Texians continued into the 1870s, when those Indians were finally removed to Oklahoma as well.

Quannah Parker was the son of Comanche chief Peta Nacoma and Cynthia Ann Parker, who was captured by the Comanches in 1836. (*National Archives*)

American Settlers in the Pacific Northwest

Although sizable numbers of Americans lived in Oregon by the late 1840s, what would one day be the state of Washington was still sparsely settled by Americans, and in the Puget Sound region, only 100 or so farmers lived in and around present-day Olympia. By 1860, however, 5,000 Americans were in residence, and bustling settlements dotted the shores of Puget Sound at Port Townsend, Port Ludlow, Steilacoom, Seattle, and Olympia. Unlike eastern Indians, these Euro-American settlers came of their own volition. Like

Texians, they sought economic opportunity, and many were farmers. What really drove Puget Sound settlement, however, was the development of a lumber industry, and many immigrants sought economic opportunity, not in farming, but in lumber milling, entrepreneurial pursuits, and promotional schemes for the region's economic development. Although the Hudson's Bay Company had developed a limited Pacific trade in Northwest lumber, it was gold rush California that stimulated the growth of a lumber industry in the Pacific Northwest, especially on Puget Sound. Gold was discovered in the spring of 1848, and by late 1849, San Francisco was the most booming of all boom towns, but there was little accessible timber close at hand to meet its building needs. Legend has it that ships from San Francisco first entered Puget Sound in 1850 seeking ice to cool the champagne of thirsty gold rush millionaires. They were sorry to discover that Puget Sound was ice-free, but the ships' captains soon recovered at finding a vast inland sea with forests of easily harvested timber growing to the water's edge. Here was the answer to California's lumber needs; forget the champagne!

While this story is surely apocryphal, by 1851, ships were sailing regularly from San Francisco to Puget Sound and returning laden with cargoes of squared timbers—costing eight cents a foot shipside and selling for $1 a foot in San Francisco. San Franciscans soon saw even greater potential for profits in establishing lumber mills at harvest point, and in the next few years, numerous lumber mills were built on Puget Sound. These cargo mills—as opposed to mills that produced for local use—were initially intended to serve California's needs, but owners quickly moved to develop markets around the Pacific Rim. By decade's end, the mills were producing millions of board feet in lumber products and employing hundreds of mill workers. Small towns sprang up around the mills, typically including a wharf for loading lumber, sawmill buildings, housing for employees and their families, a general store, a hotel, and a saloon or two. There were shipbuilding firms in some of the mill ports, and throughout the forested hinterlands, small logging companies ventured from the shoreline to work the woods from logging camps, some of which eventually became permanent settlements. This industry then provided both large-scale economic opportunities for capital investment in the mills and larger shipyards and small-scale opportunities in small boat-building, logging, construction, shop and saloon keeping, and available skilled and unskilled wage labor.

The lumber industry gave rise to another: shipping. Port Townsend, founded in 1851 and the region's customs port of entry, demonstrates how shipping provided entrepreneurial settlers with economic opportunities. All shipping had to stop at Port Townsend, and a growing collection of businesses catered to shipping: warehouses, wharves, shipping agencies, chandlers who sold merchandise necessary to shipping, butchers who sold salted meat to ship captains, bakeries that advertised ship's bread, hotels and sailors' boardinghouses, restaurants, public bathhouses, and barber shops. Also flourishing were saloons and seedier establishments, such as brothels and gambling dens.

There were other perceived economic opportunities. Some Port Townsendites believed the town might develop into the economic center of Puget

Port Townsend, located on Puget Sound in the Washington Territory, was an important port for goods entering the Pacific Northwest. (*Library of Congress*)

Sound, and with this goal in mind, they became boosters, promoting settlement and capital investment in Port Townsend and its hinterlands. Boostering was very much a phenomenon of the nineteenth century, when the acquisition of immense reaches of land by the United States and the movement of increasingly larger numbers of people westward encouraged popular thinking about economic development on the frontier. During the Jacksonian period and beyond, boosters' theories of economic growth were commonly accepted wisdom with regard to frontier development, and booster literature was widely read. Boosters expressed the nineteenth-century belief in the inevitability of expansion and frontier development. Such development would naturally provide individuals with economic opportunity; and some settlers sought their own economic future through taking part in the development of a specific region or town, such as Port Townsend.

Some of the earliest American ideas about expansion centered on finding the Northwest Passage, which would connect Europe and North America to the riches of Asia. However, by the late Jacksonian period when Puget Sound was being settled, this search had long since been replaced by plans for building transcontinental railroads that would connect North America, Asia, and Europe. Also important to this thinking was the acquisition of Pacific Coast ports. During negotiations over Oregon, diplomats were determined that Puget Sound should be American. Boosters also emphasized the importance of cities as transportation and commercial hubs for the exploitation of western resources: timber, agricultural lands, minerals, and so on. Thus, urban development was an essential aspect of economic development. Because boosterist goals were necessarily projected onto the future, an important task for boosters was to predict where a city might develop and then to convince people to immigrate and/or invest capital there. Thus, in Port Townsend, there were settlers who saw economic opportunities not only in the development of the lumber industry and other businesses but also of the town itself. They believed their future was tied to that of Port Townsend and its hinterlands, and some of these settlers actively sought to effect boosterist goals. They produced promotional books, newspaper and magazine articles, pamphlets, flyers, and maps and even letters written back home, all pitched to appeal to potential immigrants and capitalists. They also made attempts to convince railroad companies that Port Townsend was ideal as a transcontinental railroad terminus; they courted San Francisco investment in the development of local iron deposits; they funded a locally owned lumber mill; and they released lobsters into Port Townsend waters to seed a lobster fishery. Ultimately, Port Townsend boosters failed (the town never became a city), but their search for economic opportunity through resource exploitation and urban development was not an uncommon frontier experience.

References and Further Reading

Abing, Kevin. "A Holy Battleground: Methodist, Baptist, and Quaker Missionaries among Shawnee Indians, 1830–1844." *Kansas History* 21 (1998): 118–137.

Binns, Archie. *The Roaring Land*. New York: R. M. McBride, 1942.

Boag, Peter G. *Environment and Experience: Settlement Culture in Nineteenth-Century Oregon*. Berkeley: University of California Press, 1992.

Bristler, Louis E. "Eduard Ludecus's Journey to the Texas Frontier: A Critical Account of Beales's Rio Grande Colony." *Southwestern Historical Quarterly* 108 (2005): 368–385.

Britton, Diane F. *The Iron and Steel Industry in the Far West: Irondale, Washington*. Niwot: University of Colorado Press, 1991.

Bunting, Robert. *The Pacific Raincoast: Environment and Culture in an American Eden, 1778–1900*. Lawrence: University Press of Kansas, 1997.

Bunting, Robert. "Michael Luark and Settler Culture in the Western Pacific Northwest, 1853–1899." *Pacific Northwest Quarterly* 96 (2005): 198–205.

Calloway, Colin G. *One Vast Winter Count: The Native American West before Lewis and Clark*. Lincoln: University of Nebraska, 2003.

Campbell, Randolph B. *Gone to Texas: A History of the Lone Star State*. New York: Oxford University Press, 2003.

Clark, Jerry E. *The Shawnee*. Lexington: University Press of Kentucky, 1977.

Coman, Edwin T., Jr., and Helen M. Gibbs. *Time, Tide and Timber: A Century of Pope and Talbot*. Stanford: Stanford University Press, 1949.

Cox, Thomas R. *Mills and Markets: A History of the Pacific Coast Lumber Industry to 1900*. Seattle: University of Washington Press, 1974.

Doig, Ivan. *Winter Brothers: A Season at the Edge of America*. New York: Harcourt, 1980.

Edmunds, R. David. "Indians as Pioneers: Potawatomis on the Frontier." *Chronicles of Oklahoma* 65 (1987–1988): 340–353.

Edwards, G. Thomas. "'Terminus Disease': The Clark P. Crandall Description of Puget Sound in 1871." *Pacific Northwest Quarterly* 70 (1979): 163–177.

Exley, Jo Ella Powell. *Frontier Blood: The Saga of the Parker Family.* College Station: Texas A&M University Press, 2001.

Fehrenbach, T. R. *Lone Star: A History of Texas and the Texans.* Toronto, ON: Macmillan, 1968.

Ficken, Robert E. *The Forested Land: A History of Lumbering in Western Washington.* Seattle: University of Washington Press, 1988.

Ficken, Robert E., and Charles P. LeWarne. *Washington: A Centennial History.* Seattle: University of Washington Press, 1988.

Grimes, Richard S. "The Early Years of the Delaware Indian Experience in Kansas Territory, 1830–1845." *Journal of the West* 41 (2002): 73–82.

Herring, Joseph B. *The Enduring Indians of Kansas: A Century and a Half of Acculturation.* Lawrence: University Press of Kansas, 1990.

Hine, Robert V., and John Mack Farragher. *The American West: A New Interpretive History.* New Haven, NJ: Yale University Press, 2000.

May, Dean L. *Three Frontiers: Family, Land, and Society in the American West, 1850–1900.* New York: Cambridge University Press, 1994.

McCurdy, James G. *By Juan de Fuca's Strait: Pioneering along the Northwestern Edge of the Continent.* Portland, OR: Metropolitan Press, 1937.

McDonald, Lucile. *Swan among the Indians: Life of James G. Swan, 1818–1900.* Portland, OR: Binford and Mort, 1972.

Miner, Craig. *Kansas: The History of the Sunflower State, 1854–2000.* Lawrence: University Press of Kansas, 2002.

Miner, Craig, and William E. Unrau. *The End of Indian Kansas: A Study of Cultural Revolution, 1854–1871.* Lawrence: Regents' Press of Kansas, 1978.

Nackman, Mark E. "The Making of the Texan Citizen Soldier, 1835–1860." *Southwestern Historical Quarterly* 78 (1975): 231–253.

Napier, Rita, ed. *Kansas and the West: New Perspectives.* Lawrence: University Press of Kansas, 2003.

Newell, Gordon. *Ships of the Inland Sea: The Story of the Puget Sound Steamboats.* Portland, OR: Binford and Mort, 1951.

Nobles, Gregory H. *American Frontiers: Cultural Encounters and Continental Conquest.* New York: Hill and Wang, 1997.

Prucha, Francis Paul. *American Indian Treaties: The History of a Political Anomaly.* Berkeley: University of California Press, 1994.

Robbins, William G. *Landscapes of Promise: The Oregon Story: 1800–1940.* Seattle: University of Washington Press, 1997.

Sale, Roger. *Seattle: Past to Present.* Seattle: University of Washington Press, 1976.

Schwantes, Carlos Arnaldo. *The Pacific Northwest: An Interpretive History.* Rev. and enl. ed. Lincoln: University of Nebraska Press, 1996.

Throckmorton, Arthur L. *Oregon Argonauts: Merchant Adventurers on the Western Frontier.* Portland: Oregon Historical Society, 1961.

Warren, Stephen A. "The Baptists, the Methodists, and the Shawnees: Conflicting Cultures in Indian Territory, 1833–34." *Kansas History* 17 (1994): 148–161.

West, Eliot. *The Way to the West: Essays on the Central Plains.* Albuquerque: University of New Mexico Press, 1995.

White, Richard. *"It's Your Misfortune and None of My Own": A History of the American West.* Norman: University of Oklahoma Press, 1991

Women, Taverns, and Travel | 5

Kirsten E. Wood

Taverns abounded at the crossroads and street corners of antebellum America. Americans gathered in taverns to celebrate national holidays like the Fourth of July and George Washington's birthday. They listened to concerts, danced at balls, and gawked at traveling menageries in taverns. They bought and sold goods, traded stories, met friends, and cast their ballots in elections. Perhaps above all, they drank—especially whiskey. Many of these tavern-based activities were heavily associated with men. Women did not vote, for example, and they rarely appeared among those bidding at auctions or buying and selling commodities. Yet women were regular and even essential parts of the tavern environment.

Some women kept taverns in their own names, especially in more suburban and rural areas. In taverns run by men, women did much of the work. In most taverns, women cooked, cleaned, and waited on the patrons. Often, these women were tavern keepers' wives or daughters, and the tavern was really a family business. Men without female kin, or with larger taverns to run, relied on hired women or on female slaves for their domestic labor. (Tavern keepers also sometimes hired men to care for the horses or to tend bar. In the largest hotels, the cooks and waiters were men, but female labor predominated in most taverns.)

Women also entered taverns as customers. A dance or ball, such as the 1839 Stageman's Ball in Concord, New Hampshire, would be a total failure without women present. Special ladies' tickets were printed for a ball honoring Zachary Taylor at Niblo's Saloon in New York in 1850. Women went to taverns for concerts, dramatic performances, and exhibitions. In 1843, a tavern in Dover, Massachusetts, hosted a traveling menagerie and a band. According to Abram Hewitt, a law student visiting from New York City, most of the spectators were young women from the nearby textile manufactories. And in a nation on the move, thousands upon thousands of women traveled, and these women entered taverns regularly. Taverns were, in a sense, the

Women were necessary participants in the social life of taverns. (*Library of Congress*)

fast-food restaurants and the motels of their day, providing meals and over-night lodging for travelers. On a three-month trip in New York, for example, Sarah Howlands, her husband John, and daughter Martha stopped in at least seventy-five different taverns, returning to several of them twice or more. Serving travelers' needs for food and shelter had long been part of the justi-fication for having taverns in the first place. Colonial licensing procedures gave tavern keepers the right to sell alcohol by the drink in exchange for providing food and shelter to travelers and their horses.

The frequency with which women entered taverns, especially as travel-ers, is somewhat startling. If asked, most antebellum Americans would prob-ably have agreed that taverns were men's space. For their part, historians have generally considered taverns an especially masculine aspect of the American "public sphere": political or civic concerns and activities, especially those taking place outside the home. In contrast, according to countless novels, sermons, etiquette manuals, and poems, the home was women's special sphere. Women made their homes into sanctuaries against the hustle and bustle of moneymaking and politics, men's domain. In reality, even in middle- and upper-class families, which had the best chance of approximat-ing this ideal, the division between men's and women's worlds was repeat-edly broken and blurred in practice. So it was with taverns.

Still, most tavern patrons were undoubtedly men, and taverns remained slightly uncomfortable spaces for women, both as workers and as customers. This discomfort reflected not only the idea that women belonged at home, but also the nature of taverns themselves. Quite simply, taverns were often unappealing places. Some urban taverns were elegant multistory buildings with good roofs, plenty of windows, ample furniture, and decorations such as maps, mirrors, and paintings. In the countryside, however, many were rude log cabins. Some travelers complained that they could see the stars through the chinks in the roof. Others struggled with smoking chimneys or windows that either would not stay open or lacked glass altogether.

In city and country taverns alike, people often complained about the beds. In this period, it was relatively rare to get a private bedroom, and experienced travelers knew they could not even count on having a bed to themselves. Instead, they regularly doubled and even tripled up, with utter strangers as their bedmates. Usually, one shared a room or bed with people of the same sex, but sometimes, a husband and wife had to share a room, or even a bed, with a stranger. Some travelers were worse off, having to sleep in the barn, in the hayloft, or on the floor. At a tavern in Michigan, British writer Harriet Martineau observed fifteen children and two adults sleeping on chairs and on the floor. Travelers also complained that their sheets were dirty or wet. Damp sheets might inspire the hope that they had been recently washed, but they hardly made for comfortable sleeping. Worse still were the bugs. While not every traveler complained of bugs in every tavern, vermin were clearly a regular hazard for people on the road. Travelers tried to deal with the problem by sleeping on the floor or on top of their own cloaks, but many spent restless nights killing bugs and scratching their bites.

Perhaps the greatest complaint about taverns, however, was the food. Tavern meals were typically ample in size, but often lacking in other ways. Some travelers, especially city people and Europeans, could not stomach the coarse corn bread commonly found on southern tables. Others complained that the wheat bread was pasty, the butter rancid, and the milk sour. Those who expected coffee or tea often found these were unavailable or tasted foul. Some tired of the incessant ham and bacon they received, and one traveler suspected that she had been fed dog. Given this fare, travelers did not always mind being compelled to gobble up their food in fifteen minutes so that their stagecoach or train could get under way again. (European travelers, by contrast, despised Americans' haste at meals.) But sometimes, travelers who arrived at odd hours or visited taverns off the beaten track had to wait for hours or were sent away with empty stomachs because no one was willing or able to prepare a meal for them.

Women Travelers

Female travelers came to taverns for the same mix of reasons as their male counterparts. Some traveled for their health, while others journeyed for business, pleasure, or to relocate to a new section of the country. The problems of bad food and lousy beds bothered male and female tavern-goers alike, but in some ways, men's and women's experiences of travel and taverns were quite different.

Most notably, in antebellum America, it was unusual, although not impossible, for a woman to travel completely alone. While women did not need a chaperone, most preferred to travel in company, at least with another woman, and with a man if possible. For most women travelers, a man served as a kind of travel agent, arranging transportation and lodgings, taking care of the baggage, and settling the bills. Perhaps as a result, many women felt that a male escort was more of a convenience than an absolute necessity. In any case, women traveling without a man expected to get help from steamboat captains, stage drivers, and railroad conductors. Female travelers expected these men not only to look after them and their baggage, but also to book rooms in a tavern or hotel for them. When astronomer Maria Mitchell and her younger sister grew weary on the way from Knoxville, Kentucky, to Lynchburg, Virginia, for example, the conductor found them a place to spend the night. This helpfulness was not universal, however. Mitchell remarked that men in the South and West were significantly more solicitous than men in her New England home.

Once inside taverns, female travelers continued to behave and perceive differently from men. For example, middle- and upper-class women were more likely than their male peers to insist on having a private bedroom and a private parlor—and they were more likely to get them, as well. In a South Carolina tavern in 1814, Margaret Steele enjoyed a private parlor, which neither the other travelers nor the long-term boarders could enter. Such privacy was a real luxury. At this time, most taverns had only a few bedrooms, and they might have no parlors at all. Instead, they might have a single large room that served as dining room, barroom, and even kitchen. In such rooms, travelers mixed with long-term lodgers and with locals who came to drink or do business. In the 1830s, getting a room and a private parlor to oneself was still a luxury, although one that increasing numbers of well-off women felt was an essential requirement. More unusual still was a hotel that segregated its male and female travelers in separate parts of the building. By the 1850s, however, larger taverns typically had a number of private sitting rooms, while the biggest city hotels had ladies' dining rooms as well as ladies' drawing rooms.

Middle- and upper-class women expected and often got special treatment in other ways as well. An early guide to hotel management, written by a former headwaiter at the Howard House in Philadelphia, suggested that the proprietor or his immediate subordinate should escort women traveling alone to their seats at the dinner table. He should also write letters for these women to stage drivers, steamboat captains, and railroad conductors, bidding them to take care of their female passengers. In practice, some women seemed never to lack courteous assistance from tavern keepers and from their fellow travelers. In Hollidaysburg, Pennsylvania, one man found himself in a shared room with four beds because all the single rooms were reserved for female travelers. A woman got the best room in a Lancaster, South Carolina, tavern when a fellow traveler, one Colonel John Boykin, insisted that she should have it. Boykin's stepson wryly observed that Mrs. Edgar doubted her good fortune, apparently because Mr. Edgar rarely took such pains on his wife's behalf. A Mrs. Reed also received special attention in Huntingdon, Pennsylvania. After the tavern keeper learned that she was the new widow of a prominent jurist and law professor, he gave her the best his house had to offer and introduced her husband's former student to her. The student, in turn, personally escorted her to the train station the next morning and made sure her travel arrangements were in order.

Other women, however, had more difficulty in enforcing their sense that their mere presence required certain modifications to men's behavior. When Anne Royall visited Augusta, Georgia, she stayed at Mr. Shannon's tavern. Also resident were the Hull family, long-term boarders. One afternoon, while she was sitting and drinking tea in the parlor, Mr. Hull came to stare at her, pacing up and down the room without speaking. Later, Mr. Hull brought two men to her room uninvited, another liberty. At the dinner table, the rest of the Hull family "fell on me like so many wild-cats," badgering her with comments and questions, while the Shannon family looked on (Royall 1830–1831, vol. 2, p. 70). Small wonder Mrs. Royall preferred the New England custom of segregating travelers from regular boarders at the dinner table, to protect the travelers from the supposedly impertinent curiosity of the locals. A more common experience involved the sort of problem Elizabeth Willson had at a tavern near Zanesville, Ohio. Here, she was offended by the swearing of some young men who were drinking at the tavern. Even after they left the house itself, she complained that they hung around the barn, making a racket and burning her ears with their profanity.

As Mrs. Edgar's, Mrs. Reed's, and Mrs. Royall's experiences suggest, being female was not, by itself, enough to guarantee special treatment for themselves or good behavior from men. A woman had to be ready to demand the best and make a pest of herself until she got her way (Mrs. Royall's *modus operandi*), or she had to have a man willing to speak for her, as in Mrs. Edgar's case. As for Mrs. Reed, apparently the outward signs that she was a well-off woman (such as her dress) apparently were not enough to charm the Huntingdon tavern keeper, but her husband's name proved just the ticket. Visibly poor white women and black women of any appearance were far less likely to get the best rooms or any personal attentions from tavern proprietors. In Utica, New York, a poor woman who was taking her three children to meet her husband 100 miles away could not get so much as a glass of water from a tavern. In two and a half years in the United States, only once did Harriet Martineau see a black woman traveler allowed to eat her meal in the dining room alongside the white guests.

Even being well connected and white did not ensure that a female traveler would avoid rude treatment. Tavern keepers could be aggressive or insulting to their guests. In Vicksburg, Mississippi, a tavern keeper tried to throw Mrs. Royall out, threatening to eject her physically if she did not leave. In this case, she was perfectly happy to leave, since the sight of men gambling, swearing, and drinking convinced her that this tavern was the favorite haunt of robbers and pirates. A New York hotelier told Frances Trollope that if she chose to eat her meals in private, in the English fashion, she could leave his house. "Our manners are very good manners," he told her, "and we don't wish any changes from England" (Trollope 1832, p. 50).

For a woman, the hazards of staying in a tavern could go far beyond slighting words and treatment. In a Knoxville tavern, Maria Mitchell grew so suspicious of the tavern staff that she dared not leave her room for fear it

Anne Royall

Anne Royall was born in colonial Maryland in 1769. Married in 1797 and widowed sixteen years later, Anne Royall earned her living for thirty years as an author. Anne's first publishing success came from her books of travel journalism, in which she recounted her observations of the United States. As a traveling writer, Anne had extensive contact with tavern and innkeepers, and she arguably experienced the best and the worst of what taverns had to offer women in antebellum America.

Before launching her writing career in 1824, Anne lived in a Washington City hotel. There she experienced kindness well beyond the ordinary standard of special treatment for female travelers. Innkeeper Mr. M. E. Claggett not only gave her his best room, but he let her stay for six months, even though she had arrived all but penniless. Claggett also provided her with her own maid, a real luxury. Most important, he became a confidant, friend, and adviser, again far beyond the usual custom of tavern keepers providing local information and travel tips. At this point in her life, Anne was desperately looking for a way to make money. After many long conversations, Mr. Claggett knew that Anne could spin engaging tales about her travels, and he suggested that she write for her living. When she told him that she had already tried to find a publisher, he advised her to solicit subscriptions directly from readers and then self-publish (a common strategy in this era). As a hotel keeper and as Grand Master of the Alexandria Masonic Lodge, Claggett knew many important people, so he offered to write letters to promote her new project. With his help, Anne quickly collected subscriptions from John Quincy Adams, Daniel Webster, and many other luminaries.

Her first book, *Sketches of History, Life and Manners in the United States* (1826), was a popular success, and she decided to continue traveling and writing. As she toured, she made enemies as well as friends. She attacked tavern keepers by name when they treated her unkindly. She warned her readers against patronizing the Eagle Tavern in Richmond, Virginia, because its keeper charged her fifty cents for a cup of coffee (the price of a full dinner). She also wrote copiously about the growing influence of evangelical religion in American life.

would be robbed. Numerous travelers complained that their bedroom doors had neither locks nor latches, which meant that they had no way to prevent someone from entering. More specific to women was a sense of physical or even sexual danger. At a Pennsylvania tavern, three Philadelphia women could reach their private bedroom only by walking through a large barracks-style lodging room. This room contained a dozen beds full of men, some of whom probably called out to or teased the women as they passed. By the time the women reached their own room, they had become so nervous that they suspected their bedroom closet actually concealed a secret door to the lodging room, and they barricaded the closet with a heavy piece of furniture. They also insisted that their male companion take the room next door, and they frequently called out to him during the night. As it happened, the Philadelphians suffered no harm but anxiety and sleeplessness.

Other women were far less fortunate. Across the nation, a woman traveling alone ran the risk that a man who offered to be her protector or escort actually planned to bring her to a tavern or hotel and rape her. In New York

She considered their efforts to ban Sunday travel, for example, a threat to the republic and the constitutional separation of church and state. Early in 1829, her quarrel with an evangelical congregation in Washington, D.C., resulted in her conviction as a "common scold." She was sentenced to a $10 fine, and her friends had to pledge $100 for her good behavior.

This experience convinced Anne Royall that the nation needed her services more than ever, and she continued to write, publish, and travel. The attentions she had previously received on the road, first as a woman and later as a successful author, now acquired a new character. In some taverns, towns, and even entire states, Anne now faced hostility and abuse. Perhaps no clearer example can be found than her experience in Charlottesville, Virginia. When Anne Royall came to town, she wrote the president of the University of Virginia, asking for a tour. When she got no answer, she hired a carriage and driver to tour the campus on her own. While there, groups of students tried to frighten her horses into running away with her. Later, more students came to the tavern where she

was staying, "shouting and yelling like Indians" (Royall 1830–1831, vol. 1, p. 91). When Anne escaped to her bedroom, they wrote obscene notes and pushed them under her door. Next, they banged on the door, shouted, and threatened her. Meanwhile, a friend stood on the other side of the door, armed with a chair and ready to knock down anyone who broke into the room. Anne did not blame the tavern keeper for the fracas. Instead, she concluded that the evangelical-influenced faculty had encouraged the students to try to drive her out of town. Similar experiences awaited her in South Carolina, Georgia, Mississippi, and Missouri, but unlike her Charlottesville hosts, the tavern keepers she met there often proved antagonistic or even downright dangerous.

Anne Royall survived her trip, but she ultimately decided to stop traveling. Instead, she started a newspaper, called *Paul Pry*, in which she continued to tackle contentious political and social issues of the day. Anne Royall's travels had made her a national name, just as she had made—and ruined—reputations among proprietors of the nation's inns and hotels.

City, young working-class women coming home from work were sometimes lured (or kidnapped) into a tavern, where working-class "b'hoys" would gang-rape them. On at least one occasion, a policeman leered through a keyhole rather than stopping the assault. According to historian Michael Kaplan, this behavior represented a form of male bonding for New York's young working men.

Working-class white and black women were far more vulnerable to violence and rape than middle- and upper-class women, but even these more privileged women sometimes felt threatened. Schoolteacher Martha Anthony earned enough money to travel during her summer vacations, and on several occasions, she commented on the inconveniences of traveling alone. Most of these were minor, but on her return to her Philadelphia home in the spring of 1839, she mentioned "several little adventures" which all but convinced her to stop "travelling alone" (Anthony, Vacation Diary, May 24, 1839). Her coy language strongly hints at sexual danger, a threat she found too awful to describe in detail. Even without a personal experience of

Frances Trollope was
an English author who
wrote about travel
in the United States.
(*Hulton Archive/Getty
Images*)

danger, American women learned from each other and from popular travel
narratives to be wary. Harriet Martineau, for example, related a story of a
stage driver who abducted one of his female passengers, while Anne Royall
told of women murdered by their guide during a journey through Indian
territory.

Yet for all the real dangers that awaited women in taverns, women's diaries and letters reflecting their tavern visits rarely focused on them but rather
on other factors. If we look at individual women's experiences in taverns
over the course of a particular trip, for example, we get a sense of what these
women valued or found wanting in the taverns they patronized. In the
course of her 1818 tour in New York state, Sarah Howlands made brief comments on the taverns she visited in her travel diary. Howlands was generally
satisfied with the taverns she visited, but her comments were so brief that it
is usually impossible to tell what made a place good or bad in her eyes. Of
the fifty-three she rated, about a third were, in her estimation, very poor,
very unpleasant, miserable, or wretched. Only 15 percent were merely toler-
able or pretty good, while fully half were good, very good, or excellent.
When she did record details, her evaluation had a lot to do with the work of
the women in the tavern. She called Kibbe's tavern in Buffalo wretched because the food was inedible. At a Vienna tavern, "They gave us dirty cotton

sheets and bedbugs after my requesting clean linnen ones" (Howlands, Diary, [August 17,] 1818). She called other taverns miserable because they provided wet sheets, were especially dirty, or served wretched meals. In most taverns, bed linens, general cleanliness, and cooking were women's responsibility. Depending on the tavern, the tavern keeper's wife might do the cooking and cleaning. Sometimes, a tavern keeper hired a housekeeper or a cook. Much of the time, the tavern keeper's wife got help from her children, servants, or slaves. Either way, as in a private home, laundry, cleaning, and preparing meals were considered women's work, and those were the areas that caught Sarah Howlands's attention.

Other women shared Sarah Howlands's concern for cleanliness and cookery. During her 1824 tour, S. Schulling complained of a poorly kept inn, which apparently served nothing but half-rotten boiled mackerel. Another hotel was overrun with bugs, to the point that her party spent a sleepless night killing them. Yet another provided a meager meal of hard-boiled eggs and bread, but only after significant delay. Schulling called this place filthy and its keepers ignorant. Ann Sellers's strongest complaints about any tavern she visited during an 1830 trip in Pennsylvania concerned a Lehigh inn that served sour, moldy bread. She also commented on another tavern that was infested with bugs. In taverns where the basic accommodations met her standards, however, she paid more attention to the other guests than to the tavern workers. In one diary entry, she devoted several lines to describing an older woman guest, who wore stained lace and muslins, rarely spoke, and looked sour and discontented.

By the 1850s, women travelers were more commonly generally satisfied with the taverns and hotels they encountered. However, women who traveled in the western states often found fault, along the same lines as their predecessors twenty years earlier in the East. Mrs. John Reed found the Garnit House in Louisville dirty and unpleasantly crowded. She also felt the staff was too rushed and frantic to make anyone feel at home. During her travels in the West and the South, Maria Mitchell observed that St. Louis's renowned Planters' Hotel would never be considered a first-class hotel in Boston. She also suggested that southern hotels in general were inferior to northern ones, while those in eastern Tennessee and western Virginia in particular were mere hovels. Disparaging taverns in newly or sparsely settled areas of the United States was nothing new, of course. Back in 1824, S. Schulling had been pleasantly surprised by a hotel in Geneva, New York, which was large and well-maintained. In contrast, she asserted, most taverns in the eastern part of the state had horrible food and primitive accommodations.

As the Geneva hotel itself suggested, in the antebellum decades, many newly settled towns boasted ambitious and well-furnished hotels that could sleep hundreds long before there was any real need for such large establishments. This reflected a general increase in standards for domestic travel. Just as transportation had improved significantly, with the creation of well-furnished steamboats and rapidly moving trains, so too had taverns sought to attain a higher standard of furnishings, decoration, and overall comfort. Always striving to keep ahead of the competition, the largest new hotels cost hundreds of thousands of dollars to build, largely because of their size, but also because of their furnishings, decor, and use of new conveniences like piped gas for lighting. In addition, women travelers in the 1850s were probably more demanding in terms of housekeeping, both their own and others', than their predecessors had been.

Throughout the antebellum period, whether female travelers were pleased or dissatisfied, the female departments of tavern keeping were often largely responsible. Elizabeth Willson made this explicit. At the tavern where she complained of the drunken men's noise, she concluded that the place's low standards had everything to do with the death of the tavern keeper's wife and his loss of her assistance. When S. Schulling applauded Keppler's tavern, near Reading, Pennsylvania, she particularly noted the comfortable beds and the tasty food. She also observed that *"the praise belongs"* to the housekeeper (Schulling, Diary, [July 1,] 1824). Samuel B. Morris agreed, observing "Let me see *our hostess*, and I will answer for good or bad accommodations accordingly" (Morris, Diary, October 13, 1845). Dispensing blame and applause equally freely, Anne Royall claimed that southern taverns were generally poor because southern women were too proud or too lazy to attend to them properly. In contrast, their peers in the North really knew how to make a tavern cozy and homelike.

Tavern Landladies

Looking at taverns from the perspective of the women who worked there reveals a slightly different picture from the colorful but highly biased viewpoint of their customers. The first point to make about tavern workers is simply how hard they worked. Even more than most housekeepers and domestic servants, they kept incredibly long hours. In the early nineteenth century, stagecoach companies regularly scheduled their coaches to depart in the middle of the night. Long distances and poor roads made overnight travel a necessity for people in a hurry. A 2:00 or 3:00 A.M. departure was hardly unusual, much to travelers' disgust. The travelers rarely considered what this schedule meant for tavern workers. First, they had be awake themselves to rouse any guests who might be expecting to catch a stagecoach. Sometimes they were expected to prepare breakfast, or at least coffee, for these early risers. More typically, those traveling by stage would breakfast in a different tavern from where they slept, which meant that a hostess might get rid of one set of guests, and perhaps start cleaning the rooms or doing some laundry, only to have to stop her work to cook breakfast for a coach-load of hungry and grumpy passengers.

Since stages rarely arrived exactly when they were expected and had variable numbers of passengers, tavern landladies could not easily prepare a meal in advance. Some stage drivers blew their horns as they approached a tavern, indicating the number of passengers by the number of blasts they blew, but short of that, a hostess usually had little or no specific warning about what might be expected of her. Once breakfast was over, preparations for dinner had to be started. Dinner was the main meal of the day, eaten in the early to midafternoon. The same problems about timing and numbers plagued women preparing this meal as well. Only the larger city taverns and hotels could insist on serving meals on their own schedule. Tavern keepers sometimes had to provide two additional meals to their guests, tea and supper. These were generally smaller meals than dinner, and they often involved similar dishes, so harried hostesses might have saved some time by reheating foods prepared for a previous meal. Still, tavern women had to accommodate the tastes of a wide range of travelers, from drovers and wagoners to wealthy and refined city folk. A tavern housewife in Virginia told Martha Cocke that she had to keep separate dining tables, as "genteel travellers would not like to eat with waggoners . . . neither would it be reasonable to expect it" (Martha Cocke, Letter, November 19, 1810).

Beyond the problems of timing, numbers, and tastes, tavern women faced other obstacles in preparing meals. Except in the better-appointed city taverns, they did some if not most of their cooking over open fires in the fireplace, or with an early version of a cast-iron stove. Cooking in this manner was more of an art than a science, as it was very difficult to maintain a constant temperature, especially important for baking bread. In addition to watching a temperamental fire or oven, they might also have to haul in the firewood from the woodpile, as well as bring bucket after bucket of water from the well or the spring. Slaughtering and cleaning chickens for dinner took more time still, as did milking cows and churning butter. Some women also engaged in more seasonal food-related work, like making hams, bacon, and sausage from a freshly slaughtered pig. Moreover, like farmwives, rural tavern wives engaged in a range of handicrafts, all intended to provide the family with necessities while limiting the number of items they had to buy at the store. Many travelers observed tavern women keeping busy at all times, picking up their knitting or sewing as soon as their guests were fed. Samuel B. Morris observed one woman still busily knitting at 11:00 P.M.

Exterior view of a tavern with horse-drawn carriages in front at Blackwoodtown, New Jersey, 1851. (*Library of Congress*)

Further competition for their time came from the piles of laundry that a busy tavern generated, even when sheets got used by more than one visitor. Laundry meant hauling many gallons of washing water, as well as the firewood needed to boil it, washing and wringing the sheets, and then hanging them out to dry. In addition, some tavern landladies found that their female guests demanded their attention at odd moments. Some women summoned their hostess to open or close windows for them, disdaining to do even so much for themselves.

Adding to their burdens, tavern women, like American women in general in this period, typically had several children. If they were lucky, at least one girl was old enough to help with the cooking, washing, and sewing. But even so, a tavern-keeping mother with a small child had more than enough work to drive anyone to distraction. Frances Wright encountered one such woman in her travels. "Worked out of strength, and almost out of temper" by her nursing infant, this woman was trying to cook while coping with a "tribe of young urchins" underfoot and an "unusual inundation of travellers" (Wright 1821, p. 172). Charmed by the pink-cheeked baby, and perhaps hungry for her supper, Wright held it long enough for her hostess to prepare the meal.

Given all this, it was no wonder that tavern guests sometimes encountered sheets that were either dirty or still damp. Nor was it strange that meals sometimes came to the table late, missing some element that guests expected or poorly prepared. At times, tavern hostesses even had to turn would-be guests away. One woman told James Flint she could not give him breakfast that morning. Once she explained that she had no bread ready and that thirty highway construction workers were already waiting for their meal, he took it reasonably well, especially since she directed him to a less crowded inn nearby. Tavern landladies also turned visitors away if they were preoccupied with sick children.

More surprising than disagreeable incidents like these were the number of truly lavish meals that taverns provided. James Flint observed during his travels that "wheaten and Indian corn breads, beef, pork, venison, wild turkey, geese, and poultry, are staple articles; with a profusion of vegetables, such as cucumbers, onions, cabbages, beans, and preserved fruits" (Flint 1822, p. 36). In Indian country, the Duke of Saxe-Weimar enjoyed a more unusual meal of turnip soup, roast venison, bear, and turkey, chickens, and pork with sweet potatoes. In another tavern, he marveled that a woman heavily pregnant with her sixth child could prepare an excellent supper and manage the entire tavern alone while her husband and the household's one slave were away. At a tavern in Montgomery, Harriet Martineau decided that a well-prepared breakfast of corn bread, buckwheat cakes, chicken, bacon, eggs, rice, hominy, fish, and beef made up for an unmade bed, a dirty room, an unhelpful servant, and mice.

A rare respite in the tavern-keeping woman's day came from the custom that the lady of the house should sit with her guests and pour out the tea. This practice met with consternation from some British travelers. They expected the hostess to serve the meal and disappear. In other words, they expected her to act like a servant. Instead, they were often surprised to find her either joining them at table or staying in the room to pick up some other work, such as the ever-present knitting. In contrast, Americans usually took their hostess's presence in stride. Both they and foreigners noted that the seats nearest her were places of honor. Even at the table, however, the hostess was hardly at leisure. If she was not hopping up every other minute to satisfy a demand for more tea or to quiet a fussy child, she was answering questions about the area or giving directions on how to find a particular place or person. Occasionally she might have to figure out how to handle the gallantry of a man like Colonel John Boykin of South Carolina, who seemed to think the day was wasted if he had not flirted with at least one woman. Unlike Boykin, some guests preferred to limit their interaction with their hosts, and some absolutely hated being quizzed, considering any questions an invasion of their privacy. But most preferred a cordial, attentive hostess who made them feel at home through her friendly conversation.

A tavern-keeping woman's work was nearly done once the last meal of the day had been served, but "last" was something of a flexible concept, because late arrivals might expect to be fed. In the Florida territory near Pensacola, a Mr. Pollard made his sick wife get out of bed to make up beds and prepare supper for the Duke of Saxe-Weimar and his servant. Even if late-comers just wanted a place to sleep, tavern women sometimes had to scramble to find them a place on chairs, in the hayloft, or on the floor. Particularly accommodating women sometimes gave up their own beds to their guests. During a drenching storm outside of Pittsburgh, Édouard Montulé took refuge at an inn, where the hostess offered him her own bed, as her guest beds were already full. Harriet Martineau found another hostess similarly generous, giving up her bed for Martineau and her female companion. The same evening, two other guests offered up their beds to the men traveling with Martineau, but they demurred, taking their rest in the barn instead.

Not all tavern housekeepers were so accommodating, of course. In addition to those women who refused to serve additional customers when their houses were already packed to the rafters or because their families were ill, there were women whose ideas about how to treat guests differed significantly from travelers' own views. At a newly opened tavern in Mobile, Alabama, Anne Royall was shocked to find the landlady dressed in white, sitting at her leisure in the parlor. Royall thought she belonged in the kitchen and should dress and act in a manner that showed her readiness to serve her guests. Clearly, this woman had her own ideas. Other landladies refused to rush a meal to the table to accommodate impatient travelers, or simply did things in their own way. Even when female patrons were not always satisfied with their tavern experiences, however, some did at least acknowledge how hard tavern women worked. Lucy Battle gave back-handed recognition to the work of tavern keeping when she thanked God that she had never had to run a hotel or a boardinghouse. And as Harriet Martineau understood, women worked in public houses more from necessity than from choice. A tavern-keeper's wife and daughters had no particular reason to enjoy having their homes invaded by a steady stream of often ungrateful guests.

Tavern Servants and Slaves

Tavern-keepers' wives were not the only women who worked hard in taverns, of course. In many taverns, servants and slaves did much of the dirtiest and most tiring work, such as cleaning the rooms and doing laundry. Travelers disagreed about whether American tavern servants were in general lazy or helpful, rude or polite, but it seems safe to say that theirs was usually a hard lot. The tavern landlady whom Samuel Morris saw knitting at eleven o'clock at night had servants who were busy scrubbing out tubs and cleaning up indoors and out, far more strenuous labor. And while the activity and company in tavern households could be exciting, tavern customers were often very demanding. British travelers typically expected a degree of servility that Americans disdained to offer. Frances Trollope found the level of service better in the slave states, in part because the supposedly dangerous notion of equality had so little purchase there. Returning to the free state of Pennsylvania, she moaned that they had to extort clean bed linens and a fire from the surly chambermaid. For her part, the servant grumbled about the difficulty of pleasing English visitors. She also implied that guests should address her like they would any young lady. But even an American democrat like Anne Royall found it strange that a chambermaid would expect to be called "miss" or considered a "lady."

Like landladies, servants regularly came into conflict with guests over how to conduct themselves and their work. In American hotels and taverns, meals were usually served at a set table with a fixed menu rather than the à la carte system of modern restaurants. Like hotel keepers, servants sometimes refused guests' requests to dine in their rooms, probably because such special arrangements made extra work for the servants themselves. Many of the servants and slaves whom travelers called lazy and stupid were in fact neither, but chose to work at their own pace, or even slowed down in reaction to travelers' more obnoxious demands. A suggestion of just how exacting some customers could be comes from Anne Royall, who remarked that she preferred taverns without a landlady because then she could be mistress of the servants. In addition to more passive forms of resistance, some servants openly criticized tavern patrons. In one tavern, when a guest asked for coffee before the rest of her slow-moving party had come to the breakfast table, the servant first ignored the request and then berated the lady for sitting down before the others had arrived. In this house, the traveler observed, the host and staff were united in promoting their idea of good manners.

More serious than these quarrels was the constant potential for servants and slaves to be abused. Female domestics in any household were at risk for physical and sexual abuse. In a tavern, the large number of strange men coming and going aggravated the problem. So did the plentiful consumption of alcohol and the general notion that women in a public house might be "public women," or prostitutes. Anne Royall simply took it for granted that every tavern had a quasi-prostitute on the premises. That kind of assumption could dishonor any woman who worked in a tavern, no matter how she behaved. When Andrew Jackson named John Eaton to his cabinet, Washington gossips delighted in equating his new wife's former work as a barmaid in her father's tavern with prostitution. Black women had the least protection against insult, especially if they were enslaved. A light-skinned slave mother working in a disorderly tavern in South Carolina—that is, a tavern with a reputation for impropriety—begged a traveler to buy her young daughter and remove her from this immoral environment. At only eight years old, this little girl had perhaps so far escaped harassment or molestation, but her worried mother could not count on her youth to protect her for much longer. Whether servants or slaves, tavern workers had little or no recourse against assault. This was especially true for taverns with lots of travelers, who might be on their way before a woman spoke of or anyone discovered their crimes.

For all the trouble that servants and slaves had with tavern guests, some had even more difficulty with the tavern keeper. In private houses, housekeepers and servants regularly argued over matters like the proper way to cook or clean, leisure time, and compensation. The same conflicts happened in taverns, with the added complication of competing demands from guests. For example, in one New York hotel, when an Irish servant volunteered to serve a private meal to newly arrived British travelers, her employer took offense at the implied criticism of American customs, upbraiding his guests and most likely the accommodating Irishwoman as well. In antebellum northern cities like New York, domestic servants were increasingly likely to be either Irish immigrants or free African Americans. Native-born white American women typically shunned domestic service if they could find work in manufacturing. In northern and southern hotels, the housekeeping staff—chambermaids, scullery maids, and waiters—was usually black, free or enslaved depending on the region, while the proprietor, barman, and housekeeper were usually white. As a result, tensions between employers and servants often had broad cultural as well as class dimensions.

Such was the case in Mr. Melton's tavern in Alabama, where the cook was an enslaved woman from Baltimore and the tavern keeper's wife was a Cherokee woman. Mr. Melton had paid a high price for the slave woman because she was known to be an excellent cook. Yet Mrs. Melton wanted authority over the kitchen for herself, so she repeatedly tried to force the cook out and prepare her own Cherokee-style meals. Arguing that she was accountable not to Mrs. Melton but to her husband, the slave woman refused to cede the kitchen to her. Mr. Melton repeatedly had to wade into the fray and restore order. At a Fayetteville tavern, where the innkeeper's mother did the cooking, she and a slave woman also disagreed about how to conduct the business. According to one traveler, Mrs. Wells was a cross sort of woman who did not believe in putting herself out for her guests. When she grudgingly agreed to share the family's dinner of cabbage, bacon, and cornbread with some lately arrived travelers, the slave woman pointed out that she should also offer tea or coffee. Mrs. Wells refused, saying that the strangers could take what they were given or go hungry. The slave then protested that Mr. Wells would not approve. Mrs. Wells replied that she did not care a fig either for her son's opinion or for the bondwoman's. With such obvious animosity between mother and son as well as between mistress and slave, this cannot have been a comfortable, smooth-running tavern.

Conclusion

In terms of the sheer numbers of people who entered their doors, antebellum American taverns were clearly male-dominated spaces. The overwhelming majority of tavern *drinkers* were men. Tavern account books rarely indicate that a woman came in to buy a drink. Even if some of the men listed in the account books bought drinks for women who accompanied them, the evidence clearly indicates that women did not generally go to taverns to drink. Even though women came to taverns for balls, concerts, and sometimes for auctions and other commercial business, most tavern customers were still men. In addition, the vast majority of tavern keepers were men. Women had composed a substantial minority of tavern keepers in colonial and early republican America—from 10 percent to 25 percent, by some estimates—but their numbers had declined significantly by the antebellum decades. In 1819 in New York City, for example, only 8 percent of the tavern-keepers' recognizances were sworn by women. (These recognizances were promises to follow the regulations governing taverns or forfeit a certain sum of money.)

Yet despite the numerical predominance of men among tavern customers and keepers, and despite the cultural pressures that made many women reluctant to enter taverns, women were essential parts of antebellum American tavern life. Few taverns could have stayed in business without women's labor. While some men were trained as cooks, and while the era's famous chefs were always men, the vast majority of taverns relied on women not only in the kitchen but also for the wide range of other domestic tasks, like doing laundry and cleaning. Most also had a female housekeeper—often the tavern-keeper's wife, sometimes a kinswoman or a hired assistant—who

Taverns often served as more than places to drink; in some instances, they were voting places. (*Library of Congress*)

oversaw the other female workers. Many of these women had more contact with traveling guests than did male tavern keepers. In part, this stemmed from Americans' tendency to associate domestic comfort with women in this period. Most simply liked to see a woman in charge of the house. But this pattern also reflected the reality that many tavern-keeping men had other occupations as well. Some were farmers, others were artisans, and some held political office. All of these activities took them away from their taverns, which meant that some tavern-goers encountered only the lady of the house.

Finally, as members of a restless generation, women made up a substantial portion of the tavern's customers. While only a privileged few could travel for leisure or "go on vacation," as we might now say, many women traveled to seek work, conduct business, or preach the gospel. Still more women journeyed as migrants, whether from the countryside to the city or from the eastern regions to the new western territories and states. Many of these women traveled with their families, rather than alone, but even so, their presence shaped taverns. Women travelers, more than men, demanded and increasingly got private bedrooms and parlors. Their presence imposed at least some restraint on other patrons' behavior as well. Drinking and swearing did not automatically cease when a woman entered the door. However, some men felt constrained to act differently in front of women guests, even if they felt little pressure to change their behavior in front of their hostess or female servants. More temperate men were even relieved when women's sobering presence freed them from having to act like one of the boys. Some taverns were probably 99 percent male most of the time, and often fairly homogeneous in terms of class and culture. This was especially true in the nation's cities. All in all, however, antebellum American taverns remained a surprisingly mixed venue, bringing together not just the two sexes, but also people of different classes, religions, regions, political affiliations, and tastes. Women were thus one source of variety among many, although an extremely important one. And as participants in this key institution in American economic, political, and social life, women were also necessarily part of the antebellum "public sphere."

References and Further Reading

Anthony, Martha Hampton. Vacation Diary, 1834. Historical Society of Pennsylvania, Philadelphia, PA.

Aron, Cindy Sondik. *Working at Play: A History of Vacations in the United States.* New York: Oxford University Press, 1999.

Bernard, Duke of Saxe-Weimar Eisenach. *Travels through North America, during the Years 1825 and 1826.* Philadelphia: Carey, Lea and Carey, 1828.

Campbell, Tunis G. *Never Let People Be Kept Waiting: A Textbook on Hotel Management. A Reprint of Tunis G. Campbell's Hotel Keepers, Head Waiters, and Housekeepers' Guide.* Edited with an introduction by Doris Elizabeth King. 1848. Raleigh: King Reprints in Hospitality History, 1973.

Clapp, Elizabeth J. "'A Virago-Errant in Enchanted Armor?': Anne Royall's 1829 Trial as a Common Scold." *Journal of the Early Republic* 23 (Summer 2003): 207–232.

Cocke Family Papers. Virginia Historical Society, Richmond, VA.

Cohen, Patricia Cline. "Safety and Danger: Women on American Public Transport, 1750–1850." In *Gendered Domains: Rethinking Public and Private in Women's History: Essays from the Seventh Berkshire Conference on the History of Women*, ed. Dorothy O. Helly, 110–122. Ithaca: Cornell University Press, 1992.

Cohen, Patricia Cline. "Women at Large: Travel in Antebellum America." *History Today* 44, no. 12 (1994): 44–50.

Flint, James. *Letters from America, Containing Observations on the Climate and Agriculture of the Western States*. Edinburgh: W. & C. Tait, 1822.

Garvin, Donna-Belle, and James L. Garvin. *On the Road North of Boston: New Hampshire Taverns and Turnpikes, 1700–1900*. Hanover and London: University Press of New England, 1988.

Houstoun, Matilda Charlotte (Jesse) Fraser. *Texas and the Gulf of Mexico: Or, Yachting in the New World*. London: J. Murray, 1844.

Howlands, Sarah (Hazard). Diaries, 1818–1882. New-York Historical Society, New York, NY.

Kaplan, Michael. "New York Tavern Violence and the Creation of Male Working Class Identity." *Journal of the Early Republic* 15 (Winter 1995): 592–617.

Lewis, Charlene M. Boyer. *Ladies and Gentlemen on Display: Planter Society at the Virginia Springs, 1790–1860*. Charlottesville: University Press of Virginia, 2001.

Martineau, Harriet. *Retrospect of Western Travel*. London: Saunders and Otley, 1838.

Martineau, Harriet. *Society in America, in Two Volumes*. New York: Saunders and Otley, 1837.

Maxwell, Alice S., and Marion B. Dunlevy. *Virago! The Story of Anne Newport Royall*. Jefferson, NC: McFarland, 1985.

Montulé, Édouard de. *A Voyage to North America, the West Indies, and the Mediterranean*. London: Sir Richard Phillips, 1821.

Morris, Samuel Buckley. Diary, 1845. Historical Society of Pennsylvania, Philadelphia, PA.

Ripley, Dorothy. *The Bank of Faith and Works United*. Philadelphia: J. H. Cunningham, 1819.

Royall, Anne Newport. *Letters from Alabama on Various Subjects: To Which Is Added, an Appendix, Containing Remarks on Sundry Members of the 20th & 21st Congress, and Other High Characters, &c. &c. at the Seat of Government. In One Volume*. Washington: [No publisher given], 1830.

Royall, Anne Newport. *Mrs. Royall's Southern Tour, or, Second Series of the Black Book*. 3 Volumes. Washington: [No publisher given], 1830–1831.

Royall, Anne Newport. *Sketches of History, Life and Manners in the United States. By a Traveler.* New Haven: Printed for the author, 1826.

Sandoval-Strausz, Andrew K. *Hotel: An American History.* New Haven: Yale University Press, 2006.

Schulling, S. Diary, 1824. Historical Society of Pennsylvania, Philadelphia, PA.

Trollope, Frances. *Domestic Manners of the Americans.* London, New York: Whittacher, Treacher. In New York, reprinted for the booksellers, 1832.

White, Wm., *Annual Stageman's Ball.* [Broadside]. New York Historical Society, New York, NY, 1839.

Wright, Frances. *Views of Society and Manners in America: In a Series of Letters from That Country to a Friend in England, during the Years 1818, 1819, and 1820. By an Englishwoman.* New York: E. Bliss and E. White, 1821.

Religious Sects and Social Reform | 6

David J. Voelker

During the three decades prior to 1860, Americans experienced unprecedented religious diversification and growth, embracing new religious leaders and styles of worship as well as a variety of reform activities. The years around 1830 encapsulated the tumult of the period. In that year, the innovative preaching of Charles Grandison Finney sparked a revival in the booming canal town of Rochester, New York, thus igniting urban revivals across the North. Also in upstate New York, Joseph Smith, Jr., published the *Book of Mormon* and began organizing a controversial new church. While Finney and Smith presaged new religious developments, William Lloyd Garrison opened a new era for reform in January of 1831 with the publication of *The Liberator*, a newspaper devoted to advocating the immediate emancipation of American slaves. Garrison's clarion call followed upon David Walker's *Appeal to the Coloured Citizens of the World* (1829). A free black Methodist living in Boston, Walker called for violent action, if necessary, to destroy the oppressive system of slavery. Although Garrison repudiated violence, the rising antislavery movement in the North angered white southerners, who feared rebellion. Nat Turner, enslaved in Virginia, confirmed their worst fears in the summer of 1831, when he led several dozen slaves as they killed about sixty white men, women, and children, before their plans to start a large-scale rebellion were thwarted. In response, southern whites tightened control over the slave population, in part by strictly monitoring their religious worship.

Historians once believed that the evangelical and reform movements of this era constituted primarily an attempt at "social control" exercised by society's economic elites. According to this line of argument, employers in towns and cities promoted revivals and reforms, such as temperance, to mold a more obedient and disciplined labor force. By the 1990s, however, the historical consensus shifted dramatically. Nathan Hatch's *The Democratization of American Christianity* made a compelling argument that early nineteenth-century

American religion was most characterized by a "religious populism, reflecting the passions of ordinary people and the charisma of democratic movement-builders." Christianity became a "liberating force," as people seized "the right to think and act for themselves rather than depending upon the mediations of an educated elite" (Hatch 1989, pp. 5, 11). Scholars have made similar arguments about antebellum reform movements. Daniel Walker Howe especially has contended that northern evangelicals and reformers promoted self-discipline and self-control rather than overt social control. Both Hatch and Howe recognized that religious leaders, churches, and reformers sometimes sought to exercise authority over others, especially given the dominant race and gender hierarchies of this period, but they nevertheless detected a notable impulse toward liberation.

Religion and reform constituted a complex set of interrelated social movements that had a profound impact on the Jacksonian era. The nation's churches competed in an open market that unleashed tremendous religious energy and creativity. An extended wave of revivals, swelled by new measures and millennial aspirations, helped Christianize many Americans, white and black. In this new religious climate, Methodists, especially, were able to harness the energies of laity to expand their organization, while new sects such as the Mormons attracted followers by offering a restored, authoritative church. Out of this religious ferment evolved a series of reform movements aimed at cooperating across denominational lines to build God's kingdom on earth. Most radically, northern abolitionists challenged the institution of slavery, spurring reaction in the South. In a variety of ways, these interlocking social movements thus contributed to the cultural and political polarization that portended civil war.

Religious Liberty and Religious Conflict

In 1833, the state of Massachusetts ended tax support for the last remaining established church in the nation, thus completing the revolutionary American overthrow of the traditional European practice of state-supported churches. After the American Revolution, political leaders influenced by the Enlightenment—joined by evangelical dissenters weary of the established churches—had seized the moment to begin separating churches and religious belief from the state and politics. Most notably, James Madison helped push Thomas Jefferson's "Statute for Establishing Religious Freedom" through the Virginia legislature in 1786, thus defeating an attempt to provide general tax support for churches. Jefferson's bill included three key features. First, it stated that "no man shall be compelled to frequent or support any religious worship, place, or ministry whatsoever." Second, it stated that "all men shall be free to profess, and by argument to maintain, their opinion in matters of religion." Finally, it established that civil rights and privileges depended in no way on one's religious opinions (Gaustad 1993, pp. 149–151).

Although Baptists and other dissenters from the established church held very different religious beliefs from those of Jefferson, they strongly supported the move away from a tight bond between churches and government, as they had suffered years of persecution under the Anglican regime. The Jeffersonian definition of religious freedom did not immediately dominate, but it did influence several other states that had also considered some sort of general establishment of religion. Furthermore, again with the help of Madison, this Jeffersonian definition was essentially embedded in the United States Constitution with the ratification in 1791 of the First Amendment, which declared that "Congress shall make no law respecting an establishment of religion, or prohibiting the free exercise thereof." By the early 1800s, then, the churches across the nation were on their own, competing for supporters and funds. In the words of Methodist minister James Quinn, Americans "were left free to choose their own course, and worship God . . . standing, sitting, or kneeling, in silence or with a loud voice, with or without [a] book" (Wigger 2001, p. 9). In short, they could worship however they pleased.

In this new environment, there was no legal barrier to stop men and women from preaching on their own authority or from organizing new churches of their own design. But when religious "outsiders" crossed certain social and cultural lines, they could find themselves harassed by the state or, more perilously, by vigilantes. Throughout the 1830s and 1840s, for instance, Mormons suffered repeated violence at the hands of mobs. Anti-Mormon rioters helped drive the "Saints" out of Ohio and Missouri, and the Mormon founder Joseph Smith, Jr., and his brother Hyrum were killed by a mob in 1844, an event that led Mormons to relinquish their community in Illinois as well. Anti-Mormon violence derived from religious intolerance, as well as from concerns about their collective power wherever they settled en masse. Mormons, nevertheless, experienced the attacks as a form of bigotry, as the social, political, and economic cohesiveness that made them seem threatening to non-Mormons ultimately derived from their distinctive religious identity and the imperatives of their faith.

Roman Catholics also became a target of hatred during the Jacksonian period. Catholics seemed especially threatening because of their growing numbers and their presumed allegiance to a foreign pope. Between 1845 and 1855, almost 3 million immigrants poured into the country, including large numbers of German and Irish Catholics. Many of the Irish immigrants were impoverished, and they clustered together in visible groups in the northern cities, where they generated the resentment of native-born white Americans. By the 1850s, it was mistakenly believed that there were over 3 million Catholics in the United States, which would have made them the single largest church group in the country. More recent estimates, however, suggest that there were just over a million adult Catholics in 1850, compared with 2.7 million Methodists. Given unreasonable fears about their potential dominance, Catholics suffered from occasional outbursts of violence, which they sometimes reciprocated. In 1834, fed by sensational rumors that a young woman had been held captive by nuns, a Boston working-class mob burned a Roman Catholic convent outside the city. Ten years later, nativist (anti-immigrant) mobs burned two Catholic churches in Philadelphia. By the time the conflict ended, twenty-four people had been killed in the violence.

These sometimes fierce religious conflicts revealed an underlying tension. Many American Christians felt uncomfortable with the extraordinary religious diversity made possible by American openness. In the words of historian Robert Abzug, it seemed that "a spiritual free-for-all had replaced cosmic order" (Abzug 1994, p. 5). Some believers dwelled in this discomfort by refusing to join any of the churches. Others worked for unity by participating in ecumenical missionary, educational, and reform activities. Still others—most notably the "Christians" and the Disciples of Christ—rejected the established denominations and sought to restore the "primitive" or original Christian church. Despite occasional outbreaks of repression and violence, the free religious market fostered an unprecedented growth of new religious groups. Each year, the churches counted an ever larger percentage of the population as members or adherents. The groups that fared best in this new climate, including evangelical groups such as Baptists and Methodists, deployed a variety of new strategies to reach out to new members and fostered hopes of establishing the Kingdom of Heaven on earth—starting with their own nation.

Revivalism and Millennial Hopes

Evangelicalism came to dominate the United States—North, South, and West—between the American Revolution and the Civil War. During that period, Methodists and Baptists grew to outnumber all other evangelicals by far, leaving Presbyterians and Congregationalists lagging behind. These evangelical churches differed substantially in terms of theology, church structure, and liturgy, but they shared several key elements. Evangelicals looked to the Bible as their fundamental authority, they emphasized the importance of the conversion experience, and they expected members to lead a righteous life while helping to spread the Gospel message. Early nineteenth-century revivals fused many of these concerns into an intense event. Historians have often used the phrase "the Second Great Awakening" to refer to a series of religious revivals that swept across regions of the United States between the 1790s and the 1840s. More a decades-long religious movement than a discrete event, the Second Great Awakening made evangelical Protestantism a key historical force during the Jacksonian era. The revivals of the period recruited new church members and energized existing believers, drawing them into the project of building God's kingdom.

Although revivalists usually shunned abstract theology, they deployed certain ideas to good effect. Revivalists tended to dispense with the Calvinistic notion that God had predestined all souls for salvation or damnation, along with the corollary belief that individuals were powerless to pursue salvation—the doctrines that Charles Finney dismissed as "cannot-ism." Although some Presbyterian and Baptist revivalists still retained vestiges of Calvinism, most revivalists preached what amounted to the Methodist doctrine of "free grace," which meant that God freely offered saving grace to everyone. To be saved, one simply had to accept God's grace and thus be spiritually reborn. This "Arminian" theology placed the power of decision in the hands of potential converts. It dramatized the role of personal choice in the salvation process. The free grace doctrine thus complemented the increasingly individualistic and democratic American culture, and it aided revivalists in search of converts.

In both rural and urban settings, revivalists used a new combination of techniques to bring converts into their churches. At rural camp meetings, hundreds and sometimes thousands of people gathered for days at a time for sermonizing, praying, and hymn singing. At such events, preachers from several denominations, including especially Methodists, Baptists, and Presbyterians, sometimes put aside their doctrinal differences and worked together to reap a harvest of new church members. Described as "festivals of democracy" in 1839 by Michael Chevalier, a French visitor to the United States, camp meetings empowered common people in their worship (Hatch 1989, p. 58).

Most revival preachers came from humble backgrounds; they were "of the people" rather than from the theological centers of Harvard, Princeton, and Yale. Usually lacking degrees in divinity, they worried little about the niceties of theological orthodoxy. Unlike the orthodox ministers of old, they preached extemporaneously rather than reading from carefully prepared texts. Their spontaneous preaching was grounded in personal religious experience and personal emotions. Their message of free grace meant that anyone present could grasp salvation by choosing to accept Jesus. The personal spiritual experience promoted by popular preachers invited interaction with the laity, who might spontaneously break into hymn or prayer.

Camp meetings offered revivalists the opportunity to help the converted and unconverted experience the emotions associated with evangelical religion. (*Library of Congress*)

Charles Finney took such revivals, enriched with his "New Measures," to the growing towns and cities of the North. Many of Finney's "new" techniques had been practiced by Methodists for years, but Finney's carefully engineered tactics for raising a revival bore his own stamp. Finney was an ex-lawyer, not a theologian, and he preached in the popular idiom, the better to reach the widest possible audience. He frequently made his preaching personal, mentioning potential converts by name and offering prayers for his opponents. Making a spectacle out of struggling souls, he called forward those who felt conviction of their sins to sit on the "anxious bench" near the pulpit. He violated some sensibilities by asking women to testify publicly about their spiritual experiences before women and men alike. In his influential *Lectures on Revivals* (1835), Finney used a democratic metaphor to describe the goal of revivalism: "The object of the ministry is to get all the people to feel that the devil has no right to rule this world, but that they ought all to give themselves to God, and vote in the Lord Jesus Christ as the Governor of the universe" (Finney 1960, p. 181). In sum, Finney argued, revivals should center on the spiritual experiences and needs of ordinary people.

Critics of the revivals were dismayed by the emotional and physical chaos that routinely broke out. One opponent, for instance, described the "Bedlam" that erupted at a camp meeting: "They literally . . . jumped and yelled, and barked, groaned and grunted, howled and screamed, cried and laughed, and tumbled and rolled over one another, men, women, and children, as if reason had been entirely dethroned and the mind had become a chaos" (Bratt 2006, p. 6). Orthodox Presbyterians and Congregationalists were joined by rationalistic Unitarians in condemning the disorder of the revivals.

The defenders of the revivals, however, remained convinced of the righteousness of their cause, which they tied closely to their expectation that revivals could help usher in the millennium. American Protestants of the Jacksonian era were well schooled in the idea that the millennium was on the horizon if not actually at hand. Through God's grace and human agency, they believed, the world would undergo a gradual process of perfection, leading to a 1,000-year period of harmony, which would set the stage for the triumphal "Second Coming" of Christ to earth. Such millennial beliefs became ubiquitous during the early republic period, when American Protestants wed Christian expectation with nationalism. In sermon after sermon, American ministers forecast a future in which the United States would become the center of the progressive millennium. This hopeful vision, known as "postmillennialism," did not entail a simple-minded faith in inevitable progress. Beneath the optimistic surface lay anxiety that the young United States, like so many civilizations before it, might decline or collapse, thus failing to fulfill its potential.

Postmillennialists thus did not take the millennium for granted—they expected to strive long and hard to achieve it. Finney, for instance, defended the necessity of revivals for claiming more converts to Christianity, warning of dire consequences should the ministry default on its duties:

If revivals do cease in this land, the ministers and churches will be guilty of all the blood of all the souls that shall go to hell in consequence of it. . . . If the Church will do all her duty, the millennium may come in this country in three years. But if . . . two-thirds of the church will hang back and do nothing but find fault in time of revival, the curse of God will be on this nation, and that before long. (Finney 1960, p. 306)

While postmillennialists saw themselves as ushering in the millennium with revivals and reform societies, the followers of William Miller became convinced that Christ's return was imminent. Using the biblical book of Daniel, Miller calculated that the Second Coming would take place within a year of March 1843. Convinced by Miller's figures and a major publicity campaign, thousands of Millerites anticipated the Second Coming, with some going so far as to sit on their rooftops, robed in white, to await ascension into heaven. When Christ did not appear, Miller revised his estimates—to no avail. In the absence of the Second Coming, most American Christians continued to express postmillennial beliefs, at least until the Civil War.

Methodism and the Limits of Egalitarianism

As skilled practitioners of revivalism and popular preaching techniques, Methodists dominated the field during the Jacksonian era. Methodism was not an American-born movement, but the theology and organization developed by Englishman John Wesley allowed it to thrive in America. Methodism originated as an outgrowth of the Church of England in the mid-eighteenth century, and the Methodist Episcopal Church came into existence in the United States as an independent denomination in 1784. Initially, Methodism experienced brisk growth, claiming nearly 58,000 adherents by 1790. But during the early nineteenth century, Methodism grew astonishingly quickly. By 1830, this upstart movement held numerical dominance in more U.S. counties than every other denomination combined. During the 1840s, the various Methodist church organizations claimed over a million members, and by 1850, Methodists made up about one-third of American church members. By mobilizing an efficient ministry and empowering the laity, Methodists sustained not simply a church but a democratic social movement throughout much of the Jacksonian era.

Taking advantage of the new religious openness of the young United States, Methodists proved better than others at keeping up with the rapidly expanding and westward-moving American population, largely because of their ability to recruit and efficiently deploy ministers. The Methodist Episcopal Church maintained a small army of itinerant ministers, each of whom rode lengthy "circuits," covering large territories on horseback. Circuit riders recruited new members, organized "class meetings," and raised funds to support their missionary efforts. Most circuit riders were young men from humble backgrounds, trained through apprenticeships but lacking formal education. They often studied the Bible and other religious texts privately to build their knowledge, but little social or cultural distance separated them

Zilpha Elaw

Zilpha Elaw was born to free African American parents in 1790, somewhere near Philadelphia. Most of what historians know about Elaw derives from her only published work, *Memoirs of the Life, Religious Experience, Ministerial Travels and Labours of Mrs. Zilpha Elaw, An American Female of Colour*, which was published in London in 1846. The extraordinary experiences of this ordinary woman illustrate the democratizing tendencies of Jacksonian-era religion, along with the limits to change.

Elaw's youth was unexceptional. After her mother died when she was twelve, she lived as a servant for a Quaker family until she was eighteen. As a teenager, she began attending Methodist services, and she experienced conversion upon seeing a vision of Jesus, with his arms open. This experience—her first of many visions—qualified her to join a Methodist class meeting, which she promptly did.

At the age of twenty, she married Joseph Elaw, with whom she had one daughter. Although she did not question her husband's authority over her, she had a very troubled marriage, because her husband was an "unbeliever" who disapproved of her piety. Several years after her marriage, while attending a camp meeting, Elaw experienced another vision, and "the Lord opened [her] mouth in public prayer." Not long after this experience, her dying sister reported being visited by an angel who told her that "Zilpha . . . must preach the gospel" (Elaw 1986, pp. 67, 73).

After operating a school for black children and becoming a widow, Elaw finally answered her call and began preaching in 1827. Her listeners soon provided her with enough funds to allow her to visit Philadelphia, New York City, and the South, where she preached extensively to white and black audiences. Referring to her-

from their audiences. Peter Cartwright, a famous Methodist preacher who compared over-educated ministers to under-grown heads of lettuce, exclaimed in his 1856 memoir that "the illiterate Methodist preachers actually set the world on fire . . . while [the orthodox ministers] were lighting their matches!" (Cartwright 1984, p. 64).

While the circuit rider linked Methodists to the larger church, local organizations fostered a strong sense of community. Many communities had voluntary local ministers, who preached with some regularity. Perhaps more important, however, were the local class meetings, which met on a weekly basis, preacher or no preacher. Becoming a full member of the Methodist church meant joining a class meeting by demonstrating that one had experienced a conversion, or "new birth." The class meeting thus formed an intimate community of Christian converts. Class meetings combined worship, through prayers and hymns, with Christian discipline. Like other evangelicals, Methodists demanded that their members lead godly lives that excluded alcohol, dancing, gambling, sexual improprieties, and frivolity. Enforcing this moral code, Methodists disciplined their members, some with more rigor, some with less. Class members were expected to police the morality of one another and to confess their own sins to their peers, thus joining themselves together into a moral community.

Class meetings and other Methodist institutions embodied a democratic, participatory spirit. Although the church had a hierarchical top-down struc-

self as "the dark coloured female stranger," she emphasized her own weakness but vehemently defended her right to preach, as she believed that she had been called to preaching by God (Elaw 1986, p. 92).

Elaw endured many hardships for daring to preach. Some observers treated her more as a curiosity than as a legitimate preacher. One unreceptive woman closed a door in Elaw's face, rather than invite her into the meetinghouse. Elaw entered anyway. And she occasionally faced down a critic who denied her right to preach. Although Elaw did not seek the backing of any church organization, everywhere she went she was able to find a willing and supportive audience. In her memoir, Elaw expressed deep suspicion of material prosperity and declared money to be the root of all evil. She resented the fact that well-off white Christians looked down on

their black fellow Christians because of their simplicity. She was particularly sharp when criticizing the "covetousness and worldly pride" of the white "polished Christians," whose sins "too often flow[ed] in a deep and mighty under current." Elaw explicitly rejected the emphasis on "respectability or pride of life of much of the present-day Christianity" (Elaw 1986, p. 118).

In 1840, believing that she had been called to preach abroad, Elaw left the United States for England, where she preached widely until 1845. Historians do not know whether she returned home, as planned, because there is no record of her later activities. If she did return to the United States, she did so at a time when women's preaching was increasingly under attack, because of the very emphasis on "respectability" that she decried—she may well have faced an unwelcome reception.

ture, local class meetings, worship, and camp meetings empowered the lay members of the church. At all of these events, prayers and preaching were informal, unscripted, and personal. Hymn singing, a very participatory form of worship, held special popularity among Methodists. Meetings and services began and ended with hymns, which revealed the laity's "core of consensus beliefs." The most commonly reprinted hymns before 1860 show a popular preoccupation with Christian conversion, God's grace, and Christ's sacrifice of his own life in order to redeem sinners. Hymns represented the Methodist "message set to music" (Hempton 2005, p. 74). Frequent hymn singing, in other words, allowed Methodists (and other evangelicals) to reinforce and celebrate their shared beliefs.

Class meetings also called upon their members to testify—to recount their spiritual experiences—or even to exhort, which often amounted to an informal or unofficial mode of preaching. With some frequency, women and African Americans, who were normally excluded from the "public sphere" of American society, testified or exhorted before mixed-sex and mixed-race audiences. More strikingly, during the early nineteenth century, a small number of Methodist women assumed the role of itinerant preacher. Beginning in 1819 and continuing well into the 1830s, for instance, Jarena Lee, a free African American woman, traveled around the country preaching to varied audiences. Zilpha Elaw did the same, and she remained active as a preacher in America until 1840, when she shifted her efforts to England.

Female ministers, such as Juliann Jane Tillman, played important roles in the democratization of Jacksonian religion. (*Library of Congress*)

Despite these striking examples of successful female preachers, many Methodist leaders began to frown on female preaching by the 1830s, and by the middle of the 1840s, there were very few evangelical women still preaching. Harriet Livermore preached in the House of Representatives for the fourth and final time in 1843, but by that time, women who spoke publicly were becoming associated with radical movements such as abolitionism and women's rights. Many Americans felt that respectable women did not speak in public, and Methodists increasingly agreed.

Methodism prospered in part because of its ability to create a sense of Christian community. Methodists (and other evangelicals) often called each other "brother" and "sister," even across racial lines, and they believed that Christ saw all human beings as equal. In theory at least, piety, rather than sex, race, or social class, provided a new egalitarian measuring stick that applied to all. Nevertheless, the church could not remove believers from the social frameworks in which they lived. Although the Methodist church utilized black preachers and made many converts among free blacks, some African American Methodists sought independence from white control and created two independent denominations during this period: the African Methodist Episcopal Church (1816) and the African Methodist Episcopal Zion Church (1821). By the time of the Civil War, these two churches together claimed over 80,000 members. Most black Methodists remained within the Methodist Episcopal Church, but these instances of racial separation hinted at the limits of Methodist egalitarianism.

Methodism's phenomenal success during the Jacksonian period had the effect of making the movement less distinctive and less democratic. What began as a countercultural movement in the eighteenth century was by the Jacksonian era part of the dominant culture. Responding to the church's evolution, during the 1840s and 1850s a number of "croakers" (usually retired ministers) began to show concern about the decline of their beloved church. Croakers complained that the energetic itinerant ministers were being replaced by a more settled, complacent ministry. More and more Methodists worshipped in handsome churches, and the church had helped found dozens of colleges. Croakers worried that this prosperity and refinement came at the price of spiritual vigor. Gradually, class meetings and the enforcement of Christian discipline were disappearing, and it seemed possible that Methodism would lose its distinctiveness by over-accommodating mainstream American culture.

Mormonism

As Jacksonian-era evangelicalism increasingly blended into the dominant culture, a significant minority of Americans sought alternatives that promised more radical personal and social transformation. The most successful such alternative was Mormonism. In July 1830, the Reverend John P. Greene, a Methodist minister living in upstate New York, answered his door to encounter Samuel Smith, the younger brother of Joseph Smith. Earlier that year, Joseph Smith had published the first 5,000 copies of the *Book of Mormon* and founded the Mormon church. Samuel became one of the first members. Although the Reverend Greene showed little interest in the Mormon message, he accepted a copy of the *Book of Mormon* to try to sell it. Greene failed to find any buyers, but he and his wife, Rhoda Young, began reading the book out of mere curiosity. They found it so compelling that they passed it along to Rhoda's family, including her brother Brigham, who later became the leader of the largest branch of the Mormon church after Joseph Smith's murder. Greene himself left the Methodists for the Mormons in 1832, convinced that Mormonism offered access to both a new scripture and to an authoritative, divinely appointed church.

Joseph Smith and his family had been battered by the forces that transformed the United States during the early nineteenth century. Born in Vermont in 1805, Smith moved with his family to upstate New York in 1816. Rather than finding opportunity in the region's rapidly developing economy, Smith's family found hardship and instability. And rather than achieving spiritual peace in a region that was being "burned over" by the fires of revival, Smith and his family experienced turmoil and uncertainty. While Smith's mother and some of his siblings joined a Presbyterian church, Smith and his father remained aloof from the churches. According to his own account of his youth, Smith felt most attracted to the Methodists, but he realized that, being young and unlearned, he was unable to discern which sect

Joseph Smith was the founder of the Church of Jesus Christ of Latter-Day Saints, known informally as the Mormons. (*Library of Congress*)

possessed the truth. Smith told of experiencing a series of visions, beginning in 1820, in which he was forbidden to join any religious sect, as all were wrong. In a vision of 1823, an angel revealed to him the location of a book of golden plates. Soon afterward, Smith found the engraved plates, along with two "seer" stones, buried in a hillside near his family's farm. Smith reported that he was required to wait four years, until 1827, before he was permitted to carry away the plates and the seer stones. With the help of his wife Emma and several other supporters, Smith used the seer stones to translate the plates, thus producing the *Book of Mormon*. This addition to the Hebrew and Christian scriptures revealed the ancient history of North America, which had been peopled by various tribes of Israel and visited by Jesus Christ after his resurrection.

Smith also claimed to have received additional revelations, and, crucially, the authority of the priesthood. According to Smith, he and his assistant Oliver Cowdery had been visited in 1829 by John the Baptist, who had bestowed upon the two men the powers of the "Priesthood of Aaron," named after Moses' brother of the Old Testament. Smith and Cowdery thus declared that they possessed God-given authority to reestablish God's church on earth. The new Mormon church promised its converts the possibility of salvation, not only eternally, but also temporally, by means of the gathering of a new Zion—God's kingdom on earth.

Alexander Campbell, leader of the Disciples of Christ, criticized the *Book of Mormon* in an 1831 review, declaring that Smith "decides all the great controversies," from "infant baptism" to "the atonement" to "the question of freemasonry," thus addressing "every error and almost every truth discussed in New York for the last ten years." This was a serious accusation. Campbell argued that the *Book of Mormon* was a patently presentist "fabrication"—not an ancient text as Smith claimed (Campbell 1831, p. 93).

Criticisms like Campbell's were widespread, but early Mormon converts dismissed them for a variety of reasons. First, converts accepted the authority of the *Book of Mormon*, not only because of the word of the witnesses who attested to seeing the golden plates but also because of the convincing relationship that they detected between the Bible and the *Book of Mormon*. Converts also believed that the Holy Spirit had made manifest to them the truth of the *Book of Mormon*, as promised in the book of Moroni. Furthermore, Mormon missionaries tapped into a variety of popular religious impulses of the time. Like Methodists and other evangelicals, Mormons emphasized the crucial power of individual choice for attaining salvation, as well as the ability of everyone to apply his or her own reason to the scriptures. Like the Disciples of Christ, Mormons sought to restore the "primitive," or original, Christian church. Mormons also preached the imminent arrival of the millennium and the establishment of the Kingdom of God on earth, a goal that they pursued through creating successive Mormon communities in Ohio, Missouri, Illinois, and ultimately Utah. Mormonism thus incorporated individualism, primitivism, and millennialism, but it also transcended them by offering converts access to the wisdom of a new scripture and a latter-day prophet. Smith was not trying to create another "denomination." Instead, he hoped to rise above the sectarian muddle of his time by reestablishing the "Church of Christ" by divine authority.

Early Mormons embraced a number of reform measures that resonated across the North of Jacksonian America. Smith joined temperance advocates in condemning the consumption of "strong drink" in an 1833 revelation known as the "Word of Wisdom." Furthermore, when Smith ran for president in 1844, his platform called for gradual emancipation of African American slaves, thus putting him in line with the moderate wing of the antislavery movement. His support of polygamy also challenged accepted mores regarding sex, family, and marriage. Smith also questioned the dominant values of capitalism. Between 1831 and 1834, he briefly attempted to establish a community of property among Mormons by asking that members turn over their property to the church for redistribution. Smith's new religious movement thus challenged the dominant culture while simultaneously drawing energy from the democratic ethos that was transforming American society.

The early success of Mormonism was impressive, especially given re-peated episodes of persecution and dislocation. Under Smith's leadership during the 1830s, Mormons established two substantial "gatherings" in Kirt-land, Ohio, and western Missouri. By the late 1830s, both settlements were abandoned because of growing "Gentile" resentment and anti-Mormon vio-lence. By the early 1840s, many Mormons had relocated to Nauvoo, Illinois, as part of Smith's plan to gather his followers. The Mormon population around Nauvoo peaked at about 15,000 before this settlement, too, fell under attack. In 1844, Smith directed that the printing press of a Mormon splinter group be destroyed, and John Greene, as marshal, carried out the order. Joseph and Hyrum Smith were arrested for this action, and they were subsequently murdered by a large mob while being held in jail.

The death of the Mormon prophet threatened the very existence of the church, which divided into several persisting factions. Brigham Young, how-ever, emerged to take Smith's place, and he earned the loyalty of the largest portion of Smith's followers. When the Mormons were forced to leave Illi-nois in 1846, Young helped organize a mass migration westward to the des-ert of Utah, which was soon to be acquired by the United States from Mexico. Perhaps 12,000 Mormons made the 1,300-mile trek west, where they at-tempted to establish the independent state of Deseret. Although Mormons soon faced political troubles with the United States, they nevertheless man-aged to create a thriving, expanding community. By the 1860s, the Latter-day Saints were closing in on 100,000 members worldwide. Despite various setbacks, Smith's attempt to build the literal kingdom of God on earth con-stituted one of the most prominent, radical, and ultimately successful ex-pressions of the antebellum impulse toward social reform.

Social Reform Movements

Few Americans committed themselves to radical movements like Mormon-ism, but a substantial number of men and women across the North became active in a web of single-issue reform societies. Reformers organized to ad-dress a long list of problems, including alcohol, slavery, women's rights, pris-ons, and Indian removal. Jacksonian-era reform organizations built upon a variety of earlier, specifically religious movements. The social reform fer-ment was thus closely linked to the religious expansion of the early nine-teenth century.

During the 1810s and 1820s, Congregationalists and Presbyterians coop-erated to found an array of national benevolent societies dedicated to mis-sionary work and religious education, including the American Board of Commissions for Foreign Missions (1810), American Bible Society (1816), American Tract Society (1823), American Sunday School Union (1824), American Home Missionary Society (1826), and the General Union for the Promotion of the Christian Sabbath (1828). The new "American" scope of the organizations reflected not only improved means of transportation and communication, which made national organizations technically feasible, but also their sense of a God-given mission to create a Christian society. As the

Reverend Justin Edwards declared at the first meeting of the American Tract Society: "We are a great people, and if not blasted by our sins, shall become greater and greater. . . . We are called by the God of heaven to make an experiment; and one of the most momentous that was ever entrusted to mortals" (Young 2002, pp. 672–673). They sought to build a "Righteous Empire," in the words of Martin Marty.

The leaders of the early national benevolent societies tended to be educated, well-heeled, and of orthodox persuasion. After 1830, however, the "righteous empire" became a more ecumenical and popular movement, with broad support from ordinary Americans, especially in the North. During the 1830s, in fact, the American Temperance Society and the American Anti-Slavery Society became the first social reform organizations to enlist at least 1 percent of the nation as members. But as the temperance and antislavery movements grew and became more ambitious, they both moved away from moral suasion and voluntary compliance to more coercive strategies, generating substantial conflict.

In the early years of the nineteenth century, temperance reformers reconfigured the consumption of alcohol as both a personal sin and a social evil. During those years, western farmers found it efficient to convert corn into inexpensive whiskey, and average levels of alcohol consumption rose to alarming rates. Responding to this problem, the American Temperance Society (1826) became a spectacularly successful organization. In 1834, the group had over 8,000 local chapters, with 1.5 million members, which made it larger, even, than the Methodist church. Advocates directly linked their cause to the coming of the millennium. As Presbyterian minister Albert Barnes wrote in a popular pamphlet: "Intemperance . . . opposes the progress of the reign of Christ. . . . It stands in the way of revivals of religion, and of the glories of the millennial morn. Every drunkard opposes the millennium" (Barnes n.d., p. 24).

The movement made a substantial impact. Overall alcohol consumption was cut in half by 1840, and thousands of distilleries went out of business. As the temperance movement gained adherents, it also became more militant. In 1836, the American Temperance Society embraced teetotalism (total abstinence from alcohol) and reorganized as the American Temperance Union. By the 1840s, many temperance reformers decided that only legal prohibition could rein in drinking among the working and immigrant classes. Starting with Maine, in 1851, thirteen states passed laws prohibiting the manufacture and sale of alcohol. What began as a social movement to promote self-control had evolved into a campaign of legal coercion. In most states, however, prohibition did not long endure. With the collapse of the Whig Party, the rise of the Republican Party, and the growing political division over the westward expansion of slavery, prohibition mostly fell to the wayside.

The antislavery movement of the Jacksonian era took more complex and controversial forms than did temperance. By the time of the Civil War, a broad spectrum of antislavery activists had participated in reform societies, political parties, and even vigilante violence. William Lloyd Garrison, like many antislavery reformers, rooted his activism in his religious beliefs.

This famous abolitionist woodcut featured an admonition from Exodus 21:16: "He that stealeth a man and selleth him, or if he be found in his hand, he shall surely be put to death." (*Corbis*)

Embracing a radical spiritual individualism, he intended to use "moral suasion" rather than political machinery to destroy slavery. Garrison disdained political antislavery because participating in politics necessarily meant compromising, and he was not one to brook compromise. In addition to publishing *The Liberator*, Garrison helped found the American Anti-Slavery Society (1833), which supported immediate, uncompensated abolition of slavery. By 1838, the group claimed about 120,000 members, with over 1,300 chapters across the North. Unlike Garrison, most of these members continued to participate in national politics. Many of them, too, were evangelical Christians who, despite retaining racial prejudice, accepted the notion of Christian equality embodied in the question—"Am I Not a Man and a Brother?"— voiced by the chained slave pictured on their publications.

Ultimately, antislavery reformers were stymied by three intractable problems. First, pervasive racism made it difficult for most whites, whether in the North or South, to imagine how millions of African Americans could integrate into free society. Second, most southern whites feared that any criticism of slavery both threatened property rights and encouraged slaves to rebel, as Turner had in 1831. This attitude led southerners in Congress to instate a "gag rule" that prevented antislavery petitions from being read, and it made many proslavery southerners all the more zealous to make slavery as impregnable as possible by expanding the institution across the West and by passing stronger fugitive slave legislation. Finally, the antislavery movement itself became seriously divided. In 1840, the American and Foreign Anti-Slavery Society broke off from Garrison's group. The leaders of the new group opposed the rising participation of women in the American Anti-Slavery Society and sought to support the antislavery Liberty Party. Despite these divisions, the knowledge that 200,000 northerners had joined antislavery organizations increasingly alarmed proslavery southerners, who mobilized to defend their "peculiar institution."

Southern Evangelicalism and Reform

As the Jacksonian period opened, evangelicalism was just achieving its status as a dominant cultural force in the South, but such dominance did not come easily. During the early decades of the republic, most southern whites saw Methodists and Baptists as subversives who threatened both patriarchal values and slavery. To Christianize the South, evangelicals had to reconcile their movement with white, male "mastery" while making peace with slavery. They did both. In 1844 and 1845, the national Methodist and Baptist organizations each split into northern and southern fragments over the issue of slavery, leaving the two dominant southern evangelical organizations to pursue their courses without northern interference. Southern evangelicals did not relinquish their goal of creating a Christian community, but they pursued that goal within the context of a patriarchal, slave society.

Southern white Christians did not embrace the popular reform movements of the North. Although postmillennialism was popular among them, it did not necessarily challenge the status quo. As Jack Maddex has argued: "The deepest faith they could invest in their social system was to believe that God was shaping it into the form of the future millennial society"—with slavery intact (Maddex 1979, p. 46). Their vitriolic rejection of antislavery tended to undercut other reform movements as well. Although temperance advocates managed to attract a substantial following in some southern states, many southern white men decried temperance as a scheme concocted by radical Yankees ultimately intent on attacking slavery. Furthermore, many northern reform projects, including dozens of attempts to establish cooperative, utopian communities, responded directly to industrialization and urbanization and therefore had little relevance across the rural South. Other movements, such as the campaign for women's rights, evolved out of abolitionism, which did not exist in the South.

Far from opposing slavery, by the 1830s southern evangelicals mounted a vigorous defense of the institution. Proslavery evangelicals did not stop at arguing that the Bible sanctioned slavery. They pushed further to insist that good slaveholders could contribute to a Christian civilization, and they pointed to their regional prosperity as evidence. Proslavery evangelicals thus conflated the status quo with God's providential plan. Southern prosperity, viewed as a gift from God, became evidence of God's approval of the basic social order in the South. They believed that southern slavery could be and usually was a benevolent and Christian institution.

As they defended slavery in the 1830s, southern evangelicals simultaneously organized missionary efforts to convert enslaved African Americans to Christianity. This timing was no coincidence. The Nat Turner rebellion of

1831, which was led by a self-styled African American prophet, revealed the perils of leaving slaves to their own religious devices. The multifaceted "Mission to Slaves," as Donald Mathews has argued, constituted the evangelicals' attempt at "saving the South" by remaking it in their image (Mathews 1977, pp. 137, 144).

To carry out the mission, evangelicals had to persuade masters, not all of whom were church members, that Christianity would improve the institution of slavery, making it both safer and more effective. Ministers believed that they could renovate and protect slavery by Christianizing it, thus making it live up to its ideal as a paternalistic institution. They believed that they could save the souls of the masters and slaves alike. They could do so without threatening slavery by teaching slaves that the racial hierarchy of the South was a God-given order that should not be questioned. In other words, they would teach the virtue of obedience.

The "Mission to Slaves" failed on numerous fronts. Few masters, even those who were church members, were willing and able to come to terms with the notion that their slaves had souls and were thus every bit as human as whites. Racism thus poisoned the mission. Furthermore, the mission did not put an end to the worst atrocities of slavery: the violence of rapes and beatings. Slaves also recognized the mission as an attempt to reassert control. For generations, African Americans in the South, enslaved and free, had been creating their own distinctive form of evangelical Christianity, with their own black preachers. They did not share the postmillennial ethos of the masters and ministers. Instead, as Mathews has argued, "Black Christians became of necessity premillennial quietists" (Mathews 1977, p. 223). For the tens of thousands of enslaved African Americans who became Christians prior to the Civil War, their religion was not about accepting their place in the hierarchy—it was about transcending their place in the hierarchy by finding what liberty could be had within the context of slavery, while imagining a world in which the chains of slavery would be broken.

After the Nat Turner rebellion, southern whites in power could no longer countenance this relatively autonomous form of black evangelicalism. As part of their campaign to tighten their control, southern masters tried to prevent African American preachers from preaching and sometimes approved the deployment of white missionaries to replace them. Such efforts at control failed to destroy black evangelicalism, but they largely drove it underground, creating an "invisible" black Christianity that reemerged with great vigor after the Civil War.

Conclusion

As President Abraham Lincoln recognized in his second inaugural address in 1865, Americans, North and South, read the same Bible and prayed to the same God, yet some supported slavery while others denounced it. While northern reformers could not persuade southern whites of the evil of slavery, neither could proslavery missionaries reform slavery to make it stable and enduring. Democratic religious and reform movements had reshaped the nation during the early nineteenth century, but they had not created a unified culture. Nor had these movements managed to resolve the great contradiction that threatened the nation's future. The success of the Republican Party, which took a very moderate stance regarding slavery and even countenanced white supremacy, precipitated the secession of southern states that led to civil war, immense bloodshed, and emancipation. Thus it was soldiers—not reformers—who destroyed slavery. Still, there can be little doubt that Jacksonian-era evangelical and reform movements played a crucial role in precipitating the conflict.

References and Further Reading

Abzug, Robert H. *Cosmos Crumbling: American Reform and the Religious Imagination.* New York: Oxford University Press, 1994.

Ahlstrom, Sydney E. *A Religious History of the American People.* New Haven: Yale University Press, 1972.

Arrington, Leonard J., and Davis Bitton. *The Mormon Experience: A History of the Latter-Day Saints.* 2nd ed. Urbana: University of Illinois Press, 1992.

Barnes, Albert. "Barnes on the Traffic in Ardent Spirits." In *Select Temperance Tracts.* New York: American Tract Society, n.d.

Bratt, James D., ed. *Antirevivalism in Antebellum America: A Collection of Religious Voices.* New Brunswick: Rutgers University Press, 2006.

Brekus, Catherine A. *Strangers & Pilgrims: Female Preaching in America, 1740–1845.* Chapel Hill: University of North Carolina Press, 1998.

Bringhurst, Newell G. "Joseph Smith, the Mormons, and Antebellum Reform—A Closer Look." In *The Prophet Puzzle: Interpretive Essays on Joseph Smith,* ed. Bryan Waterman, 113–140. Salt Lake City: Signature, 1999.

Bushman, Claudia Lauper, and Richard Lyman Bushman. *Building the Kingdom: A History of Mormons in America.* New York: Oxford University Press, 2001.

Bushman, Richard L. *Joseph Smith and the Beginnings of Mormonism.* Urbana: University of Illinois Press, 1984.

Butler, Jon. *Awash in a Sea of Faith: Christianizing the American People.* Cambridge: Harvard University Press, 1990.

Campbell, Alexander. "The Mormonites." *Millennial Harbinger* 2 (February 7, 1831): 85–96.

Cartwright, Peter. *The Autobiography of Peter Cartwright.* Introduction by Charles L. Wallis. Nashville: Abingdon Press, 1984.

Carwardine, Richard. "The Second Great Awakening in the Urban Centers: An Examination of Methodism and the 'New Measures.'" *Journal of American History* 59 (September 1972): 327–340.

Daly, John Patrick. *When Slavery Was Called Freedom: Evangelicalism, Proslavery, and the Causes of the Civil War.* Lexington: University Press of Kentucky, 2002.

Elaw, Zilpha. *Memoirs of the Life, Religious Experience, Ministerial Travels and Labours of Mrs. Zilpha Elaw.* In *Sisters of the Spirit: Three Black Women's Autobiographies of the Nineteenth Century,* ed. and intro. by William L. Andrews. Bloomington: Indiana University Press, 1986.

Finke, Roger, and Rodney Stark. *The Churching of America, 1776–1990: Winners and Losers in Our Religious Economy.* New Brunswick: Rutgers University Press, 1992.

Finney, Charles Grandison. *Lectures on Revivals of Religion.* Ed. and intro. by William G. McLoughlin. Cambridge: Harvard University Press, 1960.

Frey, Sylvia R., and Betty Wood. *Come Shouting to Zion: African American Protestantism in the American South and British Caribbean to 1830.* Chapel Hill: University of North Carolina Press, 1998.

Garrison, William Lloyd. *William Lloyd Garrison and the Fight against Slavery.* Ed. William E. Cain. Boston: Bedford Books, 1995.

Gaustad, Edwin Scott. *Neither King nor Prelate: Religion and the New Nation 1776–1826.* Grand Rapids: Eerdmans, 1993.

Gaustad, Edwin Scott, and Philip L. Barlow. *The New Historical Atlas of Religion in America.* New York: Oxford University Press, 2001.

Harper, Steven C. "Infallible Proofs, Both Human and Divine: The Persuasiveness of Mormonism for Early Converts." *Religion and American Culture* 10 (Winter 2000): 99–118.

Hatch, Nathan O. *The Democratization of American Christianity.* New Haven: Yale University Press, 1989.

Hempton, David. *Methodism: Empire of the Spirit.* New Haven: Yale University Press, 2005.

Heyrman, Christine Leigh. *Southern Cross: The Beginnings of the Bible Belt.* New York: Knopf, 1997.

Howe, Daniel Walker. "The Evangelical Movement and Political Culture in the North during the Second Party System." *Journal of American History* 77 (March 1991): 1216–1239.

John, Richard R. "Taking Sabbatarianism Seriously: The Postal System, the Sabbath, and the Transformation of American Political Culture." *Journal of the Early Republic* 10 (Winter 1990): 517–567.

Johnson, Paul E. *A Shopkeeper's Millennium: Society and Revivals in Rochester, New York, 1815–1837.* New York: Hill and Wang, 1978.

Maddex, Jack P., Jr. "Proslavery Millennialism: Social Eschatology in Antebellum Southern Calvinism." *American Quarterly* 31 (Spring 1979): 46–62.

Marini, Stephen. "Hymnody as History: Early Evangelical Hymns and Recovery of American Popular Religion." *Church History* 71 (July 2002): 273–306.

Marty, Martin. *Righteous Empire: The Protestant Experience in America.* New York: Dial Press, 1970.

Mathews, Donald G. *Religion in the Old South.* Chicago: University of Chicago Press, 1977.

Mathews, Donald G. "The Second Great Awakening as an Organizing Process, 1780–1830: An Hypothesis." *American Quarterly* 21 (1969): 23–43.

Mathews, Donald G. "United Methodism and American Culture: Testimony, Voice, and the Public Sphere." In *The People(s) Called Methodist: Forms and Reforms of their Life*, vol. 2, ed. William B. Lawrence, Dennis M. Campbell, and Russell E. Richey, 279–304. Nashville: Abingdon Press, 1998.

Mintz, Steven. *Moralists & Modernizers: America's Pre–Civil War Reformers.* Baltimore: Johns Hopkins University Press, 1995.

Moore, R. Laurence. *Religious Outsiders and the Making of Americans.* New York: Oxford University Press, 1986.

Moorhead, James H. "Between Progress and Apocalypse: A Reassessment of Millennialism in American Religious Thought, 1800–1880." *Journal of American History* 71 (December 1984): 524–542.

Pegram, Thomas R. *Battling Demon Rum: The Struggle for a Dry America, 1800–1933.* Chicago: Ivan R. Dee, 1998.

Prince, Carl E. "The Great 'Riot Year': Jacksonian Democracy and Patterns of Violence in 1834." *Journal of the Early Republic* 5 (Spring 1985): 1–19.

Scriptures: Internet Edition. Church of Jesus Christ of Latter-day Saints. http://scriptures.lds.org/contents.

Shipps, Jan. *Mormonism: The Story of a New Religious Tradition.* Urbana: University of Illinois Press, 1987.

Stewart, James Brewer. "Reconsidering the Abolitionists in an Age of Fundamentalist Politics." *Journal of the Early Republic* 26 (Spring 2006): 1–23.

Tyrrell, Ian R. "Drink and Temperance in the Antebellum South: An Overview and Interpretation." *Journal of Southern History* 48 (November 1982): 485–510.

Wigger, John H. *Taking Heaven by Storm: Methodism and the Rise of Popular Christianity in America.* Urbana: University of Illinois Press, 2001.

Wood, Gordon. "Evangelical America and Early Mormonism." *New York History* 61 (October 1980): 359–386.

Young, Michael P. "Confessional Protest: The Religious Birth of U.S. National Social Movements." *American Sociological Review* 67 (October 2002): 660–688.

New England Industry and Workers | 7

Michael J. and Mary Beth Fraser Connolly

Prior to the large-scale New England manufacturing and "economies of scale" that emerged after 1820, small-scale, household, and village manufacturing enterprises dominated the region. Most towns had a host of small mills and businesses catering to local, county, and regional demand. These businesses also employed relatively small numbers of people. After 1820, the industrial manufacturing system that developed encompassed various river and canal systems that powered factories. New towns and cities sprang up around mills in areas like the Merrimack River Valley in Massachusetts and New Hampshire, the Blackstone River Valley in Massachusetts, and the Connecticut River Valley in both Massachusetts and Connecticut. These centers of industry included cities and towns such as Manchester and Nashua, New Hampshire; Lowell, Lawrence, Haverhill, and Worcester, Massachusetts; and Hartford, Connecticut.

Early Industrialization in New England

New Hampshire in 1810, for example, bragged of 12 cotton and wool cloth mills, 236 tanneries, 19 linseed oil mills, 18 distilleries, 14 nail factories, and 6 paper mills, among other establishments, producing over $5 million in goods. By the 1820s, after the war with Britain and a highly protective tariff helped nurture American industry, the state experienced a large increase in industrial growth. In 1823, New Hampshire listed 46 cotton and wool cloth mills, 304 tanneries, 20 linseed oil mills, 22 distilleries, and 12 paper mills. Mills in Nashua and Manchester already in existence since the 1820s saw the addition of more, larger factories by the 1840s. Manchester's Amoskeag Manufacturing Company, which predated the incorporation of the city itself (1847), produced cotton cloth. The industrial development of Manchester expanded to include other industries, such as the Amoskeag Locomotive Works. Small hamlets far removed from major cities boasted some form of rural industry. Hancock, with a population of 1,178 people in 1820, had two mills and a gun factory; Alstead, with a population of 1,611 in 1820, had a host of mills and a shoe factory employing 15 men; Deering, with a population of 1,415 in 1820, had establishments producing bricks and hoes. Even Coos County in the far north, with a total population of 5,549 in 1820, had four distilleries, six clothing mills, and three tanneries.

Massachusetts showed a similar but much more impressive trend. In 1838, there were 282 cotton mills in the Commonwealth employing 19,754 workers. By 1845 (after a severe economic depression), there were 302 cotton mills with 20,710 workers. These increases signaled a fundamental shift in the American economy, as markets began to widen from local and regional to national and international. Rather than producers shipping goods to stores and consumers in neighboring counties and states (market areas were usually confined because of transportation difficulties), goods were now being marketed in entirely different regions and nations with the development of turnpike, canal, and railroad networks The inclination toward profit, self-interest, and self-improvement did not change in these years; the change was in the size of markets.

With industrial growth, the nature of American manufacturing began to change from a widely dispersed producing region to concentrated pockets of production located in the region's cities. Much of this occurred to take advantage of waterpower along major waterways, such as the Merrimack and Blackstone rivers. Where river levels dropped precipitously, mill cities popped up, harnessing the power of falling water to turn their machinery. Even older port cities like Newburyport and Salem slowly shifted from maritime and

Methuen, Massachusetts, was one of many New England towns that saw its future tied to industrialization. (*Library of Congress*)

commercial centers to prominent mill cities. The Merrimack River city of Haverhill was transformed into a major shoe-manufacturing center, even sending its wares to the cotton-oriented South to shoe that region's enslaved labor force. Entirely new industrial cities were built from scratch, an early type of planned community. The most important of these were Lowell and Lawrence. In the 1820s, Lowell developed on what was once quiet farm country along a bend of the Merrimack River in northeastern Massachusetts and was soon the leading cotton textile–manufacturing hub in the United States—a model mill town meant to "correct" and avoid the industrial blight of British factory towns like Birmingham. Lawrence grew up in the 1840s downriver from Lowell along a series of rapid falls and by 1860 was the nation's leading woolen textile center. Cloth manufactured in these two cities could be found in nations around the world. In contrast to the growth of Lowell and Lawrence, Worcester's industrial growth did not match these "new" centers of manufacturing because of its lack of waterpower. Worcester's Blackstone Canal, built in 1828, did not solve this problem, and it was not until the combined canal and railroad development of the 1840s that this section of the Blackstone River Valley saw growth. The region became known for shoe and textile factories, as well as rubber works and agricultural machinery firms.

Labor in the Industrial Revolution

As this tremendous industrial growth took place throughout New England, the demand for factory labor rose correspondingly. The trouble was locating a supply, since labor was increasingly scarce and the immigrants who would later dominate American industrial labor had not yet arrived in force. As the lands west of the Appalachian Mountains were progressively opened up to settlement after 1800, many farmers left the fickle weather and rocky, substandard soil of New England and emigrated to fertile lands in Ohio (statehood granted in 1803), Indiana (statehood in 1816), and Illinois (statehood in 1818). One nineteenth-century New Hampshire history book, remembering the particularly long winter of 1816, noted glumly, "Not a few came to the conclusion that it was vain to think of raising their bread on the cold hills of New Hampshire, and that they must hasten to the remote WEST. . . . Never was the passion for emigration, then familiarly called '*Ohio fever*,' at a greater height" (Wilton 1834, p. 189).

As farmers headed west, rural New England towns faced a demographic and economic crisis—what and who would be left after a town's young men, seeing no future for themselves in their ancestral homes, left the region? The aforementioned Hancock, New Hampshire, nearly doubled in population between 1790 and 1810, but then lost six townspeople by 1820. Acworth slipped from 1,523 citizens in 1810 to 1,479 by 1820, Epping from 1,182 to 1,158, and Greenfield from 980 to 974. Many rural towns began to age and decline.

Industrial growth provided some of the solution, at least for a time. Since farmers' sons were leaving for opportunities in the West, many families were

Charles Storer Storrow

In American industrial history, little mention is made of Charles S. Storrow. Traditionally overshadowed by men such as Lowell, Cabot, and Lawrence, he occupies space as a footnote rather than as a major player in the plot of the American Industrial Revolution. Yet that estimation fails to credit Storrow with a central role in innovating, shaping, and directing New England industrial growth, particularly in the Merrimack River Valley. Storrow was a theorist on water power, urban developer, railroad promoter, and Massachusetts politician, and his name should grace the New England industrial marquee with the other great manufacturers and boosters of the nineteenth century.

Although forever identified with New England, Storrow began life in exile—his family had been Loyalist in the American Revolution and escaped the New England colonies for life in England, the Caribbean, and Canada. He was born in Montreal and, upon returning to Boston, was educated in elite preparatory schools and at Harvard, eventually studying civil engineering in France and Great Britain. In his early twenties, he returned to Boston to become a construction engineer and manager for one of America's first railroad lines running between Boston and the new industrial city of Lowell. Simultaneously, he studied the use of waterpower at the Lowell mills and published a book on the subject.

By the mid-1840s, Storrow joined a small group of leading New England manufacturers like Abbot Lawrence and Patrick Tracy Jackson in planning out another industrial city, soon to be called Lawrence. The Essex Company was formed to complete the project, and Storrow was named company treasurer, secretary, and chief engineer. Under his direction, the city's layout and canal and dam complex

left with teenage daughters not earning income and without suitors. Thus, a ready female labor supply of prospective "mill girls" was waiting to be tapped. Industrial employment in places like Lowell offered many benefits. It allowed rural New England females to earn wages, send money back to their families, and help maintain the family farm, as well as introduce them to a wider world outside their normal rural environs. Mill cities like Lowell offered not only jobs but also entertainment, social life, and an education. Many young women stayed employed for only a couple of years, courted and married, and moved on.

Lowell mills provide an excellent example of the effect of changing industrial practices on labor, specifically women's labor. Lowell mill operators wished to create a new factory system that would provide a better working environment than existed in factories in England. This was particularly important as women worked in these new factories. At the time the Lowell mills developed, owners and operators expressed concern over the effects prolonged factory work would have on their "mill girls." Lowell mill workers in the first decades of operation were primarily from rural New England. They endured long and exhausting work days (a seventy-hour work week was common) as the girls toiled from dawn until dusk. Mill owners, when creating an ordered factory town, also constructed housing for their female workers. These boardinghouses, while initially expensive to build, enabled

were completed—in fact, for a time, the Lawrence Dam was the largest in the world. While the city was being built, he hoped to ensure future transportation and trade by returning to his earlier work: promoting railroad development. In early 1846, the Boston and Maine Railroad agreed to move its entire mainline five miles to accommodate Lawrence. The next year, Storrow anxiously wrote the Salem politician and merchant Stephen C. Phillips to encourage a line connecting Salem to Lawrence, or the "New City," as it was often called. He gushed over the railroad's potential benefits to a new industrial city like Lawrence, as well as older ocean ports like Salem: "By easy communication with this place, you will put yourselves in easy communication with the whole valley of [the] Merrimack River, covered as it is with a busy & thriving population, always in motion. . . . I see no reason why [Lawrence] may not become what Lowell is now" (Connolly, 155). Storrow was both successful and prescient in this matter; not only was the railroad built (it became known as the Essex Railroad), but Lawrence had become the nation's premier woolen manufacturing center by the time of the Civil War.

Storrow moved easily from business to politics in the 1850s, being rewarded for his hard work with election as Lawrence's first mayor. In 1860, when a mill building owned by the Essex Company collapsed and killed eighty-eight workers, he defended the company and led relief efforts to help those affected. Thereafter, he moved with his family to Boston, where he spent the rest of his life. He remained active until the 1890s, using his civil engineering expertise for various industrial and railroad projects, like the Hoosac Tunnel in western Massachusetts—for a time the world's longest railroad tunnel. He died in 1904 at age ninety-five.

the employers to keep wages low and to monitor and regiment their mill girls. This not only contributed to more efficient production of goods, but it also allowed them to ensure that female workers' moral and physical health would be maintained. As the "girls" were leaving the protection of home and going to work in factories, many operators felt required to extend paternalist protection over them. This paternalism translated into a total system of living, whereby women were required to live in boardinghouses owned by the mills with matrons to watch over the workers in their free time. Women followed strict rules of their houses. While each company had its own regulations, all generally required regular church attendance, abstinence from consumption of alcohol, and observance of a curfew. Within each boardinghouse, the matron supervised her tenants, ensuring that employees of the mills behaved morally. Companies also required that boarders keep an orderly and clean appearance, were punctual to meals served within the house, and assisted in the cleaning of the boardinghouse. Matrons were required to "report . . . the names and occupations of their boarders, also give timely warning to the unwary, and report all cases of intemperance, or of dissolute manners" (Dublin 1979, p. 79). Such reports could result in the dismissal of the offending parties.

Along with regulating the lives of their workers, companies also wished to provide social activities and endeavors that would foster cohesion and

Women and children served as important members of the industrial labor force. (*Bettmann/Corbis*)

enjoyment. While various nearby churches provided wholesome entertainments for the workers, the nature of boardinghouse living created a community in which women's only recreation and socialization was among fellow workers. The overwhelming number of native-born workers in the early decades of the companies' operation also contributed to this community life as the workers shared a common background and area of origin: rural New England. The owners helped create this cohesion through their regulation of work and leisure time. The manufactured social life of the mill girls also resulted in solidarity between the women that gave them the courage to form unions and call strikes.

Immigrants in the Workforce

By the 1850s, however, the number of immigrant workers entering textile factory work in various regions of New England, such as the factories of Lowell and Lawrence, altered the ethnic makeup of the workforce. Irish immigration of the mid-to-late 1840s resulted in a change not only in who worked in the mills, but also in what capacity. It also produced lower wages, regardless of gender. Traditionally, the paternalist corporate plan for Lowell had created a division of labor along gender lines, with female laborers rarely encountering male workers other than overseers. By the 1850s, the number of native-born American women working in the mills declined as more immigrant workers, both male and female, entered the mills. Irish men, for example, not only assumed traditionally female positions but also accepted lower wages than native-born men. The mills also saw an increase in workers under the age of fifteen.

The increase in immigrant laborers was not unique to Lowell. Other towns and industries, such as the Amesbury Flannel Manufacturing Company and Salisbury Manufacturing Company in Massachusetts, saw a shift in demographics in employment of Irish immigrants. An 1852 strike within these textile factories was thwarted when operators brought in Irish workers to replace the striking native-born workers. In these communities, the factories had historically drawn from the surrounding areas for their laborers, just as had the Lowell mills. Here, however, company housing did not exist. As the 1852 strike erupted as part of the larger "Ten Hour Movement," native-born workers, both male and female, worked together throughout the strike, with women occupying a secondary support role. Despite efforts, the strike was defeated before the year's end. Many workers left the area as more foreign-born workers moved into their vacant positions. By 1855, the immigrant population of these two towns rose to roughly 12 percent. These changes in work and demographics drove many skilled and semiskilled workers to throw their political lot in with the anti-immigrant and anti-Catholic Know-Nothing Party in 1854.

The workers in Amesbury and Salisbury struck in 1852 in reaction to the paternalistic practices of the factory employers, which included increased regulation of breaks and declining wages. They resented restrictions placed on their workday. In Lowell, the mill girls also struck against the changing working conditions as early as the 1830s. Walkouts continued in the 1840s and 1850s, but these, also a part of the Ten Hour Movement, included more male workers, like machinists from the Lowell Machine Shop in 1853. The Ten Hour Movement worked for a decrease in hours, but it also represented an effort to preserve the dignity of labor. Industrial progress had altered the means of production, which was at one point dominated by the "putting-out" system—this entailed workers finishing products from their homes. Increased dependence upon a factory system shifted the emphasis away from skilled labor toward more semiskilled and unskilled labor. The Lowell system was a means of protecting female laborers who entered this new industrial work world as wage earners. Yet by the 1850s, the paternalism of owners declined as immigration increased. Returning to the example of Lowell, church attendance was not universally required of operatives in this industrial center. Historians have argued that the shift from Yankee to Irish workers released owners from a sense of duty or obligation to protect their female workers' morality.

Growth of Railroads

Another form of industrial employment, which often caused social and political tension, was railroad work. Railroads began to expand rapidly across New England by the late 1830s, helping to enlarge further the scope of markets and aid the growth of the region's many industrial cities. Just as workers in textile mills learned to man massive machinery powered by water, many also learned to operate steam locomotives as they carried passengers and

The growth of railroads, with their promise of faster transportation and larger load capacities, coincided with the increase in industrialization. (*Library of Congress*)

freight between cities. Railroads required large numbers of workers: laborers, machinists, station agents, conductors, baggage handlers. Railroad work was increasingly a major source of industrial employment; by the early twentieth century, railroads would be the primary employer in the United States. By 1860, however, smoky railroad locomotives working a complex matrix of rail lines around mill cities like Lowell were already a common sight—they were part of the same system of industrial production and distribution that was the American Industrial Revolution.

Railroad labor was controversial in the region. Just as factory labor agitated openly for better conditions and wages, railroad workers were also a high-profile workforce, often a constant presence in many communities. The fact that so many were Irish immigrants played a major role in the rise of nativism in Massachusetts in the 1850s. Railroad building was manifestly a public activity—proceeding through town and country, digging and blasting across miles of land—and the Irish, their work, and their living habits were routinely discussed in letters and newspapers of the day. As early as the mid-1830s, when the Eastern Railroad was first being built across the Lynn salt marsh, the Irish workers gained notice and often praise. Inhabiting "shantees" near the construction sites, they lived with their families in self-contained, but highly visible, communities. Hundreds came from nearby cities and towns to observe the Irish day after day. Observations usually brought admiration. "They possess a power of labor and endurance which in general the more tenderly nurtured American cannot equal," reported the *Essex Gazette* in 1837. "It is to these qualities of the Irishman, that we are indebted for the execution of almost all the public works of our country. They dig our canals, make our railroads, and build our wharves." Working from dawn until well after dark, they never left the work sites, even in the winter when snow and frost forced a work stoppage. The Irish remained the workforce of choice for railroad construction through the whole antebellum period.

Railroad building was a brutal, difficult, loud business, however, and as much as the Irish impressed locals with their work ethic, they were also identified with construction dangers like blasting accidents. Just days before Christmas 1837, while workers blasted rock in Lynn, a fifty-pound piece of frozen earth crashed through the roof a neighboring house and nearly killed a mother and son. Two years later, while blasting in Beverly, Massachusetts, another fifty-pound piece of bedrock flew through the air and crashed through the roof of a nearby workhouse. A town meeting was convened soon after, warning the railroad contractor to be more careful. The workers were also the victims of gruesome accidents. In August 1837, two Irish workers were cut in two trying to stop a rolling gravel car near Andover, Massachusetts; three more were killed in 1854 and 1855 as embankments they were shoveling collapsed on them in Lawrence and Andover.

There were also labor problems. In 1839, the Irish workers completing the Salem Tunnel stopped construction over an "abatement" of hours dispute with the Eastern Railroad contractor. In May 1840, a riot broke out at a railroad work site in Rowley, Massachusetts, when two workers refused to work extra long hours and were docked their pay. Word quickly spread among the ranks, construction stopped, and the workers congregated in the quiet seaside town demanding payment of wages. When the "overseer" refused, the local police were called, townspeople began to gather, and a melee broke out. A local militia group finally restored peace, and two of the workers' ringleaders were arrested. With such incidents, concern, as much as praise, dominated public perceptions of Irish workers as they took a leading role in building New England railroads.

Perhaps most interesting was public interest in the drinking habits of the Irish railroad laborers. From the start, the Eastern Railroad instituted a temperance policy for its workers. That policy succeeded most of the time and gained favorable local publicity. Violations, however, were widely reported. The most blatant and tragic violation came in September 1839, when five railroad workers in Ipswich got drunk, went for a boat ride on the Ipswich River, and capsized the boat during a fight. In the frantic swim to shore, one man drowned. The others never noticed, and after sleeping on the beach all night, reported the incident to the police the next morning. The bruised body washed on shore a few days later. No charges were filed because local authorities could never establish exactly what happened. Incidents like these, combined with the high profile dangers endemic to railroad construction, gave the Irish a split personality in the public eye: good workers, but careless, violent, and drunk.

Concern about the workers' drinking was not unique to railroads or to Irish immigrants of New England. The changing nature of work has prompted historians to examine the motivations of manufacturers and businessmen who embraced the growing temperance movement of the antebellum period. As Paul Johnson argues in *Shopkeeper's Millennium*, temperance advocates in Rochester, New York, expressed their anxiety over their loss of control over workers as they moved from living with their employer to living independently. In the 1820s in Lynn, Massachusetts, shoemakers were paid along with their regular wages "a half pint of 'white eye,'" an alcoholic beverage. The Irish workers who built Worcester's Blackstone Canal and the Boston and Worcester Railroad also received whiskey with their wages. This custom of drinking while working was a part of the larger culture of work. The desire for a more ordered workplace (reminiscent of the Lowell Mill owners' paternalism) was manifested in workplace drinking bans as early as the 1830s in places like Worcester. Middle-class and upper-class native-born business men and women joined temperance movements in various industrial centers and advocated not only the regulation of alcohol but also its outright prohibition.

As railroad workers, the Irish kept a high public profile throughout the antebellum period. Essex County was Massachusetts's most densely "railroaded" region by the mid-1850s—one mile of track for every three miles of

Industrialization concerned reformers such as those in the temperance movement who believed that it was disrupting traditional American gender and social roles. (*Library of Congress*)

surface, versus the state average of one to seven. With such impressive totals, Irish laborers kept an almost constant public presence between 1835 and 1855. Railroads gave the Irish a means of support, a prominent public role, and (when railroads began to affect the local economy) a ready identification with railroad development. In many ways, railroad development and the Irish became synonymous.

The Rise of Nativism

Mixed public reception of the Irish gave added energy to nativism. Concentration of foreigners in Essex County towns increased dramatically in the early 1850s, as immigrants flooded the area looking for employment. The ratio of 12-plus foreigners for every 100 natives encompassed eleven county towns in 1850 and twenty in 1855. Such astonishing growth in such a short period must have shocked many Essex County natives familiar with the Irish railroad workers who had lived and worked in their communities for twenty years.

In 1854 and 1855, violence against the Essex County Irish was common. On July 8, 1854, a tremendous anti-Irish riot broke out in Lawrence when an upside-down American flag was discovered flying over an Irish shanty. After the mayor attended a Catholic July 4 rally, irked nativists spread rumors that the Irish hoarded arms in church basements, and the flag incident four days later sparked a 500-man march on the Irish neighborhoods. Armed with pistols and clubs and jeering the pope, they rioted with the Irish until the mayor called out the militia because the police were allied with the nativists. Later that month in Newburyport, a young Irish mill worker was grabbed off the street, gagged, and thrown in a local pond. "Let the damned Paddy drown," his abductors taunted (*Newburyport Herald*, August 4, 1854). In November, an Irish dockworker was grazed by bullets. Riots and brawls between Irish and native-born Americans broke out in Newburyport and West Newbury in the spring and summer of 1855, and the windows of a Newburyport Catholic church were smashed. The environment became so poisoned that ten Irish families left Newburyport in 1855 and relocated to Illinois, apparently because of the violence and ill will against them. As the violence increased, the political climate in Essex County swung strongly in favor of the nativist and anti-Catholic Know-Nothings, who argued for restrictions on immigrants in all facets of American life, including industry. In 1854, Know-Nothing gubernatorial candidate Henry Gardner swept the county, taking 69 percent of the vote.

Advent of the Civil War

Just as railroads and industrial workers were linked to 1850s Know-Nothingism, workers also played a prominent role in the opening days of the Civil War. As railroads expanded the markets of the Essex County shoe business across the South and West, making Lynn and Haverhill two of the biggest shoe-producing cities in the world, shoemakers became increasingly integrated into the expanding and lucrative national market. Shoemaking was one of many industries that developed in New England from a "putting-out" system where families manufactured shoes within their homes. Women in particular participated in this putting-out system by including some aspect of the shoemaking process in their daily routine of work. By the beginning of the nineteenth century, an artisan may have directed shoemaking within his home, but various members within his household, including his wife, children, and apprentices, completed the task of shoemaking. Women came to dominate the ranks of shoebinders in Massachusetts, and more women filled these jobs than those who joined the ranks of mill hands in the textile factories. Increased mechanization of the shoe industry, as in various other manufacturing completed outside of factories, enlarged the number of factory-made shoes. By the 1850s, the putting-out system could not keep up with demand. By 1852, shoe manufacturers were using modified Singer sewing machines to stitch leather rather than the hand-stitching previously done by women workers. Historians have shown that this change in the mode of production in Essex County sparked labor protest among female shoebinders, who feared that they would be replaced by machines. While not displacing them completely, sewing machines by the 1850s decreased the number of shoebinders most dramatically in the putting-out system and in factories. Despite this decline in female workers, production increased as their place was taken by male workers,

In 1857, the market for shoes declined. With this decline, manufacturers decreased wages, a move that resulted in labor agitation. Again, as with the strikes in the textile industry in the 1840s and 1850s, workers responded not only to declining wages but also to what they perceived as a devaluing of labor itself. The shoe industry still had elements of outwork (whereas the textile industry did not), and male workers voiced concerns over the destruction of traditional artisan culture. Initially, the increased mechanization brought more women into the factories and away from their more traditional position as outworkers in domestic settings, but male craftsmen were threatened by the presence of women and believed they would take their jobs.

Southern violence against the Union in 1861 struck at the heart of the emerging national market for New England boots and shoes, and hundreds of shoemakers and manufacturers did not remain idle as their economic and political life fell apart. The Civil War became a war for maintaining their work, wages, and livelihoods. Early enlistees for Civil War service were an extraordinarily small percentage of the overall eligible population. For example, the 1860 Essex County male population between the ages of fifteen and forty represented 40 percent to 60 percent of the total population. Only a very small percentage of those eligible served the Union before September 1, 1861, with no town exceeding 9 percent of its population. This early group of Union troops was a small, unique collection of men with motives and pressures for fighting different from the motives of those who came later. The industrial cities of Essex County sent most of these early troops, while the rural and fishing communities held back. Considering the reasons for

Shoemakers' strike at Lynn, Massachusetts, from an engraving published in Frank Leslie's *Illustrated Newspaper* on March 17, 1860. (*Library of Congress*)

secession and the motivations to fight for the Union, the fact that industrial workers enlisted is hardly surprising, especially in the boot and shoe industry.

The Essex County shoe business had been connected with the southern market for decades. Lynn shoe manufacturers had sales agents across the South by the early 1800s. For example, Haverhill shoemakers had connections in Richmond, Virginia, by 1808. "I think there is no doubt," one local historian chronicled, "that for many years before [1810], shoes were manufactured at odd times, in small lots, and shipped in vessels, when opportunity offered, to be sold in Southern ports" (Swett n.d.). In these early years, shoes were first sent downriver to Newburyport for shipment southward. After 1812, they were increasingly carried by road to ports like Salem and Boston for shipment. The arrival of the railroad changed shipping methods once again and by the late 1830s, many shoemakers quickly capitalized on the invention for business development. In the years after railroad shipping became available, business boomed. From 1837 to 1855, Haverhill shoe production increased from 1.4 million to 4.33 million pairs, and by 1855, 67,000 cases totaling 3.69 million pairs of shoes—85 percent of the city's shoe production—were shipped via rail to Salem and Boston for transportation to the American South. A cheaper and more efficient method of freight transportation, railroads became integral to the operations of Essex County shoe producers by the late antebellum period and helped them send vast numbers of locally made shoes to the South.

Southern secession further threatened the workers and the shoe industry by closing its primary market. The winter of 1861 was a good season for Haverhill shoemakers. Southern and western buyers came to town and conducted their business as if nothing had changed. In fact, one week in late February, over 3,400 cases of Haverhill shoes were shipped over the railroad, the largest ever in the town. This sudden burst of business was politically motivated, however. In mid-February 1861, the new Confederate government in Montgomery, Alabama, decided that all goods purchased before February 28 and delivered before March 15 would be free of tariffs. All goods shipped after March 15 would be charged. In response, there was a mad rush to clear out stock. When southern shoe customers repudiated their northern-held debt, however, the Haverhill shoe industry was plunged into a depression. "The principal business of the town is to supply the South and West with shoes," the *Haverhill Gazette* explained in February 1861, "and anything calculated to interfere with that business is sensibly felt." By May, the paper suggested that the total debt amassed in 1861 was greater than the sum of southern shoe sales over the past thirty years. "[A] deep financial gloom covers the entire business prospects of our town," a Haverhill historian wrote in 1861. "Business is almost totally suspended, and an unwonted stillness reigns in our streets. Close upon the heels of broken state faith, has followed individual repudiation, distress, and financial ruin. . . . More than one who expected ere long to be able to pass the remainder of his days in pleasant retirement from active business, has seen bright hopes of long years dashed to the ground, and their place taken by grim visions of grey-haired poverty" (Chase 1861, pp. 538–539).

For shoemakers, secession was to blame. Secession, which broke down the emerging national market and cut the shoe industry off from its primary consumers, caused terrible damage to the shoe business and threatened its future. As testimony to the importance of the South to the shoe market, shoemakers enlisted in high numbers for service in the early part of the Civil War. Even though they represented only 22 percent of the Essex County workforce in 1860, shoemakers comprised 39 percent of the early 1861 county enlistments. While mechanics and artisans enlisted in numbers comparable to their presence in the overall workforce, fishermen, farmers, laborers, and other factory workers were underrepresented, with some groups at less than half their percentage in the county workforce. Only shoemaking and leather working—two intimately related industries—were over-represented in the Union enlistment rolls. Two out of every five Essex County enlistees was in the shoe trade. In the eyes of eagerly enlisting shoemakers, secession and war threatened their livelihoods.

The landscape of New England industrial labor had changed dramatically between 1800 and 1860. Massive mill cities of concentrated production and ringed with worker housing spread across what was once farmland and a widely dispersed regional economy. A complex web of railroad lines linking these cities with other regions had replaced the earlier roads and waterways. Spread throughout was a new and growing block of laborers who played a coequal, and sometimes controversial, role with capital in spurring economic development and affecting the region's political landscape until the Civil War.

References and Further Reading

Boydston, Jeanne. *Home and Work: Housework, Wages, and the Ideology of Labor in the Early Republic.* New York: Oxford University Press, 1991.

Chase, George W. *The History of Haverhill, Massachusetts, From its First Settlement in 1640, to the Year 1860.* Haverhill: n.p., 1861.

Connolly, Michael J. *Capitalism, Politics, and Railroads in Jacksonian New England.* Columbia: University of Missouri Press, 2003.

Dalzell, Robert F., Jr. *Enterprising Elite: The Boston Associates and the World They Made.* New York: W. W. Norton, 1987.

Dublin, Thomas. *Women at Work: The Transformation of Work and Community in Lowell, Massachusetts, 1826–1860.* New York: Columbia University Press, 1979.

Newburyport Herald, August 4, 1854.

Rosenzweig, Roy. *Eight Hours for What We Will: Workers and Leisure in an Industrial City, 1870–1920.* New York: Cambridge University Press, 1983.

Rothenberg, Winifred Barr. *From Market-Places to a Market Economy: The Transformation of Rural Massachusetts, 1750–1850.* Chicago: University of Chicago Press, 1992.

Steinberg, Theodore. *Nature Incorporated: Industrialization and the Waters of New England.* Amherst: University of Massachusetts Press, 1991.

Swett, Philip C. "History of Shoemaking in Haverhill, Massachusetts." Paper read before the Fortnightly Club, in the possession of the Haverhill Public Library Special Collections, n.d.

Vickers, Daniel. *Farmers and Fishermen: Two Centuries of Work in Essex County, Massachusetts, 1630–1859.* Chapel Hill: University of North Carolina Press, 1994.

Wilton, John M. *Sketches of the History of New Hampshire, from Its Settlement in 1623 to 1833.* Concord, NH: Marsh, Capen, and Lyon, 1834.

Native American Politics and Removal | 8

Michael P. Morris

ndian removal during the age of Andrew Jackson had its roots in the Jeffersonian era. President Thomas Jefferson, who wrote about Native Americans as "noble savages" and compared them favorably with the Vikings of Northeastern Europe, was the first executive to plan eventually to use the Louisiana Territory as an area in which to dump the Southeastern Indians. Even more ironically, a later president who became the architect of Indian removal, Andrew Jackson, was the only executive to have an adopted Indian son.

Early Attempts to "Civilize" the Native Americans

In many ways, the Indian policy pursued by the United States government in the 1830s was the culmination of anger and mistrust that had been building since the American Revolution. During the war, both Patriots and Loyalists initially resisted involving the tribes. However, desperation to end the war led each side to try to engage the largest tribes by telling interesting lies or over-simplifications in order to enlist their military support. Patriots told the tribes that the war was being fought to stop the great king across the water from cheating and over-taxing the Americans. Loyalists told the tribes that the war was about stopping the Americans from taking Indian lands. Because tribes such as the Senecas of the Hodeenosaunee Confederacy in the North and the Cherokees in the South fought for Britain, patriotic citizens of the new nation often blamed all tribes for their choices in the postwar period.

Despite hard feelings on the part of many United States citizens, the government officially pursued a civilization program with these tribes. It provided them with practical and readily used materials such as farm tools and supplies and with something a bit more abstract—missionaries and other cultural agents desirous of changing them. The program mixed federal efforts at supplying basic farm equipment and model plantation-style farms along with private religious organizations that supplied missionaries and often provided boarding schools. One of the earliest private religious organizations was the American Board of Commissioners for Foreign Missions, a Boston-based organization that established missions within Cherokee country in 1816 as well as among other southern tribes. Founded in 1810 by Massachusetts Congregationalists who were Federalists, abolitionists, and Indian supporters, the organization envisioned proselytizing the roughly 65,000 Creeks, Cherokees, Choctaws, and Chickasaws living on their ancestral lands in the South.

In his first annual message to Congress, Jefferson initially reported broad successes with the civilization program in its earliest stages. He noted, "I am happy to inform you that the continued efforts to introduce among them the implements and practice of husbandry, and of the household arts, have not been without success; that they are becoming more and more sensible of the superiority of this dependence for clothing and subsistence over the precarious resources of hunting and fishing" (Jefferson 1984, p. 501). Yet Jefferson's instructions to the Indian agents through Secretary of War Henry Dearborn outlined a program of maintaining peace with the tribes while steadily obtaining land. Jefferson predicted that native conversion to small-scale farming would render the tribes' communal lands useless to them and leave them willing to sell. He indicated that trade outposts could allow native peoples to run up such debts as to make land cessions an easy alternative to settling accounts. Ultimately, Jefferson wanted the southern tribes to be squeezed between the Appalachian Mountains and the Mississippi River so that they voluntarily would request relocation. The federal government pursued, from the beginning, an Indian policy that was schizophrenic at best.

Beginnings of Indian Removal

By the time Andrew Jackson became president in March 1829, the civilization program had achieved limited results. Tribes such as the Cherokees had moved farthest toward acculturation by adopting plantation agriculture, Christianity, and the use of slave labor. Groups such as the Muskogees, the Chickasaws, and the Choctaws had achieved lesser degrees of change. The Seminoles had changed little, if any. At the time of Jackson's first inaugural address, he pledged to maintain a fair and humane policy toward Indian tribes and consider their feelings in making policy. Yet Jackson made the pledge to support native peoples with the proviso that the feelings of U.S. citizens in these matters were a major factor. Despite the altruistic words, Jackson was, in fact, already aggravated that previous administrations had not done something about the South's Indian problem. He came into office with the view that both the treaty-making process and continuing attempts to keep U.S. citizens away from Indian lands were obsolete and futile. In Jackson's mind, only a radical new policy of removing tribes from within the borders of established states would work.

The resulting national debate over Indian removal was hotly contested. Southern politicians who were pro-removal saw the political discussion as a volatile example of sectionalism provoked by northern demagogues intent on further weakening the South. Ironically, at a time when the federal relationship with states such as South Carolina was deteriorating over issues such as the import tariff, Georgia and the federal government cooperated remarkably well to carry out the removal. The government's plan to remove southeastern tribes was based on the assumption that it was the only way to ensure their continued survival. Removal was also based on the idea that only out west would further attempts at civilization of Native Americans be possible.

Georgia's role in Indian removal also began in the Jeffersonian era. While Georgians shared an antipathy for Indian peoples that was common in the post-revolutionary era, the legal basis for the coming conflict could be traced back to 1802 when Georgia agreed to surrender its western lands, the future states of Alabama and Mississippi, to the federal government in exchange for $1.25 million. The federal government promised the state that it would terminate Indian land claims within its borders in a peaceful and timely manner. The discovery of gold in 1829 at Auraria in northern Georgia added a new dimension of tension to the strain between the state's citizens and the Cherokees. Now the reasonable and peaceful land claim extinction process was accelerated by the lure of potential riches. The notion that Georgia contained a separate nation within its borders and that within the Cherokee territory lay a treasure that white Georgians could not have was inconceivable to Georgia politicians.

Jackson's Background as a Key to Removal

Andrew Jackson's background may also contain clues to the reasons for his promotion of Indian removal. Jackson was born in the backcountry at Waxhaws, South Carolina. His father died in the weeks before young Jackson was born, and so the dangers of life in the frontier environment may have seemed more threatening to the fatherless boy. An ongoing danger to family life was periodic Indian attacks from groups like the Catawbas and Cherokees. When the Revolutionary War came to the backcountry South, the level of danger increased again. Young Jackson became a courier at age thirteen for the Patriot Army. In 1781, Andrew and his brother Robert were captured by the British and transferred to a prisoner of war camp at Camden, South Carolina. Camp inmates and British guards robbed and abused the young men. Both Jacksons contracted smallpox in the camp and, although they were released in a prisoner exchange, Robert subsequently died of his illness.

Andrew Jackson had the opportunity to obtain redress from both groups, the British and Indians, later in his adult career during the War of 1812. As commanding officer at the Battle of New Orleans in January 1815, he delivered a devastating blow to the British military. Prior to that, he had made his name fighting the Creeks in Alabama. Before the Revolution, the United States government had been pressuring the Muskogees, known to some as the Creeks, for access through their lands, and the relationship had deteriorated by 1813 to open warfare. A portion of the Muskogees, the Red Stick faction,

Even as he sought to defeat them, Jackson respected the bravery of Native American leaders such as William Weatherford. (*Library of Congress*)

had accepted a call to arms by northern tribes under Tecumseh, and on August 30, 1813, had attacked Fort Mims in Alabama, killing over 250 settlers. Reports indicate that the Muskogees scalped women, killed children, and split open the stomachs of pregnant women.

The Battle of Tallushatchee was a retaliatory operation responding in kind for the Fort Mims attack. On November 3, 1813, Major General Jackson, as head of the Tennessee militia, launched his counterattack on the Muskogee village of Tallushatchee near Fort Strother on the Coosa River. One of the American combatants on the scene, Davy Crockett, noted of the day, "We shot them like dogs. No warrior escaped and 84 women and children were taken captive" (James 1938, p. 159). The victory gave the U.S. government the leverage to demand a victor's treaty, appropriately called the Treaty of Fort Jackson, which transferred 23 million acres of Muskogee land to the federal government. Jackson delivered a mortal blow to a southern tribe on the brink of launching a major Indian war within the greater war against Britain. That attack broke the power of the Red Stick faction of the Muskogees and sent a powerful warning to other tribes. The event also brought Jackson together with his future son, Lyncoya.

Jackson's Adopted Native American Son

After the battle, one of Jackson's officers observed a baby clinging to its dead mother in the ruined village. He removed the baby boy and offered it to the women among the eighty-four Muskogee survivors of Tallushatchee. The officers understood the women to say that since his clan was dead, the boy had no place and should be left for dead as well. The officer took the baby to Jackson's tent. Jackson overruled the women's suggestion and took the baby, whom he coaxed to take nourishment. Some speculate that in that moment, Jackson was holding in his hands the fate of a child who had been robbed of a normal childhood by the frontier—just as Jackson felt his own childhood had been snatched away. He subsequently adopted the boy.

Lyncoya is symbolic in the life of Andrew Jackson. He joined another adopted child in the general's family, Andrew Jackson Jr., who was one of twins born to Rachel Jackson's brother, Severn Donelson, and his wife. Rachel's sister-in-law was in poor health at the time of birth, and she and her husband did not think they could care for both babies. The surviving evidence makes it difficult to determine Lyncoya's role in the Jackson family. In some instances, he seems to have been a mere playmate for Andrew Jackson Jr. in the way that plantation owners often used a slave child to help entertain their own child. Jackson sent Lyncoya out of the war zone in the care of Major William White, who was to take the boy to the Hermitage and "present the boy as a gift to his adopted son, Andrew Jackson, Jr." (James 1938, p. 64) The Jacksons permitted Lyncoya to put on war paint and jump out with a yell to startle visitors to the Hermitage. In one letter home to Rachel, Jackson encouraged his wife to keep Lyncoya in the house "because he is savage" (James 1938, p. 64).

Contradictory evidence about Lyncoya's place in the family suggests he was more than a plaything or an amusement. Other letters home to Rachel instructed her to kiss both of the general's sons until he returned. Jackson paid for Lyncoya to attend school alongside Andrew Jackson Jr. In his teens, Jackson determined to get Lyncoya an appointment to the United States Military Academy until his political opponents in the Whig Party blocked the move. In the face of this obstacle, Lyncoya chose instead to go into the saddler's trade, a job that Jackson himself had done in his youth. Ultimately, Lyncoya did not live to see either his adopted father become president or witness Indian removal. He died on June 1, 1828. Differing reports indicate that either pneumonia or tuberculosis was the cause. Lyncoya's death may have been more symbolic for Jackson than the tragedies of the boy's infancy. One author has suggested that because Lyncoya died in "white society," Jackson came to believe that Indians in general could not survive in that culture.

Manipulating Public Opinion

In 1829, executive influence and a groundswell of public support gave Andrew Jackson the chance to handle the Indian situation once and for all. Convinced that previous presidents had failed in their duty by not eliminating the Indian problem, Jackson took his own election as a mandate to correct this deficiency. To achieve the support for a project in which he had long believed, Jackson believed it necessary to affect public opinion concerning Indians and the civilization program that had been in place since the American

Major Ridge

Born into the Cherokee in the 1770s, Kah-nung-da-tla-geh ("the man who walks on the mountaintop") became known as The Ridge. As a young man, he resided in Tennessee, eventually moving to Georgia after marrying his Cherokee wife, Sehoya, or Susanna, Wickett. The couple had two children: John and Sarah.

The Ridge family embraced President George Washington's attempt to "civilize" the various Native American groups. They abandoned the traditional Cherokee life in favor of that of the southern planter class, including the ownership of African American slaves. The Ridge also showed his loyalty to the American republic by serving in the War of 1812 under General Andrew Jackson. He was rewarded with the rank of major; from that point, he was known as Major Ridge.

Major Ridge's planter status and military experience helped him politically within the Cherokee tribe. He was instrumental in the for-

In an attempt to save his people, Cherokee leader Major Ridge supported the removal westward. (*Library of Congress*)

Revolution. Specifically, he would have to prove that the assimilation program had failed outright to justify removal. Yet such a move would not be an easy task. By Jackson's presidency, at least one of the five major southern tribes had made significant progress in readily accepting the civilization program. While the Cherokees were a model for what was possible, all that they had accomplished would have to be tarnished or blighted in some way to highlight the lack of achievement of the other four tribes.

To that end, Jackson came to the presidency prepared for battle. His secretary of war and fellow Tennessean, John Eaton, was staunchly loyal and pro-removal. Jackson's appointee as attorney general, John M. Berrien, was a Georgian who was also committed to Indian removal. Since Indian affairs were lodged within the Department of War and United States legal affairs were handled by the attorney general, Jackson was well equipped for a national discussion resulting in the desired legislation. Thomas L. McKenney, a Jackson appointee, became the head of the Indian Board for the Emigration, Preservation, and Improvement of the Aborigines of America, a benevolent-sounding organization whose job was to sway the public to accept removal as a benign inevitability. The Board was funded by monies from the annual Indian appropriation budget and pledged both to promote Indian removal as Christian policy and to cooperate with the government in Indian affairs.

mation of the Cherokee Nation in 1827; in fact, it was his protégé, John Ross, who became the nation's first principal chief. The Cherokee Nation's new constitution, alphabet, and newspaper, all attempts at assimilating with white America, proved in vain. In 1830, the United States Congress passed the Indian Removal bill, a thinly veiled attempt to force Native Americans to give up their land voluntarily. The promise of cash payments and new land west of the Mississippi River in exchange for tribal lands in the Southeast failed to entice many Cherokees, but Major Ridge thought the offer acceptable. The only other alternative was to fight, which he deemed too costly.

Major Ridge, his son, John, and his nephew, Elias Boudinot, led a group of Cherokees called the Treaty Party in opposition to John Ross, who steadfastly refused to consider capitulation to the Jackson administration's demands. In 1835, Major Ridge and other members of the Treaty Party signed an unauthorized treaty with the United States government at New Echota, the Cherokee Nation's capital in Georgia. Despite Ross's protest that a small minority (75 out of a total Cherokee population of 16,000) was speaking unconstitutionally for the majority, the United States Senate ratified the treaty.

Major Ridge and his family moved with other Cherokees, perhaps a thousand, west to the Cherokee land in present-day Oklahoma. Despite their protests, most of the other Cherokees, including John Ross, followed on the Trail of Tears in 1838–1839. A group of Ross's supporters determined to execute Major Ridge, John Ridge, and Elisa Boudinot based on a traditional Cherokee law against selling tribal land, the penalty for which was death. On June 22, 1839, Major Ridge was shot five times on his way home from a trip to Arkansas. His suffering was minimal; not so for his son, John, who was stabbed repeatedly in front of his wife and children.

McKenney was a pivotal figure in Indian removal. He had been made head of the new Bureau of Indian Affairs in 1824. He had earned a reputation both as a friend of Indian peoples and as an authority figure on Indian matters, one with an enviable amount of influence. The new Indian Board that McKenney headed had a strong Christian backing and accepted as its only mission the relocation of southern Indians. Politically, it pledged not to interfere with the operation of the federal government. Thus, Jackson was forming a powerful counterweight to the influential American Board that had worked with the southern tribes for over a decade.

Influence of the Missionaries

Andrew Jackson underestimated the opposition to his plans. Criticism of his removal policy would come from one of the cornerstones of the civilization program—the missionaries. Holding opinions that were diametrically opposed to Jackson's concerning the same group of people, the missionaries and the American Board of Commissioners for Foreign Missions bravely challenged Jackson's exercise in presidential will. The Board, unlike Jackson, was convinced that the tribes were definitely making progress and were more deserving than any foreign peoples of missionary work. It planned to continue working with the tribes in their ancestral homelands.

As damaging to Jackson as the Board's mission was its legitimacy and the source of its opinions. Not only did its members hold opinions contradictory to those of the Jackson administration, but the prior government partnership that had been in force since 1816 also lent the American Board a great deal of influence; to dismiss the Board would be difficult for the federal government without somehow damaging the government's own reputation. Before the Jackson administration, the government had made a significant investment in the civilization program and the missionaries worked under the auspices of the federal government. Board employees lived with the tribes under scrutiny, thus opening questions about who was more knowledgeable about the progress of the southeastern Indians: missionaries or Washington politicians. Perhaps their greatest power lay in their potential ability to call down Heaven's disapproval on Jackson's plan.

Legitimizing the Removal

By the time of his first annual message, Andrew Jackson had begun the war of words necessary to legitimize his agenda. He stated in December 1829 that the civilization plan had been undermined by constant and increasing land demands that had left the Southeastern Indians nomads, beyond the reach of even the civilization program. In turning to discredit the most promising tribe, the Cherokees, he noted that they had made "some progress" along the road to civilization but had misused their talents to try to erect an independent nation within the borders of Georgia (Richardson, *Messages and Papers*, 2:457).

A quick accounting of this "progress" reveals an Indian nation in the early 1800s that had tried harder than others to remake itself in the image of Euro-American culture. In the 1820s, the Cherokee people had undergone a massive literacy campaign, the first southeastern tribe to codify their language. Sequoyah, or George Gist, worked on the syllabary for several years, pulling elements from both the English and Greek alphabets for a total of eighty-five letters. Sequoyah perfected it in 1819 and, within nine years, the Cherokees published their own newspaper, the *Cherokee Phoenix*. In 1827, they produced a constitution closely modeled on that of the United States. Just like its source document, it excluded both women and African Americans from voting or holding office and forbade African Americans from even entering their nation. In 1828, the Cherokees elected John Ross to the office of principal chief, a powerful executive position armed with a veto over a Cherokee National Council. Possessing both a written language and a parliamentary government, the Cherokees hoped for equitable treatment from the United States government and the state of Georgia. These accomplishments, plus an 1819 treaty with the U.S. government and congressional passage of the Civilization Fund, convinced many Cherokees that their position within the new United States was indeed a secure one. If the missionaries had God behind them, Jackson had the Constitution on his side, stating that it was illegal to

By embracing Christianity, utilizing black slavery, and developing a written alphabet, the Cherokees were the most successful at assimilation with the white American culture. (*Library of Congress*)

create a state within an already established state without its prior consent. Giving voice to what Thomas Jefferson, James Madison, and even John Quincy Adams had hinted at years earlier, Jackson proposed removal of all Indians to western lands, where the tribes would enjoy sovereignty over themselves free of white interference. The United States' role would be reduced to that of peacekeeper when needed on the frontier.

At this stage of planning, Jackson urged that removal be voluntary; for Indians to remain on ancestral lands was possible as long as they understood they would be subject to state laws. He hinted at the loss of communal lands that would come if they agreed to remain in the Southeast, stating, "it seems to me visionary to suppose that . . . claims can be allowed on tracts of the country on which they have neither dwelt nor made improvement, merely because they have seen them from the mountain or passed them in the chase" (Richardson 1896, vol. 2, pp. 458–459).

State legislators pressured Cherokee tribal leaders for land cessions and when none were forthcoming, the Georgia legislature passed legislation in December 1828 to extend Georgia law over the Cherokees. The law, which took effect on June 1, 1830, divided Cherokee land among five counties. In March 1830, before the law went into effect, a delegation of Cherokees went to Washington to persuade the government against the dismemberment of the Cherokee nation. At the delegation's request, Samuel Worcester, a New England missionary who had lived among the Cherokees for about five years, provided Congress with a detailed report of the accomplishments of the Cherokee people. In it, Worcester noted that most Cherokee women now spun and wove cloth while their men pursued the U.S. style of agriculture (deep plowing the earth) and enjoyed the independence it brought to most families. At the same time, *Cherokee Phoenix* editor Elias Boudinot attacked in print Thomas L. McKenney, head of the Indian Board for Emigration.

That same spring, Jackson supporters in both houses of the Twenty-first Congress referenced Jackson's Indian removal plan and began to craft legislation that supported the administration's stance. Tennessee senator Hugh White and Tennessee congressman John Bell co-authored a bill calling for an even exchange of land for southeastern tribes giving up their territory to receive land in the West. For eighteen days in April 1830, the halls of the Senate became a microcosm of what had become a national debate. Jeremiah Evarts, a former president of the American Board of Foreign Missions, had close ties to anti-removal senators such as New Jersey's Theodore Frelinghuysen and Maine Senator Peleg Sprague. Frelinghuysen attacked the White Bill because it abandoned previous treaties with southern tribes that had guaranteed their lands to them. Citing failure to follow its own rules, the New Jersey freshman senator asked if skin color now affected the federal government's obligations.

Evarts had written a series of essays on the immorality of removal, and anti-removal politicians now dipped deeply into the well of his thoughts. In these writings, christened the William Penn Essays, Evarts prophesied that the world would judge the United States for what it was contemplating doing to the Indians, specifically the Cherokees. Evarts quoted Thomas Jefferson's inaugural address by asking why a nation that had land to offer ten times the population at that time needed land from tribal peoples who would be forced to abandon their ancestral homes—residency that had been guaranteed to them by treaties with the United States, such as the 1791 Treaty of Holston, which confirmed the Cherokees' land claims and made the United States liable to protect them.

Senator Sprague attacked the White Bill from another angle. He bashed the Jackson administration on corruption charges, predicting that the money set aside for removal would be used to bribe a small handful of leaders in each tribe to go along with removal against the wishes of their people. He also attacked the humanity of the proposed plan, saying that it offered nothing to help the relocated tribes once they were out West.

For the Jackson administration, one of the most valuable assets in the war of words came when the congressional debate was polarized into a classic North-South struggle. Removal proponents quickly spoke out against the Indian supporters. Georgia senator John Forsyth, former state governor, quickly accused the opposition of trying to arrest the development of the state of Georgia. Forsyth hinted that the southern states had kept quiet while northern states had taken care of their Indian problems with the Shawnees and their allies in their own way. Now, Forsyth noted, the anti-removal faction wanted to deny the South that same right. He observed that Georgia would never "submit to the intrusive sovereignty of a petty tribe of Indians" (Satz 1975, p. 24). At the end of the month, the Senate voted 28 to 19 in favor of removal.

A few days later in May, Andrew Jackson reported to the Senate that the Choctaws were ready to cede their lands and move west. Jackson was careful to note that this decision was their own and only needed the Senate's confirmation. In the report, Jackson added that the tribe was one of the larger and more powerful groups of Indians. He believed that a speedy conclusion of the treaty would have a "controlling effect upon other tribes" (Richardson 1896, vol. 2, pp. 478–479). In other words, the first tribe to give in to removal would influence other tribes, specifically the Cherokees, and hasten the completion of the political phase of removal. In the fall of 1830, the Choctaws signed the Treaty of Dancing Rabbit Creek and gave the Jackson administration the momentum it needed. Secretary of War Eaton used the army to supervise the treaty. The army required Choctaw missionaries to vacate the grounds for the duration of the event.

In the House of Representatives, John Bell's bill had not yet come up for debate by the time the White Bill came over from the Senate, so the two agreed that the latter should go through the House. As it had done in the Senate, the bill raised a storm of controversy along sectional lines. Northern congressmen attacked the bill on its humanitarian elements, asking if it was indeed humane to dump some 65,000 people in the "great American desert." Opponents of the bill, such as Massachusetts's Isaac Bates, had gone into the records of early survey missions of the Louisiana territory and pulled up reports characterizing the land as having minimal potential for productive use.

Democratic proponents of removal included Congressmen Dixon Lewis of Alabama and Wilson Lumpkin, a future governor, from Georgia. They responded to these attacks by citing former president John Adams's endorsement of such an idea in 1828. The debate caught some legislators in a true bind. Pennsylvania representative Joseph Hemphill had Quaker constituents who were decidedly anti-removal, yet he considered himself a friend and supporter of Jackson. Hemphill suggested that the government appoint impartial commissioners to visit the tribes and ascertain their true feelings about the process while challenging the government to delay removal for a year to obtain more information about living conditions in the western territory. He urged his colleagues to act in the spirit of William Penn toward the Indians. His reference was to the fact that William Penn Jr. was the only British colonizer to approach local Indians, in this case the Delawares of Pennsylvania in 1682, and ask for their permission to locate on their land before bringing settlers to North America.

Jackson's supporters carried the day. The House passed the Removal Bill by a vote of 102 to 97, and Jackson signed it into law on May 28, 1830. At this point, removal was still not a done deal. The law simply called for an even exchange of land in the East for the same amount of land in the western Indian territory. Individual treaties with each tribe would be necessary to carry out the process.

Andrew Jackson's second report to Congress in December 1830 resounded with political triumph over removal. In it, he continued to discredit the civilization program while supporting the humanitarian aspect of removal. Jackson noted that states such as Alabama and Mississippi would be

freed now from Indian occupancy while the tribes would be freed from contact with white settlements and all the deleterious effects they caused. He
noted that they would be able "to pursue happiness in their own way and
under their own rude institution." Jackson further observed that continued
government protection of them, plus wise advisers, might help them "to cast
off their savage habits and become an interesting, civilized and Christian
community" (Richardson 1896, vol. 2, p. 519). The civilization program that
Jackson had discredited had offered all these opportunities and yet, according to him, the southeastern Indians were not civilized enough to
stay. The key concept was to relocate them out west without a nearby white
settlement.

In that message, Jackson challenged a major anti-removal point—that
being dumped out west was cruel. To that statement, the president replied,
"to better their condition in an unknown land our forefathers left all that
was dear in earthly objects. Our children by thousands yearly leave the land
of their birth to seek new homes in distant regions." Jackson's analogy was
probably powerful at a time when the country was beginning to believe
strongly in Manifest Destiny, the idea that God wanted the American people
to spread their government and religion from coast to coast. However, the
comparison was faulty on two levels. While many seventeenth-century emigrants left Britain due to harassment and religious persecution, they chose
to move as opposed to being moved against their will. Native Americans
were also not expected to spread their culture and government, as white
Americans were.

The Cherokees in Georgia

While the federal government worked to remove all southeastern Indians,
Georgia Governor George Gilmer and the state legislature focused their attention on the Cherokees of Georgia. The American Board of Commissioners
for Foreign Missions stood firm in its opposition to removal and issued its
own statement against it in October 1830. Once its position was established,
Samuel Worcester felt compelled to organize the missionaries from other
denominations. To some extent, the missionaries felt secure in their position,
since the federal government had always sanctioned their work. On December 22, 1830, Worcester arranged a meeting at his home in New Echota,
Georgia. Twelve ministers signed a document denouncing removal, stating it
would damage Cherokee civilization on many levels and leave its members
vulnerable to a degree of abuse heretofore not seen. This was the very same
day that the Georgia legislature passed the new licensure law forbidding the
presence of whites on Cherokee land after March 1, 1831, if they had not
taken a loyalty oath to the state of Georgia. The new law was aimed directly
at the missionary presence. Men such as Evan Jones, Samuel Worcester, and
Elizur Butler had finally been discredited on the grounds of being northern
and of being the real malcontents behind Indian resistance to removal.

Still, the opposition continued to work. The American Board of Commissioners hired lawyers for its missionaries contemplating civil disobedience.

The Indian Removal Act of 1830, which led to the forced removal of native groups such as the Cherokees, belied Jackson's paternalistic claim that he was their "Great Father." (*Clements Library, University of Michigan*)

Samuel Worcester played an instrumental role in the Cherokees' fight against the state of Georgia and Jackson's administration. (*Library of Congress*)

These lawyers were also well versed in opposing the Jackson administration. John Sergeant was a former Pennsylvania congressman and also legal counsel for the Second Bank of the United States. Another lawyer, William Wirt, had provided legal counsel to the Cherokees in earlier cases and was a candidate for the presidency in the upcoming election.

The Georgia government was not deterred. Governor Gilmer sent Samuel Worcester a letter in the spring of 1831 notifying him that he had been dismissed from his government job as postmaster at New Echota, emphasizing that Worcester no longer had the protection of being a government employee. He intimated that Worcester and the others had driven the Cherokees to disobedience, but he wanted to give the missionaries one last chance to vacate Cherokee lands before being arrested. The missionaries did not comply, and on July 7, 1831, Gilmer sent the Georgia Guard to arrest Worcester and others.

In the end, Samuel Worcester and a small group of missionaries were the only ones to serve jail time. During the September 1831 trial, a jury quickly reached a guilty verdict against the eleven missionaries. Nine of the eleven signatories of the missionary manifesto either agreed to take the oath at the end or to leave the state of Georgia. Elizur Butler and Samuel Worcester alone refused, and Georgia officials transported them to the state penitentiary at Milledgeville, Georgia, to begin serving four years of hard labor while their attorneys worked to free them.

The year 1832 was a momentous one in the history of Indian removal. In February, Jackson again addressed both houses of Congress about Indian removal. He noted his eagerness to conclude the political phase of removal. The president mentioned that since the process had begun, he hoped that tribes that were resisting, such as the Cherokees, would capitulate and accept removal; the president's divide-and-conquer strategy among the Indians had served him well to this point. Jackson emphasized again that tribes could remain if they so chose, but they would have to accept the limitations imposed on them by the states in which they lived. In the language of states' rights, the president's statement meant that natives would lose control over their lands and would have no access to the vote or to the judicial process if they remained. They would live in a limbo status not unlike enslaved black men and women.

Also in February, the Supreme Court heard an obscure case concerning missionaries arrested by the state of Georgia. The case of *Worcester v. Georgia* was crafted to test the legitimacy of Georgia's actions and, in all truth, was probably the last legal hope at stopping removal. The chief justice, John Marshall, was sympathetic to the plight of the Cherokees. He had rejected the claim given in *Cherokee Nation v. Georgia* the previous year on the technical grounds that the tribe was not a foreign nation and could not sue a state under the Constitution.

Marshall's ruling in the *Worcester* case was perhaps the most clarion voice that joined a discordant dialogue on removal and provided a long missing element—a statement of fact defining the status of the southeastern Indians. It lacked the paternalistic, tough-love rhetoric of Jackson's public statements that merely rationalized a preconceived program. It also lacked the hell-and-brimstone revival tone of Evarts and the anti-removal politicians. In it, Marshall observed that the tribes possessed natural rights predating both U.S. authority and British power before them. He argued that the very treaties that were now being made in the removal process were proof that Indians had sovereign political power. He ended the opinion by stating that Georgia laws had no force within Cherokee territory and ordered that the two ministers held in jail be released at once.

Many historians teach that Andrew Jackson's failure to enforce the decision was an impeachable act. While Jackson may have been many things, technically he was not required to act, since neither the Georgia Supreme Court nor the state government issued a written statement of intent to disobey the federal ruling; they merely did it without advertising. He did convince Georgia's new governor, Wilson Lumpkin, to release Worcester and Butler in January 1833. If the Supreme Court ruling was not in Jackson's favor, period law at the time was.

In fact, 1832 was a banner year for Jackson. The fall presidential election brought a landslide result for the incumbent president. Voters gave him 219 electoral votes, or 77 percent of their support, reelecting the executive who had taken on both the Second Bank of the United States and Indian removal. The year also had brought more capitulation to the program. In late March 1832, the Creeks gave up their plans to litigate. The Seminoles likewise signed a removal treaty in May. One month before the presidential election, the Chickasaws agreed to removal. In Jackson's fifth annual message to Congress in December 1833, he noted that the treaty process required to carry out removal was nearly complete. The Cherokees were still holding out, though. Jackson noted his disappointment in their failure to leave, an act that he predicted would only compound their problems. Connected to that prediction was Jackson's plan to reduce to a minimum the expenditures of the Bureau of Indian Affairs once removal was complete. In other words, should the Cherokees remain, they could not expect the amenities that had been provided in the past by the civilization program.

The year 1835 proved a seminal one for the Jackson administration and the removal program. In March, a small remnant of the Cherokee nation that did not represent the majority signed a removal treaty with the United States government at New Echota, Georgia. In his December 1835 message to Congress, Jackson stated that the removal plan was rapidly approaching consummation. He reemphasized the failure of the tribes to assimilate into mainstream life, but reasserted the "moral duty" of the nation to protect the tribes once relocated. The nature of the failed civilization program had been humanitarian; the purpose of removal was to help the tribes survive and become civilized. Yet Jackson's message reveals inconsistent and insincere goals. Should they not wish to farm or be bankers out in Indian territory, Jackson stated the tribes could hunt buffalo on the Great Plains. Such an economic option would have represented a step backward for most eastern tribes that had farmed for centuries, hardly the statement of an official dedicated to progress.

Fifteen months later, Andrew Jackson wrote his farewell address to the nation, thanking them for the kindness and confidence they had shown him. Though he had never wavered in his beliefs about the necessity of Indian removal, it obviously remained paramount in his thoughts as he mentioned it in one final address. Speaking about the Choctaws, Chickasaws, Creeks, Seminoles, and Cherokees, he wrote, "This unhappy race—the original dwellers in our land—are now placed in a situation where we may well hope that they will share in the blessing of civilization and be saved from that degradation and destruction to which they were rapidly hastening" (Richardson 1896, vol. 3, pp. 293–294).

The Cost of Removal

In retrospect, removal did not achieve total assimilation in the new locale just as it had not been achieved in the East. It did pull over 65,000 native peoples out of their ancestral lands, opening the territory to use by white citizens. During the cultural upheaval that the Cherokees named the "Trail Where We Cried," some 4,000 Cherokees out of 16,000 died in transit to Indian territory. Approximately 3,500 Muskogees out of a population of 10,000 died in their move to new lands. Some 6,000 Choctaws out of 40,000 died during relocation. About 1,500 of 3,000 Seminoles died, many of whom perished in armed confrontation while resisting removal. Due to closer proximity to Indian territory and a leadership that worked to minimize relocation difficulties, the Chickasaws may have come out of removal with the fewest casualties.

In Indian territory, acculturation continued to meet with some resistance, much as it had in the East. The Indian Bureau viewed this as lack of character or laziness when in fact it was cultural. The Chickasaws resisted the idea of farming in the new territory. Back in Mississippi, they had acquired black slaves and used them to farm their acreage. Contrary to Jackson's many statements, the southeastern tribes had adopted many southern traditions quite well.

Missionaries often accompanied their host tribes out to the new Indian territory, Samuel Worcester living with the Cherokees as one example. Yet now the tribes often associated the missionaries with the homes and lives they had lost back in the East. In a sense, missionary work became more difficult in Indian country because of this negative association with authority figures.

Removal politics often left the relocated tribes more divided and violent than they had been before their move. President Martin Van Buren had to monitor events among the relocated Cherokees after they carried out the death penalty mentioned in their 1827 constitution for those who signed the Treaty of New Echota without tribal authorization. The anti-removal faction murdered Major Ridge, John Ridge, and Elias Boudinot, the leaders of the Cherokee Treaty party. Van Buren's secretary of war, Joel Poinsett, suggested creating tribunals among the Indians to deal with this kind of violence. Ironically, the violence led the Van Buren administration to conclude against

The Trail of Tears witnessed the forced removal of the Cherokees from their native lands, which resulted in the deaths of thousands. (*Woolaroc Museum, Bartlesville, Oklahoma*)

making Indian country an "Indian state" within the Union, although it did lead to more regulation of the tribes.

The Cherokees asserted their own leadership in Indian Territory when they hosted an intertribal conference at Tahlequah in the summer of 1843. There, the tribes agreed on a course of friendship among themselves while pledging to stop retributive justice, allocate a portion of their funds for education, and work to suppress the use of alcohol. Although Jackson had promised sovereignty in the new territory with minimal U.S. interference, in truth the federal government continued to regulate the tribes much as it had done before. When post-removal political violence did not cease for the Cherokees, the government imposed martial law on the tribe. In fact, Chief Justice Roger B. Taney noted in an 1846 opinion that American legal jurisdiction covered the peoples in Indian territory.

Even as the southeastern tribes began to adapt to life in their designated new homes, the federal government began plans to keep shifting them further west. During the administration of President John Tyler, Secretary of War William Wilkins began to lobby for a "safe" passage to the Pacific coast by posting soldiers along the Oregon Trail. Congressmen such as Stephen A. Douglas, who had supported removal during the Jackson administration, began to work in the 1840s to remove an "Indian barrier" from the path of westward-bound settlers.

The discovery of gold at Sutter's Mill in California in 1848 and the building of the transcontinental railroad would only increase the second wave of calls for shifting Indians out of Indian territory. In retrospect, Andrew Jackson's humane and considerate policy toward southeastern Indians created only additional hardships for them in an alien land. Jackson unwittingly created a barrier in the path of Manifest Destiny, a common nineteenth-century belief. In one sense, removal took away the one indisputable claim the southeastern tribes had—prior occupation on their ancestral lands that predated Euro-American settlement. In the western Indian territory, it reduced them to a status not unlike that of the earliest inhabitants of Jamestown or Plymouth: vulnerable and dependent colonies. One fear the tribes held before removal was that if they let the government move them once, the concession would create a precedent that would be used repeatedly. In hindsight, the rocky road before and after removal did just that.

References and Further Reading

Anderson, William L. *Cherokee Removal: Before and After.* Athens: University of Georgia Press, 1991.

Burstein, Andrew. *The Passions of Andrew Jackson.* New York: Vintage Books, 2004.

James, Marquis. *The Life of Andrew Jackson.* 2 vols. Indianapolis and New York: Bobbs-Merrill, 1938.

Jefferson, Thomas. *Writings.* New York: The Library of America, 1984.

Remini, Robert V. *Andrew Jackson and His Indian Wars.* New York: Viking Press, 2001.

Richardson, James D., ed. *The Messages and Papers of the Presidents, 1789–1897.* 10 vols. Washington, DC: GPO, 1896–1899.

Satz, Ronald N. *American Indian Policy in the Jacksonian Era.* Norman: University of Oklahoma Press, 1975.

Slave Traders | 9

Steven Deyle

The common stereotype today of an antebellum slave trader is that of the fictional trader Dan Haley in Harriet Beecher Stowe's *Uncle Tom's Cabin* (1852). As Stowe portrayed him, Haley was an uncouth and unprincipled man who, according to one character, would "sell his own mother at a good per centage—not wishing the old woman any harm either" (p. 86). The main reason for this caricature of slave traders as marginal, unscrupulous monsters is the deplorable nature of this business, which has influenced our view of the men (and they were almost all men) who worked in it. Yet it is important to look at these individuals for who they really were, in all their variety, and on their own terms, no matter how distasteful they may appear to modern eyes. That is the only way to fully appreciate the diversity of people who engaged in this trade and comprehend the important role that they played in southern society.

Slave Traders: A Diverse Lot

Simply put, there was no such thing as a typical slave trader. Also known as dealers, brokers, and speculators, these men came from all parts of the South (only a small percentage had been born outside the region) and all types of backgrounds. Some fit parts of the slave trader stereotype, while others could not have been more dissimilar. They also performed different functions and engaged in the business over varying lengths of time. The one thing they all had in common was the drive to get ahead as quickly as possible. And they understood that the surest way to do so was by speculating in their region's most important commodity.

One major reason for the many misconceptions about southern slave traders, and the role they played in American society, has been the difficulty of determining who these men actually were. Few occupations have been harder to define than that of slave trader. Even if one looks only at the inter-regional trade, and among those who engaged in the business on a regular basis, many different types of individuals could fit this label. Moreover, the vast majority of southerners who made an income from this trade, for a multitude of reasons, never identified themselves in this way. Many only participated in the slave trade seasonally or for a limited number of years. They saw themselves primarily as farmers, planters, or merchants who supplemented their income by trading in slaves. Others, such as commission brokers and auctioneers who specialized in this type of property, usually referred to themselves by their general occupation. The same was true for all of those people who worked as agents, clerks, and other salaried personnel. Finally, much of the domestic trade was financed by outside investors, who, while not directly involved in the buying and selling of slaves themselves, certainly profited from these actions by others. Therefore, to fully appreciate the importance of this trade and the number of southerners who made their living from it, one needs to look at all of the individuals involved and not just focus on those who fit a limited definition of "slave trader" or who publicly identified themselves as such.

The best-known and in many respects the most important type of slave trader was the individual who bought slaves in the Upper South (where slaves were in a surplus), transported them to the Lower South (where slaves were in demand), and then sold them for a profit. In the formative years of the domestic trade, during the late eighteenth and early nineteenth centuries, the majority of southern slave traders fit this mold. Most were small-time operators from Georgia and other southern and western states who roamed the countryside of the Upper South (especially in the area around the Chesapeake Bay) looking for bondspeople to buy and sell. When purchasing, some advertised in newspapers, but most just checked the local sales and jails and let it be known that they were looking for slaves. After acquiring enough slaves to form a "lot," the trader then led them overland on foot in a coffle, or gang held together in chains. Upon reaching their destination in the Lower South, most were sold informally wherever a buyer could be found.

Expansion of the Trade for Profit

By the 1820s, the domestic trade started to change, as innovative traders expanded their operations and made them more profitable. Taking the lead in this development was Austin Woolfolk of Augusta, Georgia. Woolfolk first began advertising for slaves in Maryland in 1815. Like many other early traders, he operated out of a well-known tavern on the eastern shore of that state. After purchasing his lot, he then carried them by coffle to Augusta where his uncle, John Woolfolk, helped him sell his human property to local farmers. By 1819, however, Woolfolk had moved his operation to Baltimore, in large part to take advantage of that city's rapidly growing port. He realized that as the nation expanded westward following the War of 1812, the demand for slaves in the new Southwest would be even greater than it was in Georgia. Therefore, instead of carrying his slaves overland in coffles, or floating them down rivers on flatboats as many western traders had done, Woolfolk became one of the first traders to extensively use oceangoing vessels to transport large cargos of slaves from the Chesapeake to New Orleans.

While shipping slaves by water was slightly more expensive than other methods of transportation (roughly $2 more per slave than overland coffle), Woolfolk and other traders realized that it provided them with several important advantages. For one thing, it greatly cut the time required for transit. Even with good roads and weather, coffles could cover only twenty to twenty-five miles a day. That meant that seven to eight weeks was required to travel from the Chesapeake to Natchez, Mississippi (a common destination for many coffles), and even longer to get to New Orleans. Vessels in the coastal trade could make it to the Crescent City in less than three weeks. Consequently, by drastically curtailing the turnaround time from purchase to resale, traders lowered their maintenance costs. Shipping was also safer. There was less chance for slaves to escape at sea, and the quick trip and protection from the elements proved healthier for their human cargo as well. Finally, the coastal trade allowed traders to transport more slaves each season. While some coffles had well over 100 bondspeople in them, most contained only thirty or forty. The larger sailing vessels could ship over 200 individuals at one time.

To run their operations, these large-scale slave traders started centralizing their offices in urban areas and forming complex business relationships. They purchased and maintained their own slave jails, or "pens," in which to house and market their human merchandise. They also took on additional partners and agents to operate their extensive enterprises. Austin Woolfolk had a slave pen behind his residence on Pratt Street in Baltimore and employed numerous agents to aid him. Such practices helped to make Woolfolk and others like him some of the wealthiest individuals in the South.

Accounts and illustrations of the slave trade from the Jacksonian Age make clear its violent and coercive nature. (*Library of Congress*)

Purchasing and Housing Slaves

As in most businesses, however, the vast majority of interregional slave traders were not large entrepreneurs but mid-range and small-scale operators who dealt in dozens of slaves instead of hundreds. While there was obviously some similarity between the larger firms and their smaller counterparts, there was also much that made the occupations of these two types of traders different from one another. For one thing, many of the smaller speculators continued to engage in the same daily work pattern as that of the early slave traders. Some employed agents of their own, but most went in search of slaves wherever they could find them and then carried them south themselves, usually by coffle.

One big difference between the majority of interregional slave traders and the handful of larger firms who dominated the trade can be seen in the way they purchased their slaves. Most had to go out and solicit their own business. Some had regular territories that they worked when purchasing, usually the area within a county or two of their homes. This gave them certain advantages, such as familiarity with their customers and knowledge of all the local sales. Others went from town to town, checking the jails and court sales for possible purchases. These itinerant traders also advertised for slaves, although not in the same way as those traders with a more permanent address, whose inserts in the newspapers often ran for months. Instead, they put out advance notices in the towns they intended to visit, stating when they would arrive, where they could be found, and how long they intended to stay in the area. Finally, there were those traders who simply went door-to-door looking for slaves.

Lacking the resources of the more established firms, the majority of smaller traders also employed less efficient methods when housing their slaves before shipment and transporting them to the importing states for sale. Only a handful owned their own jails. One such man was the early Kentucky trader Edward Stone, who had several iron-barred cellars under his house. Most, however, had to board their slaves wherever they could— on their own farms, with a local sheriff, or in the pen of a larger dealer. Many itinerant traders simply never left their new purchases or kept them under the watchful eye of one of their assistants. Their journeys south were also often quite modest. Like many early western traders, Stone just floated the men and women he bought down the Ohio and Mississippi rivers on flatboats (sometimes shipping over seventy-five at one time). Most of the others led their human property overland in coffles, spending their nights in taverns, barns, or encamped under the stars.

The smaller traders also differed from their larger urban counterparts in that many of them had no set destination when transporting their slaves. While it is true that some mid-range traders had a partner located in one of the selling states, or they had arranged to sell their slaves through one of the resident dealers in the Deep South, most country traders just set out with their human merchandise looking for purchasers. Some headed where they had heard that prices were good. Others had assistants who helped them determine the best place to go. Most just peddled their slaves wherever they could find a buyer. These men remained constantly on the move and felt little hesitation in leaving a dull market for potentially greener pastures. The country traders also sometimes brought their slaves to the major urban markets of the Deep South. Unlike the larger firms, however, who used these centers as their primary base of operation, many of the smaller traders only went there as a last resort, mainly because of the higher expenses involved in trading there. Nevertheless, they occasionally did so when sales were poor and word had reached them of greater possibilities in one of the bigger markets.

Others in the Slave Trade Business

While long-distance speculators, both large and small, were certainly the best-known type of southern slave trader, there were just as many other men, if not more, who also made at least part of their living from the slave trade. These individuals worked as commission brokers, dealers, auctioneers, financiers, and various types of agents and auxiliary personnel. Some historians of the domestic trade have not considered these men traders proper. Yet the failure to see them in this way has only obscured our understanding of the total number of people who were actually involved in this business. As part of the problem, most of these men did not identify themselves as slave traders. Although they did often engage in other business activities besides selling slaves, many of them still made a significant portion of their income from this trade, and their services proved essential for making it run as smoothly as it did. Therefore, to fully appreciate the range of people involved in this business, it is important to recognize that all of these men were slave traders as well.

Commission Brokers

Foremost among this group were those individuals who bought and sold slaves on commission. Located mostly in urban areas, these brokers played an important role in the transfer of human property from one owner to another. They purchased slaves on order and got a good price for those who wanted to sell. Like most other brokers in the new market economy, who often dealt in a variety of goods, almost all bought and sold a number of commodities besides slaves. Some sold only a handful of men and women each year, while others specialized in this trade and sold hundreds. They had their own depots where they housed the slaves they had for sale as well as provided boarding service for others. A few also held their own slave auctions. And many partook in the interregional trade: forming associations with long-distance traders, making purchases for clients in other states, and even agreeing to sell slaves for dealers from other cities who could not get a good local price.

One of the more successful of these traders was Ziba B. Oakes of Charleston, South Carolina. Like most of his broker colleagues, Oakes had a diversified

Slave auctions were often part of the larger commerical business of the Jacksonian South.
(*Library of Congress*)

business, including dealings in real estate, mortgages, insurance, and all types of stocks. But the vast majority of his business came from the buying and selling of slaves. He purchased them extensively on his own, through his agents, and from dealers in other cities. He then sold these men and women to his numerous clients, either on order or to walk-in customers from his own depot. By the end of the 1850s, he also sold increasing numbers of bondspeople by auction and even bought the slave mart complex on Chalmers Street. While much of his business was local, Oakes's reputation was such that he also sold slaves to planters as far away as Texas and Louisiana. In addition, Oakes had dealings with traders all over the South. Not only did he frequently collaborate with brokers in other South Carolina and Georgia cities, but he also conducted business with dealers in such major markets as Richmond, Montgomery, and New Orleans. Most important, he supplied a number of western traders (from a variety of states) with their human stock. Some came into his depot to pick out their goods, while others just allowed Oakes to purchase for them.

Slave Boarders

Every southern city of any size also had resident traders who made the boarding of slaves at their depots an important part of their business. Brokers like Oakes likewise provided this service, but not to the same extent as others, who made it their primary business activity. The main reason that slave owners and itinerant traders took advantage of this service was to confine their human property safely prior to their sale. The usual charge for boarding a slave was twenty-five cents a day, although Bernard Lynch in St. Louis asked thirty-seven-and-a-half cents, and John Sydnor in Galveston, Texas, got forty. This service proved quite a saving for those individuals with large numbers of slaves to confine, such as long-distance traders. According to a visitor to one of these depots in Washington, D.C., the fee of twenty-five cents a day was nine cents cheaper than that charged by the city-owned jail.

While depot-owning traders drew much of their business from local customers, most also participated in the interregional trade. In the Upper South, resident dealers played an important role in Richmond, the largest market in this part of the South. One significant branch of the domestic trade was those speculators who purchased slaves in the Chesapeake states and then brought them to Richmond for resale to traders who worked the Deep South. Some Richmond firms, like Silas and R. F. Omohundro, had their own depots from which to make these sales. But many others did not and had to conduct the majority of their business through the city's auction houses. Consequently, these individuals, as well as all those interregional buyers, needed someplace to board their human property while in the city. A few enterprising dealers set up special boarding houses and jails to cater to the needs of these itinerant traders.

The Lower South likewise had a number of resident traders who also served an important function in the interstate trade. In addition to boarding slaves for local owners, and buying and selling on commission, these dealers provided a place in the larger urban markets for interregional traders without their own depots. Some itinerant speculators found these depots useful for selling off the remainder of their stock, while others brought their lots there and stayed the entire season. They had to pay an extra expense for this service (board, commission, and city taxes), but the higher prices they usually obtained, and assistance in sales from the dealer and his staff, made it worthwhile for many smaller traders. As the largest and most important market in the importing states, New Orleans naturally had the greatest number of depot-owning brokers in the Lower South.

Auctioneers

In addition to commission brokers and depot-owning traders, most major markets also had auctioneers who specialized in the selling of slaves. Like brokers, almost all of these men dealt in a number of goods besides slaves. Every city, however, always had some auctioneers who made the sale of human property the primary focus of their business. And like the brokers who specialized in this trade, these auctioneers had depots and yards of their own for boarding slaves of local sellers and itinerant traders prior to sale. They

Slave auctions occurred in public places in large southern cities, including Richmond, Virginia, the future capital of the Confederacy. (*Library of Congress*)

also did appraisals, arranged for transportation, ran the advertising, and helped prepare the men, women, and children for sale. For this they usually received a fee of 2 to 2 and one-half percent on all sales, although some, especially those doing court-ordered sales for the state, received slightly less. Some had their own auction rooms; others used public facilities or open spaces.

Once again, these auctioneers played their biggest role in the markets of Richmond and New Orleans. In the Virginia capital, four or five firms conducted a prosperous business transferring slaves from local owners and traders to buyers for the Deep South market. During certain times of the year, they sold dozens, and even hundreds, of slaves a day, from their own auction rooms, or from public facilities like the Odd Fellows Hall on Franklin Street. To attract business, most of the major companies had their own depots. In fact, several of these facilities were quite extensive. In 1857, a local editor reported that the three largest firms employed nineteen people and had depots assessed at over $25,000.

Slave auctioneers in the Crescent City likewise performed a vital, albeit somewhat different, function in the domestic trade. Unlike Richmond, where large numbers of interregional slave sales passed through the hands of auctioneers, in New Orleans and most other southern cities, estate and other court-ordered sales made up the bulk of their business. Quite simply, long-distance speculators in New Orleans got better prices by selling out of their own (or someone else's) showrooms than they could by selling at auction. Nevertheless, the city's auctioneers still played an important role in the interregional trade. Depot sales often took time, so for those who wanted to sell out quickly, or who had difficult slaves to sell, the city's auction rooms became a valuable resource.

Silent Partners

In addition to brokers, dealers, and auctioneers, there were also those southerners who speculated in the slave-trading abilities of others. Often serving
as silent partners, these individuals engaged in the trade by bankrolling the
ventures of others. Interregional traders constantly needed large sums of
cash to make their purchases. Most large and mid-sized firms got this money
from banks and other sources at a nominal rate of interest. But many smaller
traders lacked the credit for such loans and were therefore willing to give up
a share of their profits to these outside investors. This could amount to as
much as half of all the proceeds after expenses.

Typical of these men was the famous North Carolina jurist, Thomas Ruffin. In the early 1820s, Ruffin entered into a partnership with Benjamin
Chambers to buy slaves in North Carolina and transport them to Alabama
for sale. According to their agreement, Ruffin supplied the initial $4,000 to
purchase the human property, while Chambers did all of the actual buying
and selling. Over a three-year period, the two men made more than $6,000
in profit. In addition to receiving his share of this money, Ruffin also had his
pick of all of the men and women they bought for his own plantations. This
profitable slave-trading partnership lasted five years and ended only with
Chambers's death in 1826.

Agents, Supervisors, Overseers, and Clerks

Finally, there were all those individuals who worked as agents, supervisors,
overseers, and clerks. These men performed the supporting jobs that made
the business of slave trading happen—they bought and sold slaves for others,
ran the depots and pens, and kept the books. Some worked on commission;
others were salaried personnel. Many of those who transported the coffles
across the southern countryside only received a one-time fee, usually around
$50, to take a gang from Virginia to New Orleans. A large number of these
auxiliary personnel lasted only a year or two, but some spent a lifetime in
the trade. While not actually risking their own money in the speculation of
human property, these individuals derived the majority of their income from
this trade and were certainly seen as slave traders in the eyes of many, including those of the enslaved themselves.

Profits from the Slave Trade

Uniting all of these various slave traders was their acquisitive desire to get
rich quick, or at least more quickly than they could in most other occupations. As with northern capitalists, southern slave traders were willing to
take risks for the enormous profits that could be obtained in this trade. And
some men truly did obtain great wealth, often in a short period. The Washington trader William H. Williams boasted of making $30,000 in just a few
months. While such claims may have been exaggerated, the large traders
routinely made more than that in a single year. The firm of Isaac Franklin
and John Armfield certainly bettered that amount. By 1834, Armfield was

Isaac Franklin

Isaac Franklin had long been involved in the American slave trade, shipping bondspeople and other goods with his brothers down the Mississippi River from his native Tennessee to Natchez, Mississippi, and New Orleans, Louisiana, as early as 1810. He was therefore well acquainted with the western trade when he met John Armfield, a successful trader out of North Carolina, mostly likely in Natchez in the early 1820s. The two men soon realized, however, that there was more money to be made through the coastal slave trade. Consequently, when they formed their partnership in 1828, they moved their headquarters to Alexandria, which at that time was still in the District of Columbia. Armfield, the junior partner, controlled their purchasing from that city, while Franklin did the selling in New Orleans and Natchez, the two most important slave-trading centers in the Southwest.

Three months after forming their partnership, Franklin & Armfield leased a three-story brick house for their office on Duke Street in Alexandria. While such establishments were becoming common with the larger slave-trading firms, this facility was more elaborate than most. In addition to the main building, there was a large yard of about 300 square feet surrounded by several outbuildings and a high, neatly whitewashed, wooden fence. There were separate covered yards and two-story buildings for the men and women, as well as a kitchen, a hospital, and a tailor shop where the enslaved

said to have made $500,000, and contemporaries referred to Franklin as a millionaire, which he may have been. At the time of his death, in the economically depressed mid-1840s, Franklin's estate was appraised at $750,000, most of it acquired through this trade. During the boom years of the 1850s, the most successful traders also raked in huge earnings. In Memphis, Nathan Bedford Forrest's annual profits exceeded $50,000, and most likely reached $100,000 in his best years. Even auctioneers who specialized in the selling of slaves could make that kind of money. The Richmond firm of Dickinson, Hill & Co. was reported to have sold $2 million worth of slaves in 1856. At 2 and one-half percent commission, that meant $50,000 in gross sales.

Of course, the overwhelming majority of men involved in the slave trade failed to achieve the kind of wealth enjoyed by Franklin, Armfield, or Forrest. As in any speculative endeavor, the business was filled with risks, any one of which could wipe out a season's profits and even lead to bankruptcy, or worse. The close quarters and unsanitary conditions of many of the slave pens meant that disease was always a possibility, especially in the Deep South, where outbreaks of yellow fever, smallpox, and cholera were routine. The business had other potential pitfalls that could bring economic disaster to even the most careful trader. Agents sometimes ran off with their boss's money, and accidents were likewise a possibility, especially in the coastal trade. In 1831 one brig was forced to abandon 164 slaves (most belonging to Franklin & Armfield) after it struck rocks on the Bahama Banks; four years later, weather drove another ship carrying seventy-five slaves (valued at $40,000) to Bermuda where the cargo were all set free. The commodities themselves could also cut into a trader's profits. At one time or another, almost every

each received two new suits of clothing—although these were not to be worn until they had reached their final market.

Franklin & Armfield's most important business innovation, however, involved purchasing and operating their own vessels in the coastal trade. From its beginning, the company provided shipping service on boats under its command. The firm eventually owned at least three brigs: the *Tribune*, the *Uncas*, and the self-titled *Isaac Franklin*. The money it saved on transportation allowed Franklin & Armfield to offer more for its purchases than its competitors and still make a profit. In addition, these vessels carried goods like sugar, molasses, whiskey, and cotton to eastern ports on their return trips.

One big reason for Franklin & Armfield's success was its adaptation of a shipping innovation that was transforming business in the North; it offered the relatively new service of packet lines. Unlike previous vessels that did not sail until they had a full cargo, a packet line was guaranteed to sail at a specified date, whether it was full or not. Naturally, this led to some cut in profits since few of their boats sailed full. Still, it more than made up for this loss in revenue by attracting more customers with its reliable shipping schedules. All of its business innovations and entrepreneurial skills helped make Franklin & Armfield the dominant slave-trading firm during the boom years of the mid-1830s and made its owners extremely wealthy men.

slave trader had at least a couple of individuals who successfully made their escape. While the larger firms could write off such losses as a cost of doing business, the high price of slaves meant that even one runaway could wipe out all the profits of a smaller operation. Moreover, the business was filled with danger, and dozens of slave traders lost their lives at the hands of the men and women they were hoping to sell. Finally, the greed that drove these men also sometimes led to their own undoing. Probably the most costly example in this regard was in 1840 when William H. Williams (who had earlier boasted of making $30,000 in a matter of months) was caught with twenty-seven Virginia slaves condemned for crimes; he was trying to smuggle them out of the country to be sold in New Orleans. Not only was Williams forced to forfeit the slaves, but with his fines and legal fees, this failed venture ended up costing him an estimated $48,000.

Still, despite the risks, the majority of men working in the slave trade managed to make a decent living. Economic historians have found that on average, slave traders made profits of 20 to 30 percent a year—high by antebellum standards. This was roughly equal to the profit rates of southern industrial firms. And for those individuals, such as Mr. Williams, who were willing to stretch the law, this rate could go even higher. One of the most infamous traders in New Orleans in the 1850s was Bernard Kendig, who routinely bought slaves with known faults and then sold them to unsuspecting buyers as sound. On his legitimate sales, Kendig earned an average profit of 25 percent, but on his fraudulent sales, this rate climbed to 37 percent.

Even without resorting to such tactics, however, the slave trade offered to men of ambition in the South an opportunity to make more money than

In urban areas, slaves were often kept confined like animals until a slave auction was held.
(*Library of Congress*)

they could earn in most other occupations available to them. At a time when a southern bank president's annual salary was $5,000 or less, even moderately successful slave traders could easily make twice that much, if not considerably more. And the larger firms outperformed the wealthiest cotton planters. The same was true for those at the lower end of the economic spectrum. A good annual income for southern yeoman farmers was $300, while overseers made $100 to $200 a year, and white laborers were paid even less. Even those just starting out as assistants in the slave trade could make that much, and those with experience made $600 or more per year. The reason for this disparity is that it was harder to get southern whites to work in this trade. Unlike an overseer, who was given room and board and could stay in one place with his family all year, slave traders and their assistants often spent months away from home, trudging across the country, and living outdoors in all types of weather. But for those willing to take these risks and work hard, the payoff could be rewarding.

Therefore, for many industrious white southerners, the slave trade was seen as a reasonable way to get ahead in life. While several large traders, such as the South Carolinians Thomas Gadsden, Louis DeSaussure, and John

Springs III, came from prominent southern families and used the slave trade to enhance their personal wealth, hundreds of other men from more humble origins entered the trade hoping to make their own fortunes. And there were plenty of examples of those who had done just that. Two of South Carolina's other leading slave dealers, Ziba Oakes and John Riggs, came from more modest backgrounds. Oakes was the son of a grocer, and Riggs was an Irish-born immigrant whose father was a harness maker. Yet by 1860, the slave trade had made them two of the wealthiest men in Charleston. Most important, some of the largest slave traders in the South owed their financial success almost entirely to this trade. Both Isaac Franklin and Nathan Bedford Forrest grew up under rugged conditions along the southwestern frontier, and John Armfield came from simple, North Carolina stock. The vast majority of slave traders who started out with nothing failed to achieve the kind of wealth acquired by these men. And one did need a certain amount of capital or influence to obtain the financing necessary for large-scale success. Nevertheless, for those who worked hard and lived frugally, the slave trade proved one of the quickest and surest routes for making money in the Old South.

Hard Work, Pitfalls, and Friendships

Like their northern counterparts, the various southern slave traders all embraced the hard-nosed and hyper-masculine ethos of the emerging world of commerce. Any business that promised such huge financial rewards naturally led to a great deal of competition among its practitioners. To get ahead, traders frequently tried to outsmart their competition through deception. Because so much of the success of this business depended upon the knowledge of various market conditions, speculators sought to keep the information they had hidden from others. Some deliberately planted false information; others resorted to sabotage to hinder their rivals. One tactic was running up the price at auction sales to prevent competitors from purchasing at profitable rates. It was also common to circulate false information about the business practices of other speculators or the qualities of the men and women they offered for sale.

Naturally, one needed a great deal of self-confidence to survive (much less prosper) in this rough-and-tumble, cutthroat environment. And it also took a great deal of hard work to be successful. Yet their hard work came at a personal cost for many speculators. Devotion to their business took a particularly difficult toll on slave traders' home life—especially for interregional traders, who naturally felt the loss of being absent for months from their families and loved ones. The demands of the job were the reason so many traders remained single or married later in life after they had ended their slave-trading careers. The successful trader Isaac Franklin did not marry until the age of fifty, well after he had retired from the business.

Yet many unencumbered southern men jumped at the opportunity the slave trade provided for adventure and seeing the country. The slave trade also offered them plenty of other opportunities that were not possible at home but for which places like New Orleans were well known. Moreover, given the large sums of money associated with this business, most of them had the resources to act on their indulgences, if they so desired. Consequently, many a trader lost all of his profits at the card tables or treating his friends to drinks. But the most infamous excitement for many of these young men was the unhindered access to sex. In addition to all of the prostitutes and other white women who might be drawn to men flashing large wads of cash, southern slave traders were notorious for raping the young enslaved women under their control. As abhorrent as this practice was, it did have a certain appeal to many of these sexually charged young men. It was also something common to all levels of traders. Not only did Isaac Franklin and several of his associates keep enslaved concubines, but their correspondence is peppered with sexual innuendoes. Yet, as with excessive drinking and gambling, this practice did have its perils, especially with the prevalence of sexually transmitted diseases.

Despite all of their aggressive competition and cutthroat practices, the masculine lifestyle of the trade led many speculators to develop deep and sincere friendships with one another. In large part, this was due to the work culture of slave trading and the lifestyle they shared with one another as men of business. Slave traders frequently lived together on the road and stayed in the same boardinghouses. They also experienced a certain camaraderie and male bonding as they boasted, cussed, drank, gambled, and shared women together. It is not surprising, then, that many of them also honeymooned together, named their children after one another, celebrated Christmases together, and eventually served as one another's executors. As a result, not only did the domestic slave trade provide these men with lucrative economic rewards, but it also gave them great personal satisfaction as well.

Business Practices of the Slave Trade

Most slave traders were sharp businessmen. To be successful, they had to buy wisely and hope that their final sales would exceed their expenses and leave them with a healthy return for their efforts. Interstate traders generally accepted as a fair return on their investment a $100 to $150 net on each slave sold, although they sometimes made more, and often accepted less, especially when market conditions made sales difficult. Then their profit rates could decrease considerably.

In addition to obsessing about profits and losses, slave traders employed modern accounting practices to record all their transactions. Unlike the majority of planters who just kept lists of local debts and credits, many slave traders adopted the relatively new method of double-entry bookkeeping for the most accurate accounts. While this technique had been around for centuries, it gained wide acceptance among American men of business during the early nineteenth century, and southern speculators proved no exception.

Southern slave traders likewise made frequent use of the financial instruments of the new market economy. Most important, they constantly sought funding from banks to finance their operations as well as extended their own network of credit to customers. Most speculators preferred to sell their slaves for cash, partly to pay off their own loans and partly to avoid the difficulties of collection. By necessity, however, they were often forced to accept promissory notes if they wanted to make sufficient sales. Speculators then used the cash and commercial paper that they received to pay off their own loans and obtain more credit to acquire the cash to purchase more slaves.

Furthermore, slave traders had to have a good understanding of the nation's money markets. At a time when the country's main form of currency consisted of discounted bank notes, they had to keep track of the comparative value of the various drafts so as to deal in those with the greatest acceptability. For that reason, whenever possible, they favored paper from major northern banks, which generally held its value better nationally than did that from local southern banks. To be successful, then, southern slave traders needed to follow not only the price of cotton but all of the nation's financial markets as well.

Many southern speculators also sought to protect themselves against unexpected losses by taking out insurance policies on the men and women they were shipping to the Deep South for sale. In addition, a number of traders covered themselves against losses caused by sickness and disease. They had the slaves they purchased vaccinated, especially those being shipped to unhealthy environments where contagious diseases were frequently present.

Finally, as participants in a long-distance commodity market whose profits were dependent on prices in divergent parts of the South, speculators needed a way to communicate with their colleagues about the state of one another's markets. Like other brokers, slave traders had to categorize their human merchandise so they could accurately compare their information. Usually this was done by sorting people into classes, such as first-, second-, and third-rate men and women, with boys and girls normally divided according to age or height. One Richmond firm, D. M. Pulliam & Co., even broke the market into twenty different categories, with everything from "No. 1 MEN, Extra" down to "Scrubs"—a term that traders frequently used to refer to the elderly, diseased, physically handicapped, or other hard-to-sell individuals. Much of this information was provided by the larger Richmond auctioneers, who sent out printed circulars to their regular customers (and anyone who asked for them) describing the current state of their market.

This depersonalizing of humans into objects of trade was an ever-present reality of the domestic trade, where enslaved men and women were seen as commodities and usually spoken of in market terms. It is not surprising that many speculators used animal-like images to describe the men and women they were selling. All was part and parcel of the domestic trade, where skillful businessmen trafficked in people as goods and consequently thought of them as such.

The most influential manner, however, in which southern speculators resembled modern businessmen was their use of extensive advertising to purchase and market their human commodities. One reason for the traders' success in the slave-exporting states was their heavy reliance on cash when acquiring their merchandise. In a world where most business transactions

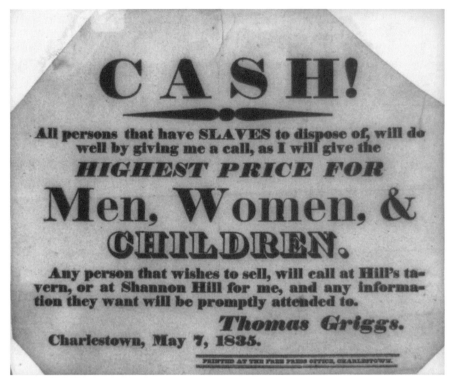

Advertisements for slaves such as this one underscored the assumption that slaves were a marketable commodity. (*Library of Congress*)

were conducted on credit, slave traders were one of the few groups in the South who dealt primarily in cash. Consequently, that became their main selling point. Throughout the Upper South, traders filled the newspapers with long-running, boldfaced advertisements that blared this point home. "CASH FOR NEGROES" or "NEGROES WANTED" were the most common headings.

While all traders stressed the promise of cash when advertising for slaves, they also needed to be creative to make their notices stand out from those of their competitors. They emphasized their reliability and made it clear that they were willing to purchase any type of enslaved person, no questions asked. And virtually all traders claimed to offer the highest prices. Speculators also caught readers' attention by making it appear that they wanted to purchase an endless number of enslaved men and women.

While calls for hundreds of slaves might have attracted attention, in the text of their notices interregional traders were much more specific about the types of men and women they wanted to purchase. Most advertised for "likely" slaves of both sexes between the ages of twelve and twenty-five, although it was not uncommon to see notices asking for children as young as eight, or even six. The main reason they wanted enslaved men and women of this type was because they were the ones most in demand in the slave-buying states. Moreover, young, healthy, unattached men and women were the safest to transport (they could most readily survive the climatic changes) and the easiest to market, and they brought the highest profits.

On arriving at their destination, interregional traders also employed the same creative advertising when selling their slaves. Almost all began their notices with boldfaced headings, such as "SLAVES FOR SALE" or "NEW AR-RIVAL OF NEGROES." Speculators also naturally emphasized that they had the types of enslaved men and women that most buyers in the Lower South wanted, which meant young, healthy slaves. Most speculators likewise mentioned the state origins of the men and women they had for sale. In part, this was because the majority of buyers desired "fresh arrivals" from outside the region who had not yet been "damaged" by the harsh realities of slave life on a Deep South cotton or sugar plantation. Finally, others went out of their way to accommodate customers, and there were always those who appealed to buyers' pocketbooks.

Attracting potential customers with good advertising was one thing; getting them to buy was another matter. Therefore, traders also needed to work their customers to make a sale. Some traders did this by offering special arrangements. In the Upper South, they persuaded owners to sell by paying them cash during the summer months and letting them keep their slaves until after the crop had been harvested in the fall. Or they let buyers take an individual home on trial before actually purchasing. Others worked their customers by befriending them through charm and alcohol. For many slave traders, working their customers also involved outright trickery and deception. The most common tactics were fixing up older individuals to look young and outfitting their slaves in new clothes. While such practices might be expected, other traders engaged in much less socially acceptable acts and pawned off individuals with known health problems as sound.

Because of the reputation that slave traders had for engaging in such unsavory practices, a number of dealers also employed creative advertising to help improve their public image as honest businessmen. Many speculators listed references in their advertisements. While most mentioned only local firms, some stressed their national reputation, such as the New Orleans dealer Seneca Bennet, who listed men in Baltimore, Mobile, Norfolk, Charleston, as well as New Orleans in his notice. Leading traders also consciously strived to project a positive image in their day-to-day dealings with the public. They both dressed and conducted themselves in a professional manner. Many traders likewise knew the importance of good customer service. Because of this public relations effort, most of the leading slave traders managed to create a reputation of honor and respect. It is important to remember that the vast majority of speculators were not leading traders, nor did they have the same resources or abilities to create such positive public images. In fact, many could not have cared less about what others thought of them. Yet the most successful traders all knew the importance of effective advertising to promote both their businesses and themselves.

While many white southerners tried to relegate slave traders to the margins of their society and blame them for all the evils associated with the trade, in reality, all elements of southern society could be found among them. Numerous speculators certainly took advantage of individual slave owners whenever they could, and all helped inflict pain and suffering on the vast majority of black southerners who came under their control. But traders did provide a vital service to the white South, and they had important marketing skills that many found useful. Therefore, few were the slave owners who did not come to them for assistance when necessary.

References and Further Reading

Bancroft, Frederic. *Slave Trading in the Old South.* 1931; reprint, New York: Ungar, 1959.

Deyle, Steven. *Carry Me Back: The Domestic Slave Trade in American Life.* New York: Oxford University Press, 2005.

Drago, Edmund L., ed. *Broke by the War: Letters of a Slave Trader.* Columbia: University of South Carolina Press, 1991.

Gudmestad, Robert H. *A Troublesome Commerce: The Transformation of the Interstate Slave Trade.* Baton Rouge: Louisiana State University Press, 2003.

Johnson, Walter. *Soul by Soul: Life inside the Antebellum Slave Market.* Cambridge, MA: Harvard University Press, 1999.

Stowe, Harriet Beecher. *Uncle Tom's Cabin; or, Life among the Lowly.* Ed. Ann Douglas. 1852; reprint, New York: Penguin, 1981.

Tadman, Michael. *Speculators and Slaves: Masters, Traders, and Slaves in the Old South.* Madison: University of Wisconsin Press, 1989.

Primary Documents

Preamble: Appeal to the Coloured Citizens of the World

David Walker's *Appeal to the Coloured Citizens of the World* provides insight into how later abolitionists would incorporate religious, economic, and social arguments into their condemnation of slavery. The preamble below (taken from the third edition, published in 1830) gives a sense of how Walker wove historical examples, religious rhetoric, and political theory together to combat what he considered the evil of human bondage.

My dearly beloved Brethren and Fellow Citizens.

Having travelled over a considerable portion of these United States, and having, in the course of my travels, taken the most accurate observations of things as they exist—the result of my observations has warranted the full and unshaken conviction, that we, (coloured people of these United States,) are the most degraded, wretched, and abject set of beings that ever lived since the world began; and I pray God that none like us ever may live again until time shall be no more. They tell us of the Israelites in Egypt, the Helots in Sparta, and of the Roman Slaves, which last were made up from almost every nation under heaven, whose sufferings under those ancient and heathen nations, were, in comparison with ours, under this enlightened and Christian nation, no more than a cypher—or, in other words, those heathen nations of antiquity, had but little more among them than the name and form of slavery; while wretchedness and endless miseries were reserved, apparently in a phial, to be poured out upon our fathers, ourselves and our children, by *Christian* Americans!

These positions I shall endeavour, by the help of the Lord, to demonstrate in the course of this *Appeal*, to the satisfaction of the most incredulous mind—and may God Almighty, who is the Father of our Lord Jesus Christ, open your hearts to understand and believe the truth.

The *causes*, my brethren, which produce our wretchedness and miseries, are so very numerous and aggravating, that I believe the pen only of a Josephus or a Plutarch, can well enumerate and explain them. Upon subjects, then, of such incomprehensible magnitude, so impenetrable, and so notorious, I shall be obliged to omit a large class of, and content myself with giving you an exposition of a few of those, which do indeed rage to such an alarming pitch, that they cannot but be a perpetual source of terror and dismay to every reflecting mind.

I am fully aware, in making this appeal to my much afflicted and suffering brethren, that I shall not only be assailed by those whose greatest earthly desires are, to keep us in abject ignorance and wretchedness, and who are of the firm conviction that Heaven has designed us and our children to be slaves and *beasts of burden* to them and their children. I say, I do not only expect to be held up to the public as an ignorant, impudent and restless disturber of the public peace, by such avaricious creatures, as well as a mover of insubordination—and perhaps put in prison or to death, for giving a superficial exposition of our miseries, and exposing tyrants. But I am persuaded, that many of my brethren, particularly those who are ignorantly in league with slave-holders or tyrants, who acquire their daily bread by the blood and sweat of their more ignorant brethren—and not a few of those too, who are too ignorant to see an inch beyond their noses, will rise up and call me cursed—Yea, the jealous ones among us will perhaps use more abject subtlety, by affirming that this work is not worth perusing, that we are well situated, and there is no use in trying to better our condition, for we cannot. I will ask one question here.—Can our condition be any worse?—Can it be more mean and abject? If there are any changes, will they not be for the better, though they may appear for the worst at first? Can they get us any lower? Where can they get us? They are afraid to treat us worse, for they know well, the day they do it they are gone. But against all accusations which may or can be preferred against me, I appeal to Heaven for my motive in writing—who knows that my object is, if possible, to awaken in the breasts of my afflicted, degraded and slumbering brethren, a spirit of inquiry and investigation respecting our miseries and wretchedness in this *Republican Land of Liberty!!!!!!*

The sources from which our miseries are derived, and on which I shall comment, I shall not combine in one, but shall put them under distinct heads and expose them in their turn; in doing which, keeping truth on my side, and not departing from the strictest rules of morality, I shall endeavour to penetrate, search out, and lay them open for your inspection. If you cannot or will not profit by them, I shall have done *my* duty to you, my country and my God.

And as the inhuman system of *slavery,* is the *source* from which most of our miseries proceed, I shall begin with that *curse to nations,* which has spread terror and devastation through so many nations of antiquity, and which is raging to such a pitch at the present day in Spain and in Portugal. It had one tug in England, in France, and in the United States of America; yet the inhabitants thereof, do not learn wisdom, and erase it entirely from their dwellings and from all with whom they have to do. The fact is, the labour of slaves comes so cheap to the avaricious usurpers, and is (as they think) of such great utility to the country where it exists, that those who are actuated by sordid avarice only, overlook the evils, which will as sure as the Lord lives, follow after the good. In fact, they are so happy to keep in ignorance and degradation, and to receive the homage and the labour of the slaves, they forget that God rules in the armies of heaven and among the inhabitants of the earth, having his ears continually open to the cries, tears and groans of his oppressed people; and being a just and holy Being will at one day appear fully in behalf of the oppressed, and arrest the progress of the avaricious oppressors; for although the destruction of the oppressors God may not effect by the oppressed, yet the Lord our God will bring other destructions upon them—for not unfrequently will he cause them to rise up one against another, to be split and divided, and to oppress each other, and sometimes to open hostilities with sword in hand. Some may ask, what is the matter with this united and happy people?—Some say it is the cause of political usurpers, tyrants, oppressors, &c. But has not the Lord an oppressed and suffering people among them? Does the Lord condescend to hear their cries and see their tears in consequence of oppression? Will he let the oppressors rest comfortably and happy always? Will he not cause the very children of the oppressors to rise up against them, and oftimes put them to death? "God works in many ways his wonders to perform."

I will not here speak of the destructions which the Lord brought upon Egypt, in consequence of the oppression and consequent groans of the oppressed—of the hundreds and thousands of Egyptians whom God hurled into the Red Sea for afflicting his people in their land—of the Lord's suffering people in Sparta or Lacedemon, the land of the truly famous Lycurgus—nor have I time to comment upon the cause which produced the fierceness with which Sylla usurped the title, and absolutely acted as dictator of the Roman people—the conspiracy of Cataline—the conspiracy against, and murder of Caesar in the Senate house—the spirit with which Marc Antony made himself master of the commonwealth—his associating Octavius and Lipidus with himself in power—their dividing the provinces of Rome among themselves—their attack and defeat, on the plains of Phillippi, of the last defenders of their liberty, (Brutus and Cassius)—the tyranny of Tiberius, and from him to the final overthrow of Constantinople by the Turkish Sultan, Mahomed II. A.D. 1453. I say, I shall not take up time to speak of the *causes* which produced so much wretchedness and massacre among those heathen nations, for I am aware that you know too well, that God is just, as well as merciful!—I shall call your attention a few moments to that *Christian* nation, the Spaniards—while I shall leave almost unnoticed, that avaricious and cruel people, the Portuguese, among whom all true hearted Christians and lovers of Jesus Christ, must evidently see the judgments of God displayed. To show the judgments of God upon the Spaniards, I shall occupy but a little time, leaving a plenty of room for the candid and unprejudiced to reflect.

All persons who are acquainted with history, and particularly the Bible, who are not blinded by the God of this world, and are not actuated solely by avarice—who are able to lay aside prejudice long enough to view candidly and impartially, things as they were, are, and probably will be—who are willing to admit that God made man to serve Him *alone,* and that man should have no other Lord or Lords but Himself—that God Almighty is the *sole proprietor* or *master* of the WHOLE human family, and will not on any consideration admit of a colleague, being unwilling to divide his glory with another—and who can dispense with prejudice long enough to admit that we are *men,* notwithstanding our *improminent noses* and *woolly heads,* and believe that we feel for our fathers, mothers, wives and children, as well as the whites do for theirs.—I say, all who are permitted to see and believe these things, can easily recognize the judgments of God among the Spaniards. Though others may lay the cause of the fierceness with which they cut each other's throats, to some other circumstance, yet they who believe that God is a God of justice, will believe that SLAVERY *is the principal cause.*

While the Spaniards are running about upon the field of battle cutting each other's throats, has not the Lord an afflicted and suffering people in the midst of them, whose cries and groans in consequence of oppression are continually pouring into the ears of the God of justice? Would they not cease to cut each other's throats, if they could? But how can they? The very support which they draw from government to aid them in perpetrating such enormities, does it not arise in a great degree from the wretched victims of oppression among them? And yet they are calling for Peace!—Peace!! Will any peace be given unto them? Their destruction may indeed be procrastinated awhile, but can it continue long, while they are oppressing the Lord's people? Has He not the hearts of all men in His hand? Will he suffer one part of his creatures to go on oppressing another like brutes always, with impunity? And yet, those avaricious wretches are calling for Peace!!!! I declare, it does appear to me, as though some nations think God is asleep, or that he made the Africans for nothing else but to dig their mines and work their farms, or they cannot believe history, sacred or profane. I ask every man who has a heart, and is blessed with the privilege of believing—Is not God a God of justice to all his creatures? Do you say he is? Then if he gives peace and tranquillity to tyrants, and permits them to keep our fathers, our mothers, ourselves and our children in eternal ignorance and wretchedness, to support them and their families, would he be to us a God of justice? I ask, O ye Christians!!! who hold us and our children in the most abject ignorance and degradation, that ever a people were afflicted with since the world began—I say, if God gives you peace and tranquillity, and suffers you thus to go on afflicting us, and our children, who have never given you the least provocation—would he be to us a God of justice? If you will allow that we are MEN, who feel for each other, does not the blood of our fathers and of us their children, cry aloud to the Lord of Sabaoth against you, for the cruelties and murders with which you have, and do continue to afflict us. But it is time for me to close my remarks on the suburbs, just to enter more fully into the interior of this system of cruelty and oppression.

Letters Concerning the Eaton Affaire (The Petticoat Affair)

The Eaton affair caused enormous turmoil within the Jackson White House. Jackson had family members there who opposed the marriage for various reasons. Most important were Andrew and Emily Donelson, Jackson's nephew and niece, who were serving as private secretary and White House hostess. The following exchange of letters between John Eaton and the Donelsons gives some indication of the personal aspects of the scandal and the way that the men involved tried, often unsuccessfully, to exert control over their wives' social relations.

John Eaton to Emily Donelson, April 8, 1829

Mrs. Donelson,

I have understood that a certain family here, have gratuitously stepped forward to become your councellors and advisers, to tell you what to do, and what not to do; and in secret whispers to slander all who are short of that standard of excellence which they deem the proper one. I have also learned amidst the variety of their gossipping tatle, that it has pleased this little nest of inquisitors, to offer some of their comments respecting me and my wife. I know not what effect they may have produced on your own mind, tho I would presume, that some recent events which gave pain in your own bosom would lead you to forbear attaching any importance to tales of slander. If fire side whispers shall have influence on intelligent minds, it is questionable whether character be worth any thing. Under such an order of things, you yourself may presently become a victim to those meddling gossips.

. . .

You are young and uninformed of the ways and of the malice and insincerity of the world, therefore do I speak to you. You may take it for a certain rule that those whom you hear abusing others, will by and by when occasion offers, abuse you too. Let your Uncle from any cause get out of his place, and those butterflies who now infest you, will be amongst the first to find out how entirely they have been deceived in you, and your character, and seek to reduce it to a level with their own. These people care nothing about you. They are eternally haunting your house, and bringing you tales and rules, only that your Uncle is in power, and they hope to give themselves consequence thro the smiles they may pick up in your doors.

. . .

Now Mrs Donelson take these hints and profit by them. Lay them by, and my life upon it, you will one day thank me for what I have said. You have known me long and well, and well know that in nothing have I ever deceived you or your friends. Appreciate therefore what is written frendly as it is intended; for your own benefit, not mine. Let your uncle get out of office, and I greatly mistake it if you do not have cause to repent that ever you nestled to your bosom such frends and such councellors.

Emily Donelson to John Eaton, April 10,1829

It was with some surprise that I recd your letters of yesterday and the day before, and it was not much relieved by a perusal of their contents. With regard to those who are understood to have "stepped forward to become my counselors and advisers and to direct me what to do and what not to do," I must say I am totally unacquainted with such; and I thank God in all cases where I have need of the council and advice of a friend I have one who is competent to judge for me. . . .

I take this opportunity to assure you that I do not wish to decide upon any person's character here, nor controul in any way the etiquette of this place, and that so far from arrogating to myself any honour or privilege from the circumstance of my being in the Genls [Jackson's] family, I shall act as if

I was not a member of it, nor expect to be considered in any other light, than the proper one as a private individual, and when Uncle has no further use of my Husband's services I can return home without expecting either honor or profit, cheerful and happy if I have been enabled to perform my duty.

Andrew J. Donelson to John Eaton, April 10, 1829

Dear Sir,

Upon my return home last night from General Macomb's, Mrs Donelson shew[ed] me two letters, which you had addressed to her, requesting a disclosure of the allegations against the character of Mrs Eaton and yourself supposed to have been raised by a family in the city. This request is doubtless based upon the impression, that Mrs D had given credence to these allegations, and of course the communication of them to you, was but an act of justice which you had a right to expect from her, and lest she may not have been explicit enough in the avowal of it, I have taken the liberty to accompany her note herewith enclosed, with this explanation.

And I take pleasure in adding as an individual that no one can be more ready than myself to pay to yourself and to Mrs Eaton every proper mark of respect, and by my example to recommend the sentiment which justifies it to my family. But beyond this my regard for them, and my duty to society does not require me to go. Upon this principle perceiving that the circle in which Mrs D had been accidentally thrown when she arrived in the city had embarrassed little her disposition to be social and free with your lady, I thought it better to rely on that corrective which I knew would be found in a longer acquaintance with society here, than on that which by seeking to oppose the sentiments of others, would have drawn her into endless dispute.

Selected Lessons from the McGuffey Reader

William H. McGuffey (1800–1873) was an educator and president of Miami University best remembered for writing the *McGuffey Readers*. These six textbooks taught American students how to read and write, while also instilling in them lessons about patriotism, virtue, and Christianity. Most public school students in the nineteenth century learned from these readers. The selections below are from the First Revised Reader, originally published in 1836.

LESSON 34

"Papa, may we have the big flag?" said James.

"What can my little boy do with such a big flag?"

"Hoist it on our tent, papa. We are playing Fourth of July."

"Is that what all this noise is about? Why not hoist your own flags?"

"Oh! they are too little."

"You might spoil my flag."

"Then we will all join to pay for it. But we will not spoil it, papa."

"Take it, then, and take the coil or rope with it."

"Oh! Thank you. Hurrah for the flag, boys!"

LESSON 39

See my dear, old grandma in her easy-chair! How gray her hair is! She wears glasses when she reads.

She is always kind, and takes such good care of me that I like to do what she tells me.

When she says, "Robert, will you get me a drink?" I run as fast as I can to get it for her. Then she says, "Thank you, my boy."

Would you not love a dear, good grandma, who is so kind? And would you not do all you could to please her?

LESSON 58

When the stars at set of sun
Watch you from on high,
When the morning has begun,
Think the Lord is nigh.
All you do and all you say,
He can see and hear:
When you work and when you play,
Think the Lord is near.
All your joys and griefs He knows,
Counts each falling tear,
When to Him you tell your woes,
Know the Lord will hear.

Excerpt from Personal Memoirs of a Residence of Thirty Years with the Indian Tribes on the American Frontiers

Henry Rowe Schoolcraft (1793–1864) was a noted American ethnologist, geographer, and geologist. He spent several years as an Indian agent and legislator in the Michigan Territory. He recorded his observations about the area and its indigenous peoples in *Personal Memoirs of a Residence of Thirty Years with the Indian Tribes on the American Frontiers*. The excerpt below is from a trip that Schoolcraft made in 1832.

1832. *June 7th*. It was not until this day that the expedition was ready to embark at the head of the portage at St. Mary's. I had organized it strictly on temperance principles, observation having convinced me, during frequent expeditions in the wilderness, that not only is there no situation, unless administered from the medicine-chest, where men are advantaged by its use, but in nearly every instance of fatigue or exhaustion their powers are enfeebled by it, while, in a moral and intellectual sense, they are rendered incapable, neglectful, or disobedient. This exclusion constituted a special clause in every verbal agreement with the men, who were Canadians, which I thought necessary to make, in order that they might have no reason to complain while inland of its exclusion. They were promised, instead of it, abundance of good wholesome food at all times. The effects of this were apparent even at the start. They all presented smiling faces, and took hold of their paddles with a conscious feeling of satisfaction in the wisdom of their agreement.

The military and their supplies occupied a large Mackinack boat; my heavy stores filled another. I traveled in a *canoe-elège*, as being better adapted to speed and the celerity of landing. Each carried a national flag. We slept the first night at Point Iroquois, which commands a full view of the magnificent entrance into the lake. We were fifteen days in traversing the lake, being my fifth trip through this inland sea. We passed up the St. Louis River by its numerous portages and falls to the Sandy Lake summit, and reached the banks of the Mississippi on the third of July, and ascertained its width above the junction of the Sandy Lake outlet to be 331 feet. We were six days in ascending it to the central island in Cass Lake. This being the point at which geographical discovery rests, I decided to encamp the men, deposit my heavy baggage, and fitted out a light party in hunting canoes to trace the stream to its source. The Indians supplied me with five canoes of two fathoms each, and requiring but two men to manage each, which would allow one canoe to each of the gentlemen of my party. I took three Indians and seven white men as the joint crew, making, with the sitters, fifteen persons. We were provisioned for a few days, carried a flag, mess-basket, tent, and other necessary apparatus. We left the island early the next morning, and reached the influx of the Mississippi into the Lake at an early hour. To avoid a very circuitous bay, which I called Allen's Bay, we made a short portage through open pine woods.

Fifty yards' walk brought us and our canoe and baggage to the banks of Queen Anne's Lake, a small sylvan lake through which the whole channel of the Mississippi passed. A few miles above its termination we entered another lake of limited size, which the Indians called Pemetascodiac. The river winds about in this portion of it—through savannas, bordered by sandhills, and pines in the distance—for about fifteen miles. At this distance, rapids commence, and the bed of the river exhibited greenstone and gneissoid boulders. We counted ten of these rapids, which our guide called the Metoswa, or Ten Rapids. They extend about twenty miles, during which there is a gradual ascent of about forty feet. The men got out at each of these rapids, and lifted or drew the canoes up by their gunwales. We ascended slowly and with toil. At the computed distance of forty-five miles, we entered a very handsome sheet of water, lying transverse to our course, which the Indians called Pamidjegumag, which means crosswater, and which the French call *Lac Traverse*. It is about twelve miles long from east to west, and five or six wide. It is surrounded with hardwood forest, presenting a picturesque appearance.

We stopped a few moments to observe a rude idol on its shores; it consisted of a granitic boulder, of an extraordinary shape, with some rings and spots of paint, designed to give it a resemblance to a human statue. We observed the passenger-pigeon and some small fresh-water shells of the species of unios and anadontas.

A short channel, with a strong current, connects this lake with another of less than a third of its dimensions, to which I gave the name of Washington Irving. Not more than three or four miles above the latter, the Mississippi exhibits the junction of its ultimate forks. The right hand, or Itasca branch, was represented as by far the longest, the most circuitous, and most difficult of ascent. It brings down much the largest volume of water. I availed myself of the geographical knowledge of my Indian guide by taking the left hand, or what I had occasion soon to call the Plantagenian branch. It expanded, in the course of a few miles, into a lake, which I called Marquette, and, a little further, into another, which I named La Salle. About four miles above the latter, we entered into a more considerable sheet of water, which I named Plantagenet, being the site of an old Indian encampment called Kubbakunna, or the Rest in the Path.

We encamped a short distance above the upper end of this lake at the close of the day, on a point of low land covered with a small growth of gray pine, fringed with alder, tamarisk, spruce, and willow. A bed of moss covered the soil, into which the foot sank at every step. Long moss hung from every branch. Everything indicated a cold frigid soil. In the act of encamping, it commenced raining, which gave a double gloom to the place. Several species of duck were brought from the different canoes as the result of the day's hunt.

Early the next morning we resumed the ascent. The river became narrow and tortuous. Clumps of willow and alder lined the shore. Wherever larger species were seen they were gray pines or tamarack. One of the Indians killed a deer, of the species *C. Virginea*, during the morning. Ducks were frequently disturbed as we pushed up the winding channel. The shores were often too sedgy and wet to permit our landing, and we went on till twelve o'clock before finding a suitable spot to breakfast.

About five o'clock we came to a high diluvial ridge of gravel and sand, mixed with boulders of syenite, trap-rock, quartz, and sandstone. Ozawandib, our guide, said we were near the junction of the Naiwa, or Copper-snake River, the principal tributary of this branch of the Mississippi, and that it was necessary to make a passage over this ridge to avoid a formidable series of rapids. Our track lay across a peninsula. This occupied the remainder of the day, and we encamped on the banks of the stream above the rapids and pitched our tent, before daylight had finally departed. The position of the sun, in this latitude, it must be recollected, is protracted, very perceptibly, above the horizon. We ascended to the summit in a series of geological steps or plateaux. There is but little perceptible rise from the Cross-water level to this point—called Agate Rapids and Portage, from the occurrence of this mineral in the drift. The descent of water at this place cannot be less than seventy feet. On resuming the journey the next morning (13th) we found the water above these rapids had almost the appearance of a dead level. The current is very gentle; and, by its diminished volume, denotes clearly the absence of the contributions from the Naiwa. About seven miles above the Agate Portage we entered Lake Assawa, which our Indian guide informed us was the source of this branch. We were precisely twenty minutes in passing through it, with the full force of paddles. It receives two small inlets, the most southerly of which we entered, and the canoes soon stuck fast, amidst aquatic plants, on a boggy shore. I did not know, for a moment, the cause of our having grounded, till Ozawandib exclaimed, "O-um-a, mikun-na!" here is the portage! We were at the Southern flanks of the diluvial hills, called HAUTEUR DES TERRES—a geological formation of drift materials, which form one of the continental water-sheds, dividing the streams tributary to the Gulf of Mexico, from those of Hudson's Bay. He described the portage as consisting of twelve *pug-gi-de-nun*, or resting places, where the men are temporarily eased of their burdens. This was indefinite, depending on the measure of a man's strength to carry. Not only our baggage, but the canoes were to be carried. After taking breakfast, on the nearest dry ground, the different back-loads for the men were prepared. Ozawandib threw my canoe over his shoulders and led the way. The rest followed, with their appointed loads. I charged myself with a spy-glass, strapped, and portfolio. Dr. Houghton carried a plant press. Each one had something, and the men toiled with five canoes, Our provisions, beds, tent, &c. The path was one of the most intricate and tangled that I ever knew. Tornadoes appeared to have cast down the trees in every direction. A soft spongy mass, that gave way under the tread, covered the interstices between the fallen timber. The toil and fatigue were incessant. At length we ascended the first height. It was an arid eminence of the pebble and erratic block era, bearing small gray pines and shrubbery. This constituted our first pause, or *puggidenun*. On descending it, we were again plunged among bramble. Path, there was none, or trail that any mortal eye, but an Indian's, could trace. We ascended another eminence. We descended it, and entered a thicket of bramble, every twig of which seemed placed there to bear some token of our wardrobe, as we passed. To avoid this, the guide passed through a lengthened shallow pond, beyond which the walking was easier. Hill succeeded hill. It was a hot day in July, and the sun shone out brightly. Although we were evidently passing an alpine height, where a long winter reigned, and the vegetation bore every indication of being imperfectly developed. We observed the passenger pigeon, and one or two species of the *falco* family. There were indications of the common deer. Moss hung abundantly from the trees. The gray pine predominated in the forest growth.

At length, the glittering of water appeared, at a distance below, as viewed from the summit of one of these eminences. It was declared by our Indian guide to be Itasca Lake—the source of the main, or South fork of the Mississippi. I passed him, as we descended a long winding slope, and was the first man to reach its banks. A little grassy opening served as the terminus of our trail, and proved that the Indians had been in the practice of crossing this eminence in their hunts. As one after another of the party came, we exulted in the accomplishment of our search. A fire was quickly kindled, and the canoes gummed, preparatory to embarkation.

We had struck within a mile of the southern extremity of the lake, and could plainly see its terminus from the place of our embarking. The view was quite enchanting. The waters were of the most limpid character. The shores were overhung with hard wood foliage, mixed with species of spruce, larch, and aspen. We judged it to be about seven miles in length, by an average of one to two broad. A bay, near its eastern-end, gave it somewhat the shape of the letter y. We observed a deer standing in the water. Wild fowl appeared to be abundant. We landed at the only island it contains—a beautiful spot for

encampment, covered with the elm, cherry, larch, maple, and birch, and giving evidence, by the remains of old camp-fires, and scattered bones of species
killed in the chase, of its having been much resorted to by the aborigines.

This picturesque island the party honored me by calling after my name—
in which they have been sanctioned by Nicollet and other geographers. I
caused some trees to be felled, pitched my tent, and raised the American flag
on a high staff, the Indians firing a salute as it rose.

This flag, as the evidence of the government having extended its jurisdiction to this quarter, I left flying, on quitting the island—and presume the
band of Ozawandib, at Cass Lake, afterwards appropriated it to themselves.

Questions of geography and astronomy may deserve a moment's attention. If we assume the discovery of the mouth of the Mississippi to have been
made by Narvaez in 1527—a doubtful point!—a period of 305 years has
elapsed before its actual source has been fixed. If the date of De Soto's journey (1541) be taken, which is undisputed, this period is reduced to 290
years. Hennepin saw it as high as the mouth of the river St. Francis in 1680.
Lt. Pike, under the administration of Mr. Jefferson, ascended it by water in
1805, near to the entrance of Elk River, south of the Crow Wing Fork, and
being overtaken at this spot by frosts and snow, and winter setting in strongly,
he afterwards ascended its banks, on snow shoes, his men carrying his baggage on hand sleds, to Sandy Lake, then a post of the North-west Company.
From this point he was carried forward, under their auspices, by the Cana-
dian train *de-glis*, drawn by dogs to Leech Lake; and eventually, by the same
conveyance, to what is now denominated Cass Lake, or upper *Lac Cedre
Rogue*. This he reached in January, 1806, and it formed the terminus of his
journey.

In 1820, Gen. Cass visited Sandy Lake, by the way of Lake Superior, with
a strong party, and exploratory outfit, under the authority of the government. He encamped the bulk of his party at Sandy Lake, depositing all his
heavy supplies, and fitted out a light party in two canoes, to trace up the river
to its source. After ascending to the point of land at the entrance of Turtle
River into Cass Lake, it was found, from Indian accounts, that he could not
ascend higher in the state of the water with his heavy canoes, if, indeed, his
supplies or the time at his command would have permitted him to accomplish it, compatibly with other objects of his instructions. This, therefore,
constituted the terminal point of his journey.

The length of the river, from the Gulf of Mexico to Itasca Lake, has been
estimated at 3,160 miles. Barometrical observations show its altitude, above
the same point, to be 1,680 feet—which denotes an average descent of a
fraction over six inches per mile.

The latitude of Itasca Lake has been accurately determined to be 47° 13'
35"—which is nearly two degrees south of the position assigned to it by the
best geographers in 1783, the date of the definite treaty of peace between the
United States and Great Britain.

The reason of this geographical mistake has been satisfactorily shown in
traversing up the stream from the summit of the Pemidjegomag, or Cross-
water Lake—during which, the general course of the ascent is due south.

Excerpt from Domestic Manners of the Americans

Frances Trollope (1780–1863) was an English novelist who lived for several years in the United States. In 1832, she wrote *Domestic Manners of the Americans*, in which she described American society in largely negative terms. Her description of boardinghouses provides some insight into how women fit into the domestic world outside of their own home.

For some reason or other, which English people are not very likely to understand, a great number of young married persons board by the year, instead of "going to housekeeping," as they call having an establishment of their own. Of course this statement does not include persons of large fortune, but it does include very many whose rank in society would make such a mode of life quite impossible with us. I can hardly imagine a contrivance more effectual for ensuring the insignificance of a woman, than marrying her at seventeen, and placing her in a boarding-house. Nor can I easily imagine a life of more uniform dulness for the lady herself; but this certainly is a matter of taste. I have heard many ladies declare that it is "just quite the perfection of comfort to have nothing to fix for oneself." Yet despite these assurances I always experienced a feeling which hovered between pity and contempt, when I contemplated their mode of existence.

How would a newly-married Englishwoman endure it, her head and her heart full of the one dear scheme—

"Well ordered home, his dear delight to make?"

She must rise exactly in time to reach the boarding table at the hour appointed for breakfast, or she will get a stiff bow from the lady president, cold coffee, and no egg. I have been sometimes greatly amused upon these occasions by watching a little scene in which the bye-play had much more meaning than the words uttered. The fasting, but tardy lady, looks round the table, and having ascertained that there was no egg left, says distinctly, "I will take an egg if you please." But as this is addressed to no one in particular, no one in particular answers it, unless it happen that her husband is at table before her, and then he says, "There are no eggs, my dear." Whereupon the lady president evidently cannot hear, and the greedy culprit who has swallowed two eggs (for there are always as many eggs as noses) looks pretty considerably afraid of being found out. The breakfast proceeds in sombre silence, save that sometimes a parrot, and sometimes a canary bird, ventures to utter a timid note. When it is finished, the gentlemen hurry to their occupation, and the quiet ladies mount the stairs, some to the first, some to the second, and some to the third stories, in an inverse proportion to the number of dollars paid, and ensconce themselves in their respective chambers. As to what they do there it is not very easy to say, but I believe they clear-starch a little, and iron a little, and sit in a rocking-chair, and sew a great deal. I always observed that the ladies who boarded, wore more elaborately worked collars and petticoats than any one else. The plough is hardly a more blessed instrument in America than the needle. How could they live without it? But time and the needle wear through the longest morning, and happily the American morning is not very long, even though they breakfast at eight.

It is generally about two o'clock that the boarding gentlemen meet the boarding ladies at dinner. Little is spoken, except a whisper between the married pairs. Sometimes a sulky bottle of wine flanks the plate of one or two individuals, but it adds nothing to the mirth of the meeting, and seldom more than one glass to the good cheer of the owners, it is not then, and it is not there, that the gentlemen of the Union drink. Soon, very soon, the silent meal is done, and then, if you mount the stairs after them, you will find from the doors of the more affectionate and indulgent wives, a smell of cigars steam forth, which plainly indicates the felicity of the couple within. If the gentleman be a very polite husband, he will, as soon as he has done smoking and drinking his toddy, offer his arm to his wife, as far as the corner of the street, where his store, or his office is situated, and there he will leave her to turn which way she likes. As this is the hour for being full dressed, of course she turns the way she can be most seen. Perhaps she pays a few visits; perhaps she goes to chapel; or, perhaps, she enters some store where her husband deals, and ventures to order a few notions; and then she goes home again—no, not home—I will not give that name to a boarding-house—but she re-enters the cold heartless atmosphere in which she dwells, where hospitality can never enter, and where interest takes the management instead of affection. At tea they all meet again, and a little trickery is perceptible to a nice observer in the manner of partaking the pound-cake, &c. After this, those who are happy enough to have engagements hasten to keep them; those who have not, either mount again to the solitude of their chamber, or, what appeared to me much worse, remain in the common sitting-room, in a society cemented by no tie, endeared by no connexion, which choice did not bring together, and which the slightest motive would break asunder. I remarked that the gentlemen were generally obliged to go out every evening on business, and, I confess, the arrangement did not surprise me.

The Book of Mormon: *Testimony and Excerpts*

One of the most controversial social movements of the Jacksonian period was Mormonism, or the Church of Jesus Christ of Latter-day Saints. This church was founded by Joseph Smith Jr. and was based on the teachings contained in the Book of Mormon, first published in 1830. Smith claimed that he received this new revelation of God on golden tablets, which only he was authorized to translate. The Book of Mormon, comprising fifteen books, claimed to give an account of two groups that migrated to North America centuries before the birth of Jesus Christ, Jesus Christ's appearance to some of these people after his resurrection, and the decline of the civilizations that had developed in North American as a result of their sin.

THE BOOK OF MORMON: An Account Written by THE HAND OF MORMON UPON PLATES TAKEN FROM THE PLATES OF NEPHI

Wherefore, it is an abridgment of the record of the people of Nephi, and also of the Lamanites—Written to the Lamanites, who are a remnant of the house of Israel; and also to Jew and Gentile—Written by way of commandment, and also by the spirit of prophecy and of revelation—Written and sealed up, and hid up unto the Lord, that they might not be destroyed—To come forth by the gift and power of God unto the interpretation thereof—Sealed by the hand of Moroni, and hid up unto the Lord, to come forth in due time by way of the Gentile—The interpretation thereof by the gift of God.

An abridgment taken from the Book of Ether also, which is a record of the people of Jared, who were scattered at the time the Lord confounded the language of the people, when they were building a tower to get to heaven— Which is to show unto the remnant of the House of Israel what great things the Lord hath done for their fathers; and that they may know the covenants of the Lord, that they are not cast off forever—And also to the convincing of the Jew and Gentile that JESUS is the CHRIST, the ETERNAL GOD, manifesting himself unto all nations—And now, if there are faults they are the mistakes of men; wherefore, condemn not the things of God, that ye may be found spotless at the judgment-seat of Christ.

TRANSLATED BY JOSEPH SMITH, JUN.

****

THE TESTIMONY OF THREE WITNESSES

Be it known unto all nations, kindreds, tongues, and people, unto whom this work shall come: That we, through the grace of God the Father, and our Lord Jesus Christ, have seen the plates which contain this record, which is a record of the people of Nephi, and also of the Lamanites, their brethren, and also of the people of Jared, who came from the tower of which hath been spoken. And we also know that they have been translated by the gift and power of God, for his voice hath declared it unto us; wherefore we know of a surety that the work is true. And we also testify that we have seen the engravings which are upon the plates; and they have been shown unto us by the power of God, and not of man. And we declare with words of soberness, that an angel of God came down from heaven, and he brought and laid before our eyes, that we beheld and saw the plates, and the engravings thereon; and we know that it is by the grace of God the Father, and our Lord Jesus Christ, that we beheld and bear record that these things are true. And it is marvelous in our eyes. Nevertheless, the voice of the Lord commanded us that we should bear record of it; wherefore, to be obedient unto the commandments of God, we bear testimony of these things. And we know that if we are faithful in Christ, we shall rid our garments of the blood of all men, and be found spotless before the judgment-seat of Christ, and shall dwell with him eternally in the heavens. And the honor be to the Father, and to the Son, and to the Holy Ghost, which is one God. Amen.

OLIVER COWDERY, DAVID WHITMER, MARTIN HARRIS

****

THE TESTIMONY OF EIGHT WITNESSES

Be it known unto all nations, kindreds, tongues, and people, unto whom this work shall come: That Joseph Smith, Jun., the translator of this work, has shown unto us the plates of which hath been spoken, which have the appearance of gold; and as many of the leaves as the said Smith has translated we did handle with our hands; and we also saw the engravings thereon, all of which has the appearance of ancient work, and of curious workmanship. And this we bear record with words of soberness, that the said Smith has shown unto us, for we have seen and hefted, and know of a surety that the said Smith has got the plates of which we have spoken. And we give our names unto the world, to witness unto the world that which we have seen. And we lie not, God bearing witness of it.

CHRISTIAN WHITMER, JACOB WHITMER, PETER WHITMER, JUN., JOHN WHITMER, HIRAM PAGE, JOSEPH SMITH, SEN., HYRUM SMITH, SAMUEL H. SMITH

****

3 NEPHI 11:1–12

1   And now it came to pass that there were a great multitude gathered together, of the people of Nephi, round about the temple which was in the land Bountiful; and they were marveling and wondering one with another, and were showing one to another the great and marvelous change which had taken place.

2   And they were also conversing about this Jesus Christ, of whom the sign had been given concerning his death.

3   And it came to pass that while they were thus conversing one with another, they heard a voice as if it came out of heaven; and they cast their eyes round about, for they understood not the voice which they heard; and it was not a harsh voice, neither was it a loud voice; nevertheless, and notwithstanding it being a small voice it did pierce them that did hear to the center, insomuch that there was no part of their frame that it did not cause to quake; yea, it did pierce them to the very soul, and did cause their hearts to burn.

4   And it came to pass that again they heard the voice, and they understood it not.

5   And again the third time they did hear the voice, and did open their ears to hear it; and their eyes were towards the sound thereof; and they did look steadfastly towards heaven, from whence the sound came.

6   And behold, the third time they did understand the voice which they heard; and it said unto them:

7   Behold my Beloved Son, in whom I am well pleased, in whom I have glorified my name—hear ye him.

8   And it came to pass, as they understood they cast their eyes up again towards heaven; and behold, they saw a Man descending out of heaven; and he was clothed in a white robe; and he came down and stood in the midst of them; and the eyes of the whole multitude were turned upon him, and they durst not open their mouths, even one to another, and wist not what it meant, for they thought it was an angel that had appeared unto them.

9   And it came to pass that he stretched forth his hand and spake unto the people, saying:

10 Behold, I am Jesus Christ, whom the prophets testified shall come into the world.

11 And behold, I am the light and the life of the world; and I have drunk out of that bitter cup which the Father hath given me, and have glorified the Father in taking upon me the sins of the world, in the which I have suffered the will of the Father in all things from the beginning.

12 And it came to pass that when Jesus had spoken these words the whole multitude fell to the earth; for they remembered that it had been prophesied among them that Christ should show himself unto them after his ascension into heaven.

****

BOOK OF MORONI 10:3–5

3 Behold, I would exhort you that when ye shall read these things, if it be wisdom in God that ye should read them, that ye would remember how merciful the Lord hath been unto the children of men, from the creation of Adam even down unto the time that ye shall receive these things, and ponder it in your hearts.

4 And when ye shall receive these things, I would exhort you that ye would ask God, the Eternal Father, in the name of Christ, if these things are not true; and if ye shall ask with a sincere heart, with real intent, having faith in Christ, he will manifest the truth of it unto you, by the power of the Holy Ghost.

5 And by the power of the Holy Ghost ye may know the truth of all things.

Excerpts from "Early Factory Labor in New England"

From 1834 to 1848, Harriet Hanson Robinson worked in the famous Lowell textile mills in Massachusetts. The excerpts below appeared in Harriet H. Robinson, "Early Factory Labor in New England," in Massachusetts Bureau of Statistics of Labor, *Fourteenth Annual Report* (Boston: Wright & Potter, 1883), pp. 38082, 38788, 39192. (Courtesy of the Internet Modern History Sourcebook <http://www.fordham.edu/halsall/mod/robinson-lowell.html>)

In what follows, I shall confine myself to a description of factory life in Lowell, Massachusetts, from 1832 to 1848, since, with that phase of Early Factory Labor in New England, I am the most familiar—because I was a part of it.

In 1832, Lowell was little more than a factory village. Five "corporations" were started, and the cotton mills belonging to them were building. Help was in great demand and stories were told all over the country of the new factory place, and the high wages that were offered to all classes of workpeople; stories that reached the ears of mechanics' and farmers' sons and gave new life to lonely and dependent women in distant towns and farmhouses. . . . Troops of young girls came from different parts of New England, and from Canada, and men were employed to collect them at so much a head, and deliver them at the factories. . . .

At the time the Lowell cotton mills were started the caste of the factory girl was the lowest among the employments of women. In England and in France, particularly, great injustice had been done to her real character. She was represented as subjected to influences that must destroy her purity and selfrespect. In the eyes of her overseer she was but a brute, a slave, to be beaten, pinched and pushed about. It was to overcome this prejudice that such high wages had been offered to women that they might be induced to become millgirls, in spite of the opprobrium that still clung to this degrading occupation. . . .

The early millgirls were of different ages. Some were not over ten years old; a few were in middle life, but the majority were between the ages of sixteen and twentyfive. The very young girls were called "doffers." They "doffed," or took off, the full bobbins from the spinningframes, and replaced them with empty ones. These mites worked about fifteen minutes every hour and the rest of the time was their own. When the overseer was kind they were allowed to read, knit, or go outside the millyard to play. They were paid two dollars a week. The working hours of all the girls extended from five o'clock in the morning until seven in the evening, with one halfhour each, for breakfast and dinner. Even the doffers were forced to be on duty nearly fourteen hours a day. This was the greatest hardship in the lives of these children. Several years later a tenhour law was passed, but not until long after some of these little doffers were old enough to appear before the legislative committee on the subject, and plead, by their presence, for a reduction of the hours of labor. . . .

Those of the millgirls who had homes generally worked from eight to ten months in the year; the rest of the time was spent with parents or friends. A few taught school during the summer months. Their life in the factory was made pleasant to them. In those days there was no need of advocating the doctrine of the proper relation between employer and employed. *Help was too valuable to be illtreated.* . . .

The most prevailing incentive to labor was to secure the means of education for some *male* member of the family. To make a *gentleman* of a brother or a son, to give him a college education, was the dominant thought in the minds of a great many of the better class of millgirls. I have known more than one to give every cent of her wages, month after month, to her brother, that he might get the education necessary to enter some profession. I have known a mother to work years in this way for her boy. I have known women to educate young men by their earnings, who were not sons or relatives. There are many men now living who were helped to an education by the wages of the early millgirls.

It is well to digress here a little, and speak of the influence the possession of money had on the characters of some of these women. We can hardly realize what a change the cotton factory made in the status of the working women. Hitherto woman had always been a money *saving* rather than a money *earning*, member of the community. Her labor could command but small return. If she worked out as servant, or "help," her wages were from 50 cents to $1.00 a week; or, if she went from house to house by the day to spin and weave, or do tailoress work, she could get but 75 cents a week and her meals. As teacher, her services were not in demand, and the arts, the professions, and even the trades and industries, were nearly all closed to her.

As late as 1840 there were only seven vocations outside the home into which the women of New England had entered. At this time woman had no property rights. A widow could be left without her share of her husband's (or the family) property, an " incumbrance" to his estate. A father could make his will without reference to his daughter's share of the inheritance. He usually left her a home on the farm as long as she remained single. A woman was not supposed to be capable of spending her own, or of using other people's money. In Massachusetts, before 1840, a woman could not, legally, be treasurer of her own sewing society, unless some man were responsible for her. The law took no cognizance of woman as a moneyspender. She was a ward, an appendage, a relict. Thus it happened that if a woman did not choose to marry, or, when left a widow, to remarry, she had no choice but to enter one of the few employments open to her, or to become a burden on the charity of some relative. . . .

One of the first strikes that ever took place in this country was in Lowell in 1836. When it was announced that the wages were to be cut down, great indignation was felt, and it was decided to strike or "turn out" en masse. This was done. The mills were shut down, and the girls went from their several corporations in procession to the grove on Chapel Hill, and listened to incendiary speeches from some early labor reformers.

One of the girls stood on a pump and gave vent to the feelings of her companions in a neat speech, declaring that it was their duty to resist all attempts at cutting down the wages. This was the first time a woman had spoken in public in Lowell, and the event caused surprise and consternation among her audience.

It is hardly necessary to say that, so far as practical results are concerned, this strike did no good. The corporation would not come to terms. The girls were soon tired of holding out, and they went back to their work at the reduced rate of wages. The ill success of this early attempt at resistance on the part of the wage element seems to have made a precedent for the issue of many succeeding strikes.

Indian Removal

INDIAN REMOVAL ACT (1830)

The Indian Removal Act (1830) passed Congress in May 1830. It set aside land west of the Mississippi River (in modern-day Oklahoma) for Native Americans to receive in exchange for their land in the East. Presented as a voluntary decision, everyone involved knew that the native groups would have no choice but to take the opportunity or risk losing both their lives and their lands. Indians who had improved their land had the option of receiving an allotment of property on or near their tribal land. Congress also approved a budget of $500,000 to help finance removal.

An Act to provide for an exchange of lands with the Indians residing in any of the states or territories, and for their removal west of the river Mississippi.

Be it enacted by the Senate and House of Representatives of the United States of America, in Congress assembled, That it shall and may be lawful for the President of the United States to cause so much of any territory belonging to the United States, west of the river Mississippi, not included in any state or organized territory, and to which the Indian title has been extinguished, as he may judge necessary, to be divided into a suitable number of districts, for the reception of such tribes or nations of Indians as may choose to exchange the lands where they now reside, and remove there; and to cause each of said districts to be so described by natural or artificial marks, as to be easily distinguished from every other.

And be it further enacted, That it shall and may be lawful for the President to exchange any or all of such districts, so to be laid off and described, with any tribe or nation of Indians now residing within the limits of any of the states or territories, and with which the United States have existing treaties, for the whole or any part or portion of the territory claimed and occupied by such tribe or nation, within the bounds of any one or more of the states or territories, where the land claimed and occupied by the Indians, is owned by the United States, or the United States are bound to the state within which it lies to extinguish the Indian claim thereto.

And be it further enacted, That in the making of any such exchange or exchanges, it shall and may be lawful for the President solemnly to assure the tribe or nation with which the exchange is made, that the United States will forever secure and guaranty to them, and their heirs or successors, the country so exchanged with them; and if they prefer it, that the United States will cause a patent or grant to be made and executed to them for the same: Provided always, That such lands shall revert to the United States, if the Indians become extinct, or abandon the same.

And be it further enacted, That if, upon any of the lands now occupied by the Indians, and to be exchanged for, there should be such improvements as add value to the land claimed by any individual or individuals of such tribes or nations, it shall and may be lawful for the President to cause such value to be ascertained by appraisement or otherwise, and to cause such ascertained value to be paid to the person or persons rightfully claiming such improvements. And upon the payment of such valuation, the improvements so valued and paid for, shall pass to the United States, and possession shall not afterwards be permitted to any of the same tribe.

And be it further enacted, That upon the making of any such exchange as is contemplated by this act, it shall and may be lawful for the President to cause such aid and assistance to be furnished to the emigrants as may be necessary and proper to enable them to remove to, and settle in, the country for which they may have exchanged; and also, to give them such aid and assistance as may be necessary for their support and subsistence for the first year after their removal.

And be it further enacted, That it shall and may be lawful for the President to cause such tribe or nation to be protected, at their new residence, against all interruption or disturbance from any other tribe or nation of Indians, or from any other person or persons whatever.

And be it further enacted, That it shall and may be lawful for the President to have the same superintendence and care over any tribe or nation in the country to which they may remove, as contemplated by this act, that he is now authorized to have over them at their present places of residence: Provided, That nothing in this act contained shall be construed as authorizing or directing the violation of any existing treaty between the United States and any of the Indian tribes.

And be it further enacted, That for the purpose of giving effect to the Provisions of this act, the sum of five hundred thousand dollars is hereby appropriated, to be paid out of any money in the treasury, not otherwise appropriated.

CHEROKEE NATION V. GEORGIA (1831)

In December 1829, the state of Georgia passed legislation that declared the Cherokee Nation within its borders nonexistent beginning June 1, 1830. The Cherokee challenged this law in court; the case, *Cherokee Nation v. Georgia*, eventually reached the United States Supreme Court. The Court, under Chief Justice John Marshall, gave its decision on March 18, 1831. It declared the Cherokee Nation a "domestic, dependent nation," subject to the laws of the United States, not individual states. In effect, the decision maintained the status quo, which allowed Georgia to continue restricting the sovereignty of the Cherokee.

Mr. Chief Justice Marshall delivered the opinion of the Court:

This bill is brought by the Cherokee nation, praying an injunction to restrain the state of Georgia from the execution of certain laws of that state, which, as is alleged, go directly to annihilate the Cherokees as a political society, and to seize, for the use of Georgia, the lands of the nation which have been assured to them by the United States in solemn treaties repeatedly made and still in force.

If courts were permitted to indulge their sympathies, a case better calculated to excite them can scarcely be imagined. A people once numerous, powerful, and truly independent, found by our ancestors in the quiet and uncontrolled possession of an ample domain, gradually sinking beneath our superior policy, our arts and our arms, have yielded their lands by successive treaties, each of which contains a solemn guarantee of the residue, until they retain no more of their formerly extensive territory than is deemed necessary to their comfortable subsistence. To preserve this remnant, the present application is made.

Before we can look into the merits of the case, a preliminary inquiry presents itself. Has this court jurisdiction of the cause?

The third article of the constitution describes the extent of the judicial power. The second section closes an enumeration of the cases to which it is extended, with "controversies" "between a state or the citizens thereof, and foreign states, citizens, or subjects." A subsequent clause of the same section gives the supreme court original jurisdiction in all cases in which a state shall be a party. The party defendant may then unquestionably be sued in this court. May the plaintiff sue in it? Is the Cherokee nation a foreign state in the sense in which that term is used in the constitution?

The counsel for the plaintiffs have maintained the affirmative of this proposition with great earnestness and ability. So much of the argument as was intended to prove the character of the Cherokees as a state, as a distinct political society, separated from others, capable of managing its own affairs and governing itself, has, in the opinion of a majority of the judges, been completely successful. They have been uniformly treated as a state from the settlement of our country. The numerous treaties made with them by the United States recognize them as a people capable of maintaining the relations of peace and war, of being responsible in their political character for any violation of their engagements, or for any aggression committed on the citizens of the United States by any individual of their community. Laws have been enacted in the spirit of these treaties. The acts of our government plainly recognize the Cherokee nation as a state, and the courts are bound by those acts.

A question of much more difficulty remains. Do the Cherokee constitute a foreign state in the sense of the constitution?

The counsel have shown conclusively that they are not a state of the union, and have insisted that individually they are aliens, not owing allegiance to the United States. An aggregate of aliens composing a state must, they say, be a foreign state. Each individual being foreign, the whole must be foreign.

This argument is imposing, but we must examine it more closely before we yield to it. The condition of the Indians in relation to the United States is perhaps unlike that of any other two people in existence. In the general, nations not owing a common allegiance are foreign to each other. The term foreign nation is, with strict propriety, applicable by either to the other. But the relation of the Indians to the United States is marked by peculiar and cardinal distinctions which exist no where else.

The Indian territory is admitted to compose a part of the United States. In all our maps, geographical treaties, histories, and laws, it is so considered. In all our intercourse with foreign nations, in our commercial regulations, in any attempt at intercourse between Indians and foreign nations, they are considered as within the jurisdictional limits of the United States, subject to many of those restraints which are imposed upon our own citizens. They acknowledge themselves in their treaties to be under the protection of the United States; they admit that the United States shall have the sole and exclusive right of regulating the trade with them, and managing all their affairs as they think proper; and the Cherokees in particular were allowed by the treaty of Hopewell, which preceded the constitution, "to send a deputy of their choice, whenever they think fit, to congress." Treaties were made with some tribes by the state of New York, under a then unsettled construction of the confederation, by which they ceded all their lands to that state, taking back a limited grant to themselves, in which they admit their dependence.

Though the Indians are acknowledged to have an unquestionable, and, heretofore, unquestioned right to the lands they occupy, until that right shall be extinguished by a voluntary cession to our government; yet it may well be doubted whether those tribes which reside within the acknowledged boundaries of the United States can, with strict accuracy, be denominated foreign nations. They may, more correctly be denominated domestic dependent nations. They occupy a territory to which we assert a title independent of their will, which must take effect in point of possession when their right of possession ceases. Meanwhile, they are in a state of pupilage. Their relation to the United States resembles that of a ward to his guardian.

They look to our government for protection; rely upon its kindness and its power; appeal to it for relief to their wants; and address the president as their great father. They and their country are considered by foreign nations, as well as by ourselves, as being so completely under the sovereignty and dominion of the United States, that any attempt to acquire their lands, or to form a political connexion with them, would be considered by all as an invasion of our territory, and an act of hostility.

These considerations go far to support the opinion, that the framers of our constitution had not the Indian tribes in view, when they opened the courts of the union to controversies between a state or the citizens thereof, and foreign states.

In considering this subject, the habits and usages of the Indians, in their intercourse with their white neighbours, ought not to be entirely disregarded. At the time the constitution was framed, the idea of appealing to an American court of justice for an assertion of right or a redress of wrong, had perhaps never entered the mind of an Indian or of his tribe. Their appeal was to the tomahawk, or to the government. This was well understood by the statesmen who framed the constitution of the United States, and might furnish some reason for omitting to enumerate them among the parties who might sue in the courts of the union. Be this as it may, the peculiar relations between the United States and the Indians occupying our territory are such, that we should feel much difficulty in considering them as designated by the term foreign state, were there no other part of the constitution which might shed light on the meaning of these words. But we think that in construing them, considerable aid is furnished by that clause in the eighth section of the third article; which empowers congress to "regulate commerce with foreign nations, and among the several states, and with the Indian tribes."

In this clause they are as clearly contradistinguished by a name appropriate to themselves, from foreign nations, as from the several states composing the union. They are designated by a distinct appellation; and as this appellation can be applied to neither of the others, neither can the appellation distinguishing either of the others be in fair construction applied to them. The objects, to which the power of regulating commerce might be directed, are divided into three distinct classes—foreign nations, the several states, and Indian tribes. When forming this article, the convention considered them as entirely distinct. We cannot assume that the distinction was lost in framing a subsequent article, unless there be something in its language to authorize the assumption.

The counsel for the plaintiffs contend that the words "Indian tribes" were introduced into the article, empowering congress to regulate commerce, for the purpose of removing those doubts in which the management of Indian affairs was involved by the language of the ninth article of the confederation. Intending to give the whole power of managing those affairs to the government about to be instituted, the convention conferred it explicitly; and omitted those qualifications which embarrassed the exercise of it as granted in the confederation. This may be admitted without weakening the construction which has been intimated. Had the Indian tribes been foreign nations, in the view of the convention; this exclusive power of regulating intercourse with them might have been, and most probably would have been, specifically given, in language indicating that idea, not in language contradistinguishing them from foreign nations. Congress might have been empowered "to regulate commerce with foreign nations, including the Indian tribes, and among the several states." This language would have suggested itself to statesmen who considered the Indian tribes as foreign nations, and were yet desirous of mentioning them particularly.

It has been also said, that the same words have not necessarily the same meaning attached to them when found in different parts of the same instrument: their meaning is controlled by the context. This is undoubtedly true. In common language the same word has various meanings, and the peculiar sense in which it is used in any sentence is to be determined by the context. This may not be equally true with respect to proper names. Foreign nations is a general term, the application of which to Indian tribes, when used in the American constitution, is at best extremely questionable. In one article in which a power is given to be exercised in regard to foreign nations generally, and to the Indian tribes particularly, they are mentioned as separate in terms clearly contradistinguishing from each other. We perceive plainly that the constitution in this article does not comprehend Indian tribes in the general term "foreign nations," not we presume because a tribe may not be a nation, but because it is not foreign to the United States. When, afterwards, the term "foreign state" is introduced, we cannot impute to the convention the intention to desert its former meaning, and to comprehend Indian tribes within it, unless the context force that construction on us. We find nothing in the context, and nothing in the subject of the article, which leads to it.

The court has bestowed its best attention on this question, and, after mature deliberation, the majority is of opinion that an Indian tribe or nation within the United States is not a foreign state in the sense of the constitution, and cannot maintain an action in the courts of the United States.

A serious additional objection exists to the jurisdiction of the court. Is the matter of the bill the proper subject for judicial inquiry and decision? It seeks to restrain a state from the forcible exercise of legislative power over a neighbouring people asserting their independence; their fight to which the state denies. On several of the matters alleged in the bill, for example on the laws making it criminal to exercise the usual powers of self-government in their own country by the Cherokee nation, this court cannot interpose; at least in the form in which those matters are presented. That part of the bill which respects the land occupied by the Indians, and prays the aid of the court to protect their possession, may be more doubtful. The mere question of right might perhaps be decided by this court in a proper case with proper parties. But the court is asked to do more than decide on the title. The bill requires us to control the legislature of Georgia, and to restrain the exertion of its physical force. The propriety of such an interposition by the court may be well questioned. It savours too much of the exercise of political power to be within the proper province of the judicial department. But the opinion on the point respecting parties makes it unnecessary to decide this question. If it be true that the Cherokee nation have rights, this is not the tribunal in which those rights are to be asserted. If it be true that wrongs have been inflicted, and that still greater are to be apprehended, this is not the tribunal which can redress the past or prevent the future.

The motion for an injunction is denied.

Excerpts from Narrative of William W. Brown

William Wells Brown (1814?–1884) was a light-complexioned slave who worked for James Walker, a slave trader in St. Louis, Missouri. In his autobiography, *Narrative of William W. Brown* (1847), Brown described his job requirements in helping Walker transport slaves to New Orleans for sale.

On landing at Natchez, the slaves were all carried to the slave-pen, and there kept one week, during which time, several of them were sold. Mr. Walker fed his slaves well. We took on board, at St. Louis, several hundred pounds of bacon (smoked meat) and corn-meal, and his slaves were better fed than slaves generally were in Natchez, so far as my observation extended.

At the end of a week, we left for New Orleans, the place of our final destination, which we reached in two days. Here the slaves were placed in a negro-pen, where those who wished to purchase could call and examine them. The negro-pen is a small yard, surrounded by buildings, from fifteen to twenty feet wide, with the exception of a large gate with iron bars. The slaves are kept in the buildings during the night, and turned out into the yard during the day. After the best of the stock was sold at private sale at the pen, the balance were taken to the Exchange Coffee House Auction Rooms, kept by Isaac L. McCoy, and sold at public auction. After the sale of this lot of slaves, we left New Orleans for St. Louis. . . .

In the course of eight or nine weeks Mr. Walker had his cargo of human flesh made up. There was in this lot a number of old men and women, some of them with gray locks. We left St. Louis in the steamboat Carlton, Captain Swan, bound for New Orleans. On our way down, and before we reached Rodney, the place where we made our first stop, I had to prepare the old slaves for market. I was ordered to have the old men's whiskers shaved off, and the grey hairs plucked out, where they were not too numerous, in which case he had a preparation of blacking to color it, and with a blacking-brush we would put it on. This was new business to me, and was performed in a room where the passengers could not see us. These slaves were also taught how old they were by Mr. Walker, and after going through the blacking process, they looked ten or fifteen years younger; and I am sure that some of those who purchased slaves of Mr. Walker, were dreadfully cheated, especially in the ages of the slaves which they bought.

We landed at Rodney, and the slaves were driven to the pen in the back part of the village. Several were sold at this place, during our stay of four or five days, when we proceeded to Natchez. There we landed at night, and the gang were put in the warehouse until morning, when they were driven to the pen. As soon as the slaves are put in these pens, swarms of planters may be seen in and about them. They knew when Walker was expected, as he always had the time advertised beforehand when he would be in Rodney, Natchez, and New Orleans. These were the principal places where he offered his slaves for sale.

When at Natchez the second time, I saw a slave very cruelly whipped. He belonged to a Mr. Broadwell, a merchant who kept a store on the wharf. The slave's name was Lewis. I had known him several years, as he was formerly from St. Louis. We were expecting a steamboat down the river, in which we were to take passage for New Orleans. Mr. Walker sent me to the landing to watch for the boat, ordering me to inform him on its arrival. While there, I went into the store to see Lewis. I saw a slave in the store, and asked him where Lewis was. Said he, "They have got Lewis hanging between the heavens and the earth." I asked him what he meant by that. He told me to go into the warehouse and see. I went in, and found Lewis there. He was tied up to a beam, with his toes just touching the floor. As there was no one in the warehouse but himself, I inquired the reason of his being in that situation. He said Mr. Broadwell had sold his wife to a planter six miles from the city, and that he had been to visit her,—that he went in the night, expecting to return before daylight, and went without his master's permission. The patrol had taken him up before he reached his wife. He was put in jail, and his master had to pay for his catching and keeping, and that was what he was tied up for.

Just as he finished his story, Mr. Broadwell came in, and inquired what I was doing there. I knew not what to say, and while I was thinking what reply to make, he struck me over the head with the cowhide, the end of which struck me over my right eye, sinking deep into the flesh, leaving a scar which I carry to this day. Before I visited Lewis, he had received fifty lashes. Mr. Broadwell gave him fifty lashes more after I came out, as I was afterwards informed by Lewis himself.

The next day we proceeded to New Orleans, and put the gang in the same negro-pen which we occupied before. In a short time, the planters came flocking to the pen to purchase slaves. Before the slaves were exhibited for sale, they were dressed and driven out into the yard. Some were set to dancing, some to jumping, some to singing, and some to playing cards. This was done to make them appear cheerful and happy. My business was to see that they were placed in those situations before the arrival of the purchasers, and I have often set them to dancing when their cheeks were wet with tears. As slaves were in good demand at that time, they were all soon disposed of, and we again set out for St. Louis.

Reference

Abolitionism   A movement against slavery that originated in America during the revolutionary period and reached its apex between 1865 and 1870 with the passage of the Thirteenth, Fourteenth, and Fifteenth Amendments to the United States Constitution. Antebellum abolitionism was led by black and white men and women such as Frederick Douglass, William Lloyd Garrison, Harriet Tubman, and Sarah and Angelina Grimké. Its supporters universally advocated the end of American slavery, and many also called for racial equality.

African Colonization Society (ACS)   An organization founded in 1816 that intended to transport free blacks in the United States to free colonies in Africa. The ACS established Liberia, but it was not as successful as society members hoped. Despite the support of prominent politicians such as Henry Clay and Abraham Lincoln, abolitionists criticized the ACS for wanting to rid the United States of African Americans instead of affording them equality.

American Anti-Slavery Society   An abolitionist society founded in 1833 by Theodore Weld, Arthur and Lewis Tappan, and William Lloyd Garrison. The American Anti-Slavery Society was at the forefront of the antebellum abolitionist movement, although some members left in 1840 in a dispute with Garrison's approach to ending slavery.

American System   A comprehensive economic system proposed by Henry Clay after the War of 1812, which became the platform of the Whig party. Clay's plan, based on the economic principles of former Secretary of the Treasury Alexander Hamilton, called for the institution of a protective tariff, the chartering of a new national bank, and the funding of internal improvements across the nation. Clay and the Whigs intended the American System to unite the nation economically and promote industrialization.

Anti-Masonry   A movement against American Freemasonry during the Jacksonian period, ostensibly originating from the mysterious disappearance of William Morgan, a New York Freemason who threatened to reveal the organization's secrets. Opposition to the Freemasons, which centered on the secretive nature of their meetings and rituals and the belief that the organization was a conspiracy of elite men to control political and economic systems, eventually coalesced in the Anti-Masonic party. This political party held the first national nominating convention in the United States, selecting William Wirt as its presidential candidate in 1832. The Anti-Masonic party eventually was absorbed by the Whig party.

Arminianism   A theological belief, articulated by Jacobus Arminius in the 1600s, that argued against Calvinism and in favor of the ability of good works to help individuals attain salvation. Arminianism influenced American Protestants, particularly Methodists.

Benevolent Empire   A term referring to the reform movements of the Jacksonian period that were based on the idea that Christians should help the less fortunate through charity. These movements, which were largely middle class in origin, included temperance and prison reform.

Bleeding Kansas   The name given to the civil war that broke out in the Kansas Territory after the passage of the Kansas-Nebraska Act of 1854. Pro- and antislavery Americans moved into the territory to ensure that they could influence the writing of its application for statehood, which would specify its residents' endorsement of, or opposition to, slavery. These years in Kansas would witness the emergence of John Brown as an abolitionist and would precipitate the infamous Brooks-Sumner incident on the floor of the Senate.

Calvinism   A theological belief articulated by John Calvin during the Protestant Reformation. It posited, among other things, that God had predestined humans for salvation before creating the universe. A major tenet of Puritanism, Calvinism influenced American thought in many ways, even as its theological sway diminished.

Church of Jesus Christ of Latter-Day Saints   Also known as Mormonism, a religion that originated in the Jacksonian period. Its founder, Joseph Smith, experienced his first vision in 1820, in which he claimed to have received prophetic revelations from God that led him to try to rejuvenate New Testament Christianity in the United States. In the 1830s and 1840s, Smith and his followers moved from western New York to Illinois and Missouri, where Smith and his brother were taken from a jail and executed by a mob. Many Americans found the Mormon claims about new Christian revelations and their practice of polygamy frightening and threatening. Under the leadership of Brigham Young, many of the Mormons moved west to the Salt Lake City area. The United States government waged a short war against the Mormons in the late 1850s.

Civic Humanism   A concept that emphasized the necessity of service to government to better the society as a whole. It was an underlying tenet of the political ideology of republicanism.

Communalism   An attempt by some individuals and groups to experience utopia in the rapidly changing world of Jacksonian America. Utopian communities often sought to bring egalitarianism to their members through economic, social, and even sexual equality. Representative groups included the Shakers, the Fourierites, the Kingdom of Matthias, and Robert Owens's New Harmony community.

Companionate Marriage   The idea that marriage was a social institution based on relative equality rather than one governed by political and economic decisions and marked by patriarchal authority.

Complex Marriage   The custom of open, or nonmonogamous, marriage practiced by several utopian societies in the antebellum period. Complex marriage was often presented as a way of removing class distinctions and revolutionizing gender roles.

Corrupt Bargain   The term that Jacksonians gave to the alleged political bribe made by Henry Clay to John Quincy Adams during the 1824 presidential election. Supposedly, Clay promised Adams that he would help him win the House vote for president if, in return, Adams would appoint the Kentuckian secretary of state. While there is no credible evidence to suggest that such an offer was made, when Adams won the House vote over Jackson, who had won a plurality of the electoral vote, the Tennessean's supporters accused Adams and Clay of making a "corrupt bargain" to steal the election from the American people. Jackson's belief in this charge sparked his 1828 presidential campaign victory.

Cult of Domesticity   A term that describes antebellum expectations about female gender roles. Women were expected to tend the home, which was the "private sphere," and to remain out of the business and political worlds, which made up the "public sphere."

Democratic Party   Political party that had its antecedents in the Jeffersonian coalition of the early 1800s. Its development during the antebellum period was closely associated with the rise of Andrew Jackson to national prominence. Along with Jackson, Martin Van Buren, Amos Kendall, and Francis P. Blair, among others, were its main organizers. Democrats generally favored universal white manhood suffrage and used new populist campaign strategies and tactics to achieve political victories. It was not a wholly unified political coalition, however, as its members divided over states' rights, slavery, and various economic policies, including the Bank and the tariff. The Democrats won six presidential elections between 1828 and 1856. In 1860, the party, divided over slavery, split its support between northern and southern candidates, Stephen A. Douglas and John C. Breckinridge, respectively.

Evangelicalism   The acceptance, particularly among Protestant denominations during the First and Second Great Awakenings, of a proselytizing religion grounded in salvation by faith, freedom of worship, and emotional expressions of faith.

Filibustering   A term used to describe attempts by congressmen to delay votes on legislation and presidential nominations. During the antebellum period, the word was also used to describe the expeditions by Americans, often southerners, into Latin America for the purpose of seizing territory and expanding slavery. Notable examples include William Walker (Nicaragua and Mexico), Narciso Lopéz (Cuba), and John Quitman (Cuba).

Fire-eaters   A term used in reference to the most extreme southern supporters of states' rights and slavery. Fire-eaters tended to be the most vocal advocates of nullification and secession.

Forty-niners   The name given to American settlers who moved to California in 1849 as part of the gold rush.

Fourierism   A movement based on the theories of Frenchman Charles Fourier. Fourierism advocated socialistic cooperation instead of capitalistic competition and found expression in the formation of phalanxes, or cooperative communities in which members theoretically shared ownership and labor equally.

Free-Soil Party   A political party that had as its slogan, "Free soil, free speech, free labor, and free men." Its members, mostly northerners, opposed the expansion of slavery into the western territories, arguing that free (white) labor was superior to black slavery. The Free-Soil presidential candidate in 1848 was former president Martin Van Buren, who ran respectably in the popular vote; John P. Hale was the party's candidate in 1852, by which time it had weakened considerably. Many Free-Soilers eventually joined the Republican Party.

Fugitive Slave Law   One of the most divisive issues of the antebellum period and a main component of the Compromise of 1850. The 1850 Fugitive Slave Law strengthened the original law, passed in 1793, which allowed judges to determine the standing of alleged fugitive slaves. The 1793 law faced substantial opposition in states that abolished slavery in the late eighteenth and early nineteenth centuries. To satisfy southerners that the federal government was not threatening slave property, the 1850 law was introduced as part of the compromise legislation of 1850. It strengthened the penalties for refusing to return fugitive slaves and increased the inducements for their return.

Gag Rule   A rule by which House members, in 1836, agreed to table antislavery petitions that were introduced to their congressional chamber. This treatment of antislavery petitions, intended to quiet debate over the slavery issue, only exacerbated the sectionalism of the Jacksonian period.

Gold Rush   The large movement of Americans into California beginning in 1849 after the discovery of gold there. California's American population would grow from approximately 800 individuals in 1848 to nearly 300,000 in 1854.

Honor   A set of assumptions and rituals that governed antebellum southern society. Essentially, honor consisted of protecting one's position and reputation. For example, well-to-do white men sometimes resorted to dueling to address an insult, although they would not duel with their social inferiors, such as poor white men or slaves.

Independent Treasury System Legislation, introduced and passed in 1840 as part of Martin Van Buren's administration, that separated the Treasury from the various state banks. Van Buren intended it to keep the federal government's funds from being subjected to the vagaries of the nation's fluctuating economic cycles. The bill failed to bring about the desired effects, according to Whigs, and it was repealed during John Tyler's administration in 1841.

Indian Removal Act An act passed in 1830 that set aside land west of the Mississippi River for Native Americans to receive in voluntary exchange for their land in the East. Indians who had improved their land had the option of receiving an allotment of property on or near their tribal land. A total of $500,000 was set aside for completing removal. This legislation allowed the Jackson administration to remove most of the so-called Five Civilized Tribes of the Southeast: the Cherokee, the Chickasaw, the Choctaw, the Creek, and the Seminole. It laid the groundwork for both the Trail of Tears and the Second Seminole War.

Industrialization The implementation of the Industrial Revolution in the United States. Americans began moving to the factory system of production, using steam-driven instead of human- or animal-powered machines, and congregating in urban areas in greater numbers. Industrialization led to calls for better transportation and communication systems, often requiring government financing and oversight. The changes in work also influenced social and economic expectations, as some women found opportunities to work outside the home and individuals banded together into unions to fight for better wages and working conditions. Still, even with this industrialization, the antebellum United States remained a predominantly agricultural society.

King Cotton A reference to the importance of cotton to the antebellum American economy. The term was encapsulated by South Carolina senator James Henry Hammond in an 1858 speech, in which he claimed, "Cotton is king," as he explained how intertwined England's industrial economy was with southern cotton. This well-founded belief that cotton was crucial to the transatlantic economy gave the future Confederate States false hope that they could convince European powers to side with the Confederacy during the Civil War.

Kitchen Cabinet The label given to the formal and informal advisers who surrounded President Andrew Jackson, including Martin Van Buren, John H. Eaton, Francis P. Blair, Amos Kendall, Roger B. Taney, and Andrew Jackson Donelson. These men allegedly were the ones who shaped Jackson's policies, although recent historians have been more willing to give Jackson credit for making his own decisions.

Know-Nothing Party A political party, also known as the American Party, that focused its platform on limiting the influence of immigrants and Catholics. Its origins were found in the 1840s among nativist secret societies located in the Northeast. (The ritualistic secrecy gave the Know-Nothings their unusual name; members were supposed to respond "I know nothing" if queried about their membership.) After the collapse of the Whig party, leaders of several of the secret orders combined to form a national coalition that used the issues of nativism and anti-Catholicism to distract Americans from the divisiveness of slavery. The party's national nominating convention selected Millard Fillmore and Andrew Jackson Donelson as its presidential and vice-presidential candidates in 1856. After the Know-Nothings' failure to win the election, many of its members joined the Republican Party, although some later formed the Constitutional Union Party of 1860.

Labor Theory of Value   The economic theory that a product should be priced in relationship to the labor that went into its production and that any profit from its sale should be paid to the individual who was most responsible for its production.

Liberalism   A political theory that became more prevalent during the Jacksonian period. Liberalism valued individual choice over coercion and sought a constitutional government that enforced laws and protected political liberty. Its supporters theoretically opposed social hierarchies, although in practice this standard was often not upheld.

Liberty Party   A political party founded in the 1840s. Its supporters were abolitionists who disagreed with the radicalism of William Lloyd Garrison. The Liberty Party, which was antislavery, nominated James G. Birney as its presidential candidate in 1840 and 1844. It eventually merged with the Free-Soil party.

Manifest Destiny   The belief that God had preordained the United States to control North America from the Atlantic Ocean to the Pacific Ocean. This term was coined in an 1845 editorial written by John L. O'Sullivan, although the idea was one that Americans had subscribed to since the time of the Puritans. The belief in Manifest Destiny would strongly influence antebellum domestic and international policy making.

Market Revolution   A description used by historians to describe the economic changes that took place during the Jacksonian period. The decades between the War of 1812 and the Civil War witnessed the United States moving from a subsistence economy based on small-scale agriculture and home production of goods to a more large-scale agricultural and industrial economy that produced goods not only, or even primarily, for individual consumption, but also for sale in the national and even global marketplace.

Millerism   The religious beliefs of William Miller, a Jacksonian prophet. Using a literal reading of the Bible, Miller calculated that Jesus would return to Earth to establish a millennial kingdom in the 1840s. The date changed several times, although October 22, 1844, was considered the official date. Miller lost followers when Jesus did not return as prophesied, but he influenced the later development of an Adventist (belief in Jesus' Second Coming) movement in the United States.

Minstrelsy   A term applied to blackface performances that gained popularity during the Jacksonian period. White performers darkened their faces and dressed and acted out their stereotypical and racist perceptions of blacks. The most famous of the Jacksonian minstrel performances was Thomas D. Rice's "Jump Jim Crow," which later gave its name to the era of segregation between Reconstruction and the civil rights movement of the post–World War II era.

Miscegenation   A term applied to interracial sexual relations, which were almost universally illegal in the Jacksonian period.

Mulatto   A derogatory term often used in antebellum America to describe the children of one white and one black parent or of mixed-race parents.

Nativism   The belief during the antebellum period that the sanctity of the United States was being threatened by growing waves of immigrants from Europe. These immigrants, many of them Irish and French Catholics, came to the United States for several reasons, including the Irish potato famine and the 1848 Revolutions. Their presence elicited concerns from Protestant Americans, who feared a papal conspiracy to undermine the nation's democratic ideals, and from other Americans who feared economic competition and social conflict.

Nullification   The political theory that a state could void, or nullify, any federal law that was unconstitutional. It was articulated in the Kentucky-Virginia Resolutions of 1798 and used by South Carolinians against the Tariff of 1832, which precipitated the Nullification Crisis. The southern states used the threat of nullification repeatedly during the antebellum period.

Overseer   A white man who managed a plantation for the owner. Often, overseers served in the place of absentee owners. Their primary duties were to supervise slave labor and other plantation workers; discipline slaves, often violently; update the owner regularly; and ensure the overall success of the plantation.

Panic   A term that during the nineteenth century often referred to a severe financial depression. During the Jacksonian period, the United States suffered "panics" in 1819, 1837, and 1857.

Paternalism   An idea about social relationships that stressed the benevolence of the individual with more power in the relationship. Often applied to the antebellum South, paternalism suggests that slave owners mitigated the severity of slavery by caring for their slaves as family members, albeit inferior ones; slaves, in return, provided labor and obedience.

Perfectionism   A Jacksonian movement that stressed the ability of individuals to bring about perfection on Earth. Followers believed that Jesus had already returned to Earth, establishing his millennial kingdom, thus providing the necessary environment for human perfection. The most prominent example of perfectionism was the Oneida Community, founded in Oneida, New York, in 1848 by John Humphrey Noyes. The Oneida Community was also a communal, utopian society.

Personal Liberty Laws   Laws put into place in northern states in response to the fugitive slave laws passed by Congress in 1793 and 1850. They worked against the return of fugitive slaves by forcing slave catchers to meet a higher standard of proof in identifying runaway slaves, limiting access to state resources to pursue and hold runaway slaves, and providing accused slaves with greater legal protection. Personal liberty laws were ruled unconstitutional by the Supreme Court in *Prigg v. Pennsylvania* (1842), a case in which a slave catcher, Edward Prigg, was prosecuted under Pennsylvania law for kidnapping a slave woman named Margaret Morgan.

Polygamy   The practice of being married to more than one spouse at the same time. Typically, antebellum polygamy involved the marriage of one man to multiple wives and was associated with the Mormon religion.

Popular Sovereignty   The political theory, espoused predominantly by Lewis Cass and Stephen A. Douglas, that the residents of United States territories should be able to determine their own course on the issue of slavery without congressional interference.

Proslavery Thought   The series of arguments, often interrelated, that southerners used to justify and defend the institution of slavery. These arguments used the Bible, classical history, science, and political and economic theories to support racist assumptions about African Americans.

Republicanism   A political ideology based on that of the eighteenth-century Opposition Whig Party of Great Britain and influential in the development of eighteenth- and nineteenth-century American politics. Republicanism emphasized the struggle between liberty and power. Power was linked closely to corruption, liberty to virtue. Only conscience and civic duty upheld liberty, while self-interest and egotism energized the forces of power. In the United States political system, a republic was seen as the only form of government that could protect liberty, which was not a personal, individual absence of constraint but the collective freedom of citizens from government tyranny.

Republican Motherhood   A conception of the role of American women in the Early Republic and Jacksonian periods. Women were expected to stay at home and provide the ideal environment in which to raise virtuous sons and daughters. Sons would presumably act virtuously in the political, public sphere, thus protecting the new American republic; daughters were to replicate their mothers' example in their own families.

Republican Party   A political party, born from the remnants of the Whigs in the mid-1850s, that eventually became the main political opponent of the Democratic Party. It focused on limiting the expansion of slavery in the western territories, supported internal improvements, and called for the construction of a transcontinental railroad, among other things. In 1856, its first presidential candidate, John C. Frémont, ran respectably. In 1860, the Republicans elected their first president, Abraham Lincoln.

Secession   A political theory arguing that the Constitution had been formed by a voluntary union of the original thirteen states; therefore, they and subsequent states could voluntarily leave the Union as well. As with nullification, the southern states threatened to secede several times during the antebellum period, particularly when they perceived that slavery's future was in jeopardy from the national government. Following Abraham Lincoln's election in 1860, seven southern states seceded and formed the Confederate States of America; they were shortly joined by four more southern states.

Second Bank of the United States   The second national bank, which was given a twenty-year charter by Congress in 1816. Intended to bring financial stability to the national economy, the Bank failed to moderate the Panic of 1819, angering many westerners and southerners. During Andrew Jackson's administration, the Bank's president, Nicholas Biddle, tried to force an early recharter of the financial institution. His effort failed, precipitating the Bank War between pro- and anti-Bank politicians; this political division contributed significantly to the formation of the Whig party. The Bank failed to receive a renewal and eventually became a short-lived state bank in Philadelphia, where it was located.

Second Great Awakening   A series of revivals stretching from the late 1790s through the 1840s. It helped evangelical Protestantism grow dramatically in urban areas, largely through the work of Charles G. Finney and Peter Cartwright. It produced the Burned-Over District of western New York, from which Mormonism, the Shakers, Millerism, and other spiritual and religious groups originated. In the South, the Second Great Awakening produced the Church of Christ, founded by Alexander Campbell and Barton Stone.

Slave Narratives   Biographies written or co-written by former slaves. These life stories provided real-life exposure to the travails of southern slavery, although they were sometimes infused with romantic or religious overtones. The narratives were often edited or written by white abolitionists, who used them in the campaign against slavery. Examples include *The History of Mary Prince, a West Indian Slave* (1831), *A Narrative of the Life of Frederick Douglass, an American Slave* (1845), *Twelve Years a Slave, Narrative of Solomon Northrup* (1853), and Harriet Jacobs's *Incidents in the Life of a Slave Girl* (1861).

Slave Power Conspiracy   The belief by northerners in the antebellum period that the federal government was increasingly coming under the malevolent influence of southern slave owners. They pointed to the number of southern and proslavery presidents elected, the passage of congressional legislation that favored slavery and its defenders, such as the Fugitive Slave Law of 1850 and the Kansas-Nebraska Act of 1854, and the rendering of prosouthern decisions by the Supreme Court, including the *Dred Scott* decision.

Specie   Coins, usually gold or silver, used in financial transactions. During the Jacksonian period, they were considered superior to banknotes because specie had actual value, whereas paper currency did not.

Spoils System   Also referred to as "rotation of office," a term used by Andrew Jackson's opponents to criticize his removal of government officials after he became president. Jackson considered the change of government officials a necessity of democratic government, giving the people the comfort of knowing that those individuals were not simply holding a position to advance their own ambitions or wealth. Ironically, the term itself came from a comment made by William L. Marcy, a Jacksonian: "To the victor belong the spoils of the enemy."

States' Rights   The idea that the separate states retained significant rights as individual members of the Union. During the Jacksonian period, states' rights theory was used, usually by the southern states, in attempts to justify opposition to tariffs, support of Indian removal, and restrictions on slavery.

Tammany Hall   A Democratic political machine in New York overseen by Thurlow Weed. During the antebellum period, it served as a political force for immigrant Irish in particular.

Telegraph   An electrical means of communication across great distances developed independently in the United States by Samuel F. B. Morse. The first public message by telegraph was sent from Baltimore to Washington, D.C., in 1844.

Temperance Movement   An antebellum movement that called for the restriction on, or outright prohibition of, alcoholic consumption. Composed mostly of women, the temperance movement had strong religious elements, and it worked in conjunction with other reform movements of the Jacksonian period.

Transcendentalism   An intellectual movement in the United States, centered primarily in New England, that was strongly influenced by European Romanticism. Transcendentalists, including Ralph Waldo Emerson, Henry David Thoreau, and Margaret Fuller, valued the individual, intuition, and nature. They also criticized the industrialization of the United States and its growing capitalistic bent as well as the evils of slavery.

Uncle Tom's Cabin   A novel, written by Harriet Beecher Stowe and published in 1852, that presented southern slavery as a terrible, violent institution. Its popularity helped mold northern public opinion against slavery.

Whig Party   A political party that formed during Andrew Jackson's second administration. It began as a conglomeration of anti-Jackson politicians, ranging from nullifiers, pro-Bank men, and Native American supporters to abolitionists. The party embraced the principles of Clay's American System and supported moral reform. It eventually elected two presidents: William Henry Harrison (1840) and Zachary Taylor (1848), both of whom died prematurely in office. The Whigs disintegrated in the early 1850s from personality differences, debates over slavery, and sectionalism.

Women's Rights Movement   A movement in which women's rights advocates used the democratizing spirit of the Jacksonian period to argue for greater political and civil rights for women. These women joined political campaigns, reform movements, religious groups, and abolitionist societies to effect change in the broader American society as well as to prove the efficacy of their influence. The apex of the movement during the Jacksonian period was the Seneca Falls Convention of 1848, which listed the grievances that American women had against the dominant male institutions, including the lack of female suffrage. The movement, however, failed to bring about the desired results and found itself superseded in the 1850s by the attention given to abolitionism.

Yeoman Farmers   Non-slave-owning white farmers who usually engaged in subsistence farming on small tracts of land that they owned. Politicians such as Thomas Jefferson considered them the moral fiber of the United States.

Young America   An intellectual and cultural movement that proclaimed the need for democracy to pervade every aspect of American society. The best-known member was John L. O'Sullivan, the editor of the Young America magazine, the *Democratic Review*, and the purported originator of the term "Manifest Destiny." Young Americans particularly supported territorial expansion, accompanied by the spread of American democratic institutions.

Bibliography

Abing, Kevin. "A Holy Battleground: Methodist, Baptist, and Quaker Missionaries among Shawnee Indians, 1830–1844." *Kansas History* 21 (1998): 118–137.

Abzug, Robert H. *Cosmos Crumbling: American Reform and the Religious Imagination.* New York: Oxford University Press, 1994.

Ahlstrom, Sydney E. *A Religious History of the American People.* New Haven: Yale University Press, 1972.

Allen, Austin. *Origins of the Dred Scott Case: Jacksonian Jurisprudence and the Supreme Court, 1837–1857.* Athens: University of Georgia Press, 2006.

Allgor, Catherine. *Parlor Politics: In Which the Ladies of Washington Help Build a City and a New Government.* Charlottesville: University Press of Virginia, 2000.

Anderson, William L. *Cherokee Removal: Before and After.* Athens: University of Georgia Press, 1991.

Anonymous. *Diary of a Tour through Pennsylvania and New York, 1836–1840.* Historical Society of Pennsylvania, Philadelphia, PA.

Anthony, Martha Hampton. Vacation Diary, 1834. Historical Society of Pennsylvania, Philadelphia, PA.

Aron, Cindy Sondik. *Working at Play: A History of Vacations in the United States.* New York: Oxford University Press, 1999.

Arrington, Leonard J., and Davis Bitton. *The Mormon Experience: A History of the Latter-Day Saints.* 2nd ed. Urbana: University Illinois Press, 1992.

Bancroft, Frederic. *Slave Trading in the Old South.* 1931; reprint, New York: Ungar, 1959.

Barnes, Albert. "Barnes on the Traffic in Ardent Spirits." In *Select Temperance Tracts.* New York: American Tract Society, n.d.

Bassett, John Spencer. *Correspondence of Andrew Jackson.* 7 vols. Washington, DC: Carnegie Institution of Washington, 1926–1935.

Battle Family Papers. Southern Historical Collection. University of North Carolina, Chapel Hill, NC.

Belko, W. Stephen. *The Invincible Duff Green: Whig of the West.* Columbia: University of Missouri Press, 2006.

Benton, Thomas Hart. *Thirty Years' View.* New York: D. Appleton, 1854–1856.

Berry, Stephen W. II. *All That Makes a Man: Love and Ambition in the Civil War South.* Oxford: Oxford University Press, 2003.

Billingsley, Carolyn Earle. *Communities of Kinship: Antebellum Families and the Settlement of the Cotton Frontier.* Athens: University of Georgia Press, 2004.

Billington, Ray Allen. *The Protestant Crusade, 1800–1860: A Study of the Origins of American Nativism.* New York: Macmillan, 1938.

Binns, Archie. *The Roaring Land.* New York: R. M. McBride, 1942.

Blue, Frederick J. *No Taint of Compromise: Crusaders in Antislavery Politics.* Baton Rouge: Louisiana State University Press, 2005.

Boag, Peter G. *Environment and Experience: Settlement Culture in Nineteenth-Century Oregon.* Berkeley: University of California Press, 1992.

Boller, Paul. *American Transcendentalism, 1830–1860: An Intellectual Inquiry.* New York: Putnam, 1974.

Bordewich, Fergus M. *Bound for Canaan: The Underground Railroad and the War for the Soul of America.* New York: Amistad, 2005.

Boykin, John, and Francis P. Lee. Journal, August 15–September 5, 1833. New-York Historical Society, New York, NY.

Bratt, James D., ed. *Antirevivalism in Antebellum America: A Collection of Religious Voices.* New Brunswick: Rutgers University Press, 2006.

Braude, Ann. *Radical Spirits: Spiritualism and Women's Rights in Nineteenth Century America.* Boston: Beacon Press, 1989.

Brekus, Catherine A. *Strangers and Pilgrims: Female Preaching in America, 1740–1845.* Chapel Hill: University of North Carolina Press, 1998.

Bringhurst, Newell G. "Joseph Smith, the Mormons, and Antebellum Reform—A Closer Look." In *The Prophet Puzzle: Interpretive Essays on Joseph Smith*, ed. Bryan Waterman, 113–140. Salt Lake City: Signature, 1999.

Bristler, Louis E. "Eduard Ludecus's Journey to the Texas Frontier: A Critical Account of Beales's Rio Grande Colony." *Southwestern Historical Quarterly* 108 (2005): 368–385.

Britton, Diane F. *The Iron and Steel Industry in the Far West: Irondale, Washington.* Niwot: University of Colorado Press, 1991.

Brown, David. *Southern Outcast: Hinton Rowan Helper and The Impending Crisis of the South.* Baton Rouge: Louisiana State University Press, 2006.

Bruce, Dickson D., Jr. *Violence and Culture in the Antebellum South.* Austin: University of Texas Press, 1979.

Bunting, Robert. *The Pacific Raincoast: Environment and Culture in an American Eden, 1778–1900.* Lawrence: University Press of Kansas, 1997.

Bunting, Robert. "Michael Luark and Settler Culture in the Western Pacific Northwest, 1853–1899." *Pacific Northwest Quarterly* 96 (2005): 198–205.

Burin, Eric. *Slavery and the Peculiar Solution: A History of the American Coloniza-tion Society.* Gainesville: University of Florida Press, 2005.

Burstein, Andrew. *The Passions of Andrew Jackson.* New York: Vintage Books, 2004.

Bushman, Claudia Lauper, and Richard Lyman Bushman. *Building the King-dom: A History of Mormons in America.* New York: Oxford University Press, 2001.

Bushman, Richard L. *Joseph Smith and the Beginnings of Mormonism.* Urbana: University of Illinois Press, 1984.

Bushman, Richard L. *Joseph Smith, Rough Stone Rolling: Mormon's Founder.* New York: Knopf, 2005.

Butler, Jon. *Awash in a Sea of Faith: Christianizing the American People.* Cam-bridge: Harvard University Press, 1990.

Calloway, Colin G. *One Vast Winter Count: The Native American West before Lewis and Clark.* Lincoln: University of Nebraska, 2003.

Camp, Stephanie M. H. *Closer to Freedom: Enslaved Women and Everyday Resis-tance in the Plantation South.* Chapel Hill: University of North Carolina Press, 2004.

Campbell, Alexander. "The Mormonites." *Millennial Harbinger* 2 (February 7, 1831): 85–96.

Campbell, Randolph B. *Gone to Texas: A History of the Lone Star State.* New York: Oxford University Press, 2003.

Campbell, Tunis G. *Never Let People Be Kept Waiting: A Textbook on Hotel Man-agement. A Reprint of Tunis G. Campbell's Hotel Keepers, Head Waiters, and House-keepers' Guide.* Ed. and Intro by Doris Elizabeth King. 1848. Raleigh: King Reprints in Hospitality History, 1973.

Carter, Christine Jacobson. *Southern Single Blessedness: Unmarried Women in the Urban South.* Urbana: University of Illinois Press, 2006.

Cartwright, Peter. *The Autobiography of Peter Cartwright.* Introduction by Charles L. Wallis. Nashville: Abingdon Press, 1984.

Carwardine, Richard. "The Second Great Awakening in the Urban Centers: An Examination of Methodism and the 'New Measures.'" *Journal of American History* 59 (September 1972): 327–340.

Caughfield, Adrienne. *True Women and Westward Expansion.* College Station: Texas A&M University Press, 2005.

Chase, George W. *The History of Haverhill, Massachusetts, From Its First Settlement in 1640, to the Year 1860.* Haverhill, Mass.: n.p.,1861.

Chapin, David. *Exploring Other Worlds: Margaret Fox, Elisha Kent Kane, and the Antebellum Culture of Curiosity.* Amherst: University of Massachusetts Press, 2004.

Cheathem, Mark R. *Old Hickory's Nephew: The Political and Private Struggles of Andrew Jackson Donelson.* Baton Rouge: Louisiana State University Press, 2007.

Church of Jesus Christ of Latter-day Saints. *Scriptures: Internet Edition.* http://scriptures.lds.org/contents.

Clapp, Elizabeth J. "'A Virago-Errant in Enchanted Armor?': Anne Royall's 1829 Trial as a Common Scold." *Journal of the Early Republic* 23 (Summer 2003): 207–232.

Clark, Jerry E. *The Shawnee*. Lexington: University Press of Kentucky, 1977.

Clinton, Catherine. *Harriet Tubman: The Road to Freedom*. New York: Little, Brown, 2004.

Cmiel, Kenneth. *Democratic Eloquence: The Fight over Popular Speech in Nineteenth-Century America*. New York: William Morrow, 1990.

Cocke Family Papers. Virginia Historical Society, Richmond VA.

Cohen, Patricia Cline. "Women at Large: Travel in Antebellum America." *History Today* 44, no. 12 (1994): 44–50.

Cohen, Patricia Cline. "Safety and Danger: Women on American Public Transport, 1750–1850." In *Gendered Domains: Rethinking Public and Private in Women's History: Essays from the Seventh Berkshire Conference on the History of Women*, ed. Dorothy O. Helly, 110–122. Ithaca, NY: Cornell University Press, 1992.

Cole, Donald B. *A Jackson Man: Amos Kendall and the Rise of American Democracy*. Baton Rouge: Louisiana State University Press, 2004.

Cole, Donald B. *The Presidency of Andrew Jackson*. Lawrence: University Press of Kansas, 1993.

Coman, Edwin T., Jr., and Helen M. Gibbs. *Time, Tide and Timber: A Century of Pope and Talbot*. Stanford: Stanford University Press, 1949.

Connolly, Michael J. *Capitalism, Politics, and Railroads in Jacksonian New England*. Columbia: University of Missouri Press, 2003.

Cox, Thomas R. *Mills and Markets: A History of the Pacific Coast Lumber Industry to 1900*. Seattle: University of Washington Press, 1974.

Cutter, Barbara. *Domestic Devils, Battlefield Angels: The Radicalization of American Womanhood, 1830–1865*. DeKalb: Northern Illinois University Press, 2003.

Dain, Bruce. *A Hideous Monster of the Mind: American Race Theory in the Early Republic*. Cambridge: Harvard University Press, 2002.

Daly, John Patrick. *When Slavery Was Called Freedom: Evangelicalism, Proslavery, and the Causes of the Civil War*. Lexington: University Press of Kentucky, 2002.

Dalzell, Robert F., Jr. *Enterprising Elite: The Boston Associates and the World They Made*. New York: W. W. Norton, 1987.

Daniels, George H. *American Science in the Age of Jackson*. Tuscaloosa: University of Alabama Press, 1968.

Degler, Carl. *At Odds: Women and the Family in America from the Revolution to the Present*. Oxford: Oxford University Press, 1980.

Deyle, Steven. *Carry Me Back: The Domestic Slave Trade in American Life*. Oxford: Oxford University Press, 2005.

Doig, Ivan. *Winter Brothers: A Season at the Edge of America*. New York: Harcourt, 1980.

Donald, David. *Charles Sumner and the Coming of the Civil War*. New York: Knopf, 1960.

Douglass, Frederick. *Narrative of the Life of Frederick Douglass, an American Slave, Written by Himself*. Ed. David W. Blight. 2d. ed. New York: Bedford/St. Martin's, 2003.

Downey, Tom. *Planting a Capitalist South: Masters, Merchants, and Manufacturers in the Southern Interior, 1790–1860*. Baton Rouge: Louisiana State University Press, 2005.

Drago, Edmund L., ed. *Broke by the War: Letters of a Slave Trader*. Columbia: University of South Carolina Press, 1991.

Dublin, Thomas. *Women at Work: The Transformation of Work and Community in Lowell, Massachusetts, 1826–1860*. New York: Columbia University Press, 1979.

DuBois, Ellen C. *Feminism and Suffrage: The Emergence of an Independent Women's Movement in America, 1848–1869*. New York: Cornell University Press, 1978.

Edmunds, R. David. "Indians as Pioneers: Potawatomis on the Frontier." *Chronicles of Oklahoma* 65 (1987–1988): 340–353.

Edwards, G. Thomas. "'Terminus Disease': The Clark P. Crandall Description of Puget Sound in 1871." *Pacific Northwest Quarterly* 70 (1979): 163–177.

Elaw, Zilpha. *Memoirs of the Life, Religious Experience, Ministerial Travels and Labours of Mrs. Zilpha Elaw*. In *Sisters of the Spirit: Three Black Women's Autobiographies of the Nineteenth Century*, ed. and intro. by William L. Andrews. Bloomington: Indiana University Press, 1986.

Ely, Melvin Patrick. *Israel on the Appomattox: A Southern Experiment in Black Freedom from the 1790s through the Civil War*. New York: Knopf, 2004.

Exley, Jo Ella Powell. *Frontier Blood: The Saga of the Parker Family*. College Station: Texas A&M University Press, 2001.

Fehrenbach, T. R. *Lone Star: A History of Texas and the Texans*. Toronto, ON: Macmillan, 1968.

Feldberg, Michael. *The Turbulent Era: Riot and Disorder in Jacksonian America*. New York: Oxford University Press, 1980.

Feller, Daniel. *The Jacksonian Promise: America, 1815–1840*. Baltimore: Johns Hopkins University Press, 1995.

Ficken, Robert E. *The Forested Land: A History of Lumbering in Western Washington*. Seattle: University of Washington Press, 1988.

Ficken, Robert E., and Charles P. LeWarne. *Washington: A Centennial History*. Seattle: University of Washington Press, 1988.

Finke, Roger, and Rodney Stark. *The Churching of America, 1776–1990: Winners and Losers in Our Religious Economy*. New Brunswick: Rutgers University Press, 1992.

Finney, Charles Grandison. *Lectures on Revivals of Religion*. Ed. and Intro. by William G. McLoughlin. Cambridge: Harvard University Press, 1960.

Flint, James. *Letters from America, Containing Observations on the Climate and Agriculture of the Western States*. Edinburgh: W & C Tait, 1822.

Follett, Richard. *The Sugar Masters: Planters and Slaves in Louisiana's Cane World, 1820–1860*. Baton Rouge: Louisiana State University Press, 2005.

Forret, Jeff. *Race Relations at the Margins: Slaves and Poor Whites in the Antebellum Southern Countryside.* Baton Rouge: Louisiana State University Press, 2006.

Foster, Lawrence. *Religion and Sexuality: The Shakers, the Mormons, and the Oneida Community.* Oxford: Oxford University Press, 1981.

Fox-Genovese, Elizabeth. *Within the Plantation Household: Black and White Women of the Old South.* Chapel Hill: University of North Carolina Press, 1988.

Fox-Genovese, Elizabeth, and Eugene D. Genovese. *The Mind of the Master Class: History and Faith in the Southern Slaveholders' Worldview.* Cambridge: Cambridge University Press, 2005.

Frey, Sylvia R., and Betty Wood. *Come Shouting to Zion: African American Protestantism in the American South and British Caribbean to 1830.* Chapel Hill: University of North Carolina Press, 1998.

Friend, Craig T., and Lorri Glover, eds. *Southern Manhood: Perspectives on Masculinity in the Old South.* Athens: University of Georgia Press, 2004.

Garrison, William Lloyd. *William Lloyd Garrison and the Fight against Slavery.* Ed. William E. Cain. Boston: Bedford Books, 1995.

Gaustad, Edwin Scott. *Neither King nor Prelate: Religion and the New Nation, 1776–1826.* Grand Rapids: Eerdmans, 1993.

Gaustad, Edwin Scott, and Philip L. Barlow. *The New Historical Atlas of Religion in America.* New York: Oxford University Press, 2001.

Garvey, T. Gregory. *Creating the Culture of Reform in Antebellum America.* Athens: University of Georgia Press, 2006.

Garvin, Donna-Belle, and James L. Garvin. *On the Road North of Boston: New Hampshire Taverns and Turnpikes, 1700–1900.* Hanover: University Press of New England, 1988.

Gillespie, Michele. *Free Labor in an Unfree World: White Artisans in Slaveholding Georgia, 1789–1860.* Athens: University of Georgia Press, 1999.

Glover, Lorri. *Southern Sons: Becoming Men in the New Nation.* Baltimore: Johns Hopkins University Press, 2006.

Goodman, Paul. *Towards a Christian Republic: Antimasonry and the Great Transition in New England, 1826–1836.* Oxford: Oxford University Press, 1988.

Gorn, Elliot, ed. *The McGuffey Readers.* Boston: Bedford/St. Martin's, 1998.

Greenberg, Amy S. *Manifest Manhood and the Antebellum American Empire.* Cambridge: Cambridge University Press, 2005.

Greenberg, Kenneth S. *Honor and Slavery: Lies, Duels, Noses, Masks, Dressing as a Woman, Gifts, Strangers, Humanitarianism, Death, Slave Rebellions, the Proslavery Argument, Baseball, Hunting, and Gambling in the Old South.* Princeton: Princeton University Press, 1996.

Greenberg, Kenneth S. *Nat Turner: A Slave Rebellion in History and Memory.* Oxford: Oxford University Press, 2003.

Greven, Philip. *The Protestant Temperament: Patterns of Child Rearing, Religious Experience, and the Self in Early America.* Chicago: University of Chicago Press, 1977.

Grimes, Richard S. "The Early Years of the Delaware Indian Experience in Kansas Territory, 1830–1845." *Journal of the West* 41 (2002): 73–82.

Gudmestad, Robert H. *A Troublesome Commerce: The Transformation of the Interstate Slave Trade.* Baton Rouge: Louisiana State University Press, 2003.

Hammond, Bray. *Banks and Politics in America: From the Revolution to the Civil War.* Princeton: Princeton University Press, 1957.

Harper, Steven C. "Infallible Proofs, Both Human and Divine: The Persuasiveness of Mormonism for Early Converts." *Religion and American Culture* 10 (Winter 2000): 99–118.

Hatch, Nathan O. *The Democratization of American Christianity.* New Haven: Yale University Press, 1989.

Hawes, Joseph M. *The Children's Rights Movement: A History of Advocacy and Protection.* Boston: Twayne, 1991.

Hempton, David. *Methodism: Empire of the Spirit.* New Haven: Yale University Press, 2005.

Herring, Joseph B. *The Enduring Indians of Kansas: A Century and a Half of Acculturation.* Lawrence: University Press of Kansas, 1990.

Hessinger, Rodney. *Seduced, Abandoned, and Reborn: Visions of Youth in Middle-Class America, 1780–1850.* Philadelphia: University of Pennsylvania Press, 2005.

Hewitt, Abram S. Diary and letterpress copybooks, 1843, 1876, 1887–1888. New-York Historical Society, New York, NY.

Heyrman, Christine Leigh. *Southern Cross: The Beginnings of the Bible Belt.* New York: Knopf, 1997.

Hine, Robert V., and John Mack Farragher. *The American West: A New Interpretive History.* New Haven, CT: Yale University Press, 2000.

Hinks, Peter. *To Awaken My Afflicted Brethren: David Walker and the Problem of Antebellum Slave Resistance.* University Park: Pennsylvania State University Press, 1997.

Hoffert, Sylvia D. *Jane Grey Swisshelm: An Unconventional Life, 1815–1884.* Chapel Hill: University of North Carolina Press, 2004.

Horsman, Reginald. *Race and Manifest Destiny: The Origins of American Racial Anglo-Saxonism.* Cambridge: Harvard University Press, 1981.

Horton, James O., and Lois E. Horton. *In Hope of Liberty: Culture, Community, and Protest among Northern Free Blacks, 1700–1860.* New York: Oxford University Press, 1997.

Houstoun, Matilda Charlotte (Jesse) Fraser. *Texas and the Gulf of Mexico: Or, Yachting in the New World.* London: J. Murray, 1844.

Howe, Daniel Walker. "The Evangelical Movement and Political Culture in the North during the Second Party System." *Journal of American History* 77 (March 1991): 1216–1239.

Howlands, Sarah (Hazard). Diaries, 1818–1882. New-York Historical Society, New York, NY.

Hugins, Walter. *Jacksonian Democracy and the Working Class: A Study of the New York Workingmen's Movement, 1829–1837.* Stanford: Stanford University Press, 1960.

Hurtado, Albert L. *John Sutter: A Life on the North American Frontier.* Norman: University of Oklahoma Press, 2006.

Huston, James L. *Calculating the Value of the Union: Slavery, Property Rights, and the Economic Origins of the Civil War.* Chapel Hill: University of North Carolina Press, 2003.

Isenberg, Nancy. *Sex and Citizenship in Antebellum America.* Chapel Hill: University of North Carolina Press, 1998.

Jabour, Anya. *Marriage in the Early Republic: Elizabeth and William Wirt and the Companionate Ideal.* Baltimore: Johns Hopkins University Press, 1998.

John, Richard R. "Taking Sabbatarianism Seriously: The Postal System, the Sabbath, and the Transformation of American Political Culture." *Journal of the Early Republic* 10 (Winter 1990): 517–567.

Johnson, Paul E. *Sam Patch, the Famous Jumper.* New York: Hill and Wang, 2003.

Johnson, Paul E. *A Shopkeeper's Millennium: Society and Revivals in Rochester, New York, 1815–1837.* New York: Hill and Wang, 1978.

Johnson, Paul E., and Sean Wilentz. *The Kingdom of Matthias: A Story of Sex and Salvation in 19th-Century America.* Oxford: Oxford University Press, 1994.

Johnson, Walter. *Soul by Soul: Life Inside the Antebellum Slave Market.* Cambridge: Harvard University Press, 1999.

Joyner, Charles. *Down by the Riverside: A South Carolina Slave Community.* Urbana: University of Illinois Press, 1984.

Kaestle, Carl E. *Pillars of the Republic: Common Schools and American Society, 1780–1860.* New York: Hill and Wang, 1983.

Kaplan, Michael. "New York Tavern Violence and the Creation of Male Working Class Identity." *Journal of the Early Republic* 15 (Winter 1995): 592–617.

King, Charles R. *Children's Health in America: A History.* New York: Twayne/ McMillan, 1993.

Larkin, Jack. *The Reshaping of Everyday Life, 1790–1840.* New York: Harper and Row, 1988.

Larcom, Lucy. *A New England Girlhood.* Boston: Houghton, Mifflin, 1889.

Larson, Kate Clifford. *Bound for the Promised Land: Harriet Tubman, Portrait of an American Hero.* New York: Ballantine, 2003.

Latner, Richard. "The Kitchen Cabinet and Andrew Jackson's Advisory System." *Journal of American History* 65, no. 2 (Sept. 1978): 367–388.

Laurie, Bruce. *Beyond Garrison: Antislavery and Social Reform.* Cambridge: Cambridge University Press, 2005.

Lebsock, Suzanne. *The Free Women of Petersburg: Status and Culture in a Southern Town, 1784–1860.* New York: W.W. Norton, 1984.

Lewis, Charlene M. Boyer. *Ladies and Gentlemen on Display: Planter Society at the Virginia Springs, 1790–1860.* Charlottesville: University Press of Virginia, 2001.

Longaker, Richard. "Was Jackson's Kitchen Cabinet a Cabinet?" *Mississippi Valley Historical Review* 44, no. 1 (June 1957): 94–108.

Maddex, Jack P., Jr. "Proslavery Millennialism: Social Eschatology in Antebellum Southern Calvinism." *American Quarterly* 31 (Spring 1979): 46–62.

Marini, Stephen. "Hymnody as History: Early Evangelical Hymns and Recovery of American Popular Religion." *Church History* 71 (July 2002): 273–306.

Marszalek, John F. *The Petticoat Affair: Manners, Mutiny, and Sex in Andrew Jackson's White House.* New York: Free Press, 1997.

Martin, Jonathan D. *Divided Mastery: Slave Hiring in the America South.* Cambridge: Harvard University Press, 2004.

Martin, Scott C., ed. *Cultural Change and the Market Revolution in America, 1789–1860.* Latham, MD: Rowman and Littlefield, 2004.

Martineau, Harriet. *Retrospect of Western Travel.* London: Saunders and Otley, 1838.

Martineau, Harriet. *Society in America, in Two Volumes.* New York: Saunders and Otley, 1837.

Marty, Martin. *Righteous Empire: The Protestant Experience in America.* New York: Dial Press, 1970.

Masur, Louis P. *1831: Year of the Eclipse.* New York: Hill and Wang, 2001.

Mathews, Donald G. *Religion in the Old South.* Chicago: University of Chicago Press, 1977.

Mathews, Donald G. "The Second Great Awakening as an Organizing Process, 1780–1830: An Hypothesis." *American Quarterly* 21 (1969): 23–43.

Mathews, Donald G. "United Methodism and American Culture: Testimony, Voice, and the Public Sphere." In *The People(s) Called Methodist: Forms and Reforms of their Life.* Vol. 2. Ed. William B. Lawrence, Dennis M. Campbell, and Russell E. Richey, 279–304. Nashville: Abingdon Press, 1998.

Maxwell, Alice S., and Marion B. Dunlevy. *Virago! The Story of Anne Newport Royall.* Jefferson, NC: McFarland, 1985.

May, Dean L. *Three Frontiers: Family, Land, and Society in the American West, 1850–1900.* New York: Cambridge University Press, 1994.

May, Robert E. *Manifest Destiny's Underworld: Filibustering in Antebellum America.* Chapel Hill: University of North Carolina Press, 2002.

McCullough, David Wallace, ed. *American Childhoods: An Anthology.* Boston: Little, Brown, 1987.

McCurdy, James G. *By Juan de Fuca's Strait: Pioneering along the Northwestern Edge of the Continent.* Portland, OR: Metropolitan Press, 1937.

McCurry, Stephanie. *Masters of Small Worlds: Yeoman Households, Gender Relations, and the Political Culture of the Antebellum South Carolina Low Country.* New York: Oxford University Press, 1995.

McDonald, Lucile. *Swan among the Indians: Life of James G. Swan, 1818–1900.* Portland, OR: Binford and Mort, 1972.

McFeely, William S. *Frederick Douglass.* New York: W.W. Norton, 1991.

Meer, Sarah. *Uncle Tom Mania: Slavery, Minstrelsy, and Transatlantic Culture in the 1850s.* Athens: University of Georgia Press, 2005.

Melish, Joanne Pope. *Disowning Slavery: Gradual Emancipation and Race in New England, 1780–1860.* Ithaca, NY: Cornell University Press, 2000.

Meyer, David R. *The Roots of American Industrialization.* Baltimore: Johns Hopkins University Press, 2003.

Miller, Douglas T. *Jacksonian Aristocracy: Class and Democracy in New York, 1830–1860.* New York: Oxford University Press, 1967.

Miner, Craig. *Kansas: The History of the Sunflower State, 1854–2000.* Lawrence: University Press of Kansas, 2002.

Miner, Craig, and William E. Unrau. *The End of Indian Kansas: A Study of Cultural Revolution, 1854–1871.* Lawrence: Regents' Press of Kansas, 1978.

Mintz, Steven. *Huck's Raft: A History of American Childhood.* Cambridge: Belknap Press of Harvard University, 2004.

Mintz, Steven. *Moralists and Modernizers: America's Pre–Civil War Reformers.* Baltimore: Johns Hopkins University Press, 1995.

Montulé, Édouard de. *A Voyage to North America, the West Indies, and the Mediterranean.* London: Sir Richard Phillips, 1821.

Moore, R. Laurence. *Religious Outsiders and the Making of Americans.* New York: Oxford University Press, 1986.

Moorhead, James H. "Between Progress and Apocalypse: A Reassessment of Millennialism in American Religious Thought, 1800–1880." *Journal of American History* 71 (December 1984): 524–542.

Morris, Samuel Buckley. Diary, 1845. Historical Society of Pennsylvania, Philadelphia, PA.

Murray, Gail S. *American Children's Literature and the Construction of Childhood.* New York: Twayne/McMillan, 1998.

Nackman, Mark E. "The Making of the Texan Citizen Soldier, 1835–1860." *Southwestern Historical Quarterly* 78 (1975): 231–253.

Napier, Rita, ed. *Kansas and the West: New Perspectives.* Lawrence: University Press of Kansas, 2003.

Newell, Gordon. *Ships of the Inland Sea: The Story of the Puget Sound Steamboats.* Portland, OR: Binford and Mort, 1951.

Newman, Richard S. *The Transformation of American Abolitionism: Fighting Slavery in the Early Republic.* Chapel Hill: University of North Carolina Press, 2002.

Nissenbaum, Stephen. *Sex, Diet, and Debility in Jacksonian America: Sylvester Graham and Health Reform.* Westport, CT: Greenwood Press, 1980.

Nobles, Gregory H. *American Frontiers: Cultural Encounters and Continental Conquest.* New York: Hill and Wang, 1997.

Oakes, James. *The Ruling Race: A History of American Slaveholders.* New York: Knopf, 1982.

O'Brien, Michael. *Conjectures of Order: Intellectual Life and the American South, 1815–1860.* 2 vols. Chapel Hill: University of North Carolina Press, 2004.

Owsley, Frank L. *Plain Folk of the Old South.* Baton Rouge: Louisiana State University Press, 1949.

Pace, Robert F. *Halls of Honor: College Men in the Old South.* Baton Rouge: Louisiana State University Press, 2004.

Parish, Peter J. *Slavery: History and Historians.* New York: Westview, 1989.

Parton, James. *Life of Andrew Jackson.* New York: Mason Brothers, 1860.

Pegram, Thomas R. *Battling Demon Rum: The Struggle for a Dry America, 1800–1933.* Chicago: Ivan R. Dee, 1998.

Perry, Lewis. *Boats against the Current: American Culture between Revolution and Modernity, 1820–1860.* New York: Oxford University Press, 1993.

Pessen, Edward. *Jacksonian America: Society, Personality, and Politics.* Homewood, IL: Dorsey Press, 1969.

Pierson, Michael D. *Free Hearts and Free Homes: Gender and American Antislavery Politics.* Chapel Hill: University of North Carolina Press, 2003.

Portnoy, Alisse. *Their Right to Speak: Women's Activism in the Indian and Slave Debates.* Cambridge: Harvard University Press, 2005.

Prince, Carl E. "The Great 'Riot Year': Jacksonian Democracy and Patterns of Violence in 1834." *Journal of the Early Republic* 5 (Spring 1985): 1–19.

Prucha, Francis Paul. *American Indian Treaties: The History of a Political Anomaly.* Berkeley: University of California Press, 1994.

Prucha, Francis Paul. *The Great Father: The United States Government and the American Indians.* 2 vols. Lincoln: University of Nebraska Press, 1984.

Raboteau, Albert J. *Slave Religion: The "Invisible Institution" in the Antebellum South.* Oxford: Oxford University Press, 1978.

Rael, Patrick. *Black Identity and Black Protest in the Antebellum North.* Chapel Hill: University of North Carolina Press, 2002.

Ratner, Lorman A., and Dwight L. Teeter Jr. *Fanatics and Fire-Eaters: Newspapers and the Coming of the Civil War.* Urbana: University of Illinois Press, 2003.

Recognizances. Taverns, New York City, 1819. New-York Historical Society, New York, NY.

Remini, Robert V. *The Legacy of Andrew Jackson: Essays on Democracy, Indian Removal, and Slavery.* Baton Rouge: Louisiana State University Press, 1988.

Remini, Robert V. *Andrew Jackson and the Course of American Freedom.* New York: Harper and Row, 1981.

Remini, Robert V. *Andrew Jackson and His Indian Wars.* New York: Viking Press, 2001.

Renier, Jacqueline. *From Virtue to Character.* New York: Twayne, 1996.

Reséndez, Andrés. *Changing National Identities at the Frontier: Texas and New Mexico, 1800–1850.* Cambridge: Cambridge University Press, 2005.

Richards, Leonard L. *"Gentlemen of Property and Standing": Anti-Abolition Mobs in Jacksonian America.* New York: Oxford University Press, 1970.

Richards, Leonard L. *The Slave Power: The Free North and Southern Domination, 1780–1860.* Baton Rouge: Louisiana State University Press, 2000.

Ripley, Dorothy. *The Bank of Faith and Works United.* Philadelphia: J. H. Cunningham, 1819.

Robbins, William G. *Landscapes of Promise: The Oregon Story: 1800–1940.* Seattle: University of Washington Press, 1997.

Robertson, Stacey M. *Parker Pillsbury: Radical Abolitionist, Male Feminist.* Ithaca, NY: Cornell University Press, 2000.

Rogin, Michael Paul. *Fathers and Children: Andrew Jackson and the Subjugation of the American Indian.* New York: Knopf, 1975.

Rorabaugh, William J. *The Alcoholic Republic: An American Tradition.* Oxford: Oxford University Press, 1979.

Rose, Anne C. *Voices of the Marketplace: American Thought and Culture, 1830–1860.* New York: Twayne, 1995.

Rosenzweig, Roy. *Eight Hours for What We Will: Workers and Leisure in an Industrial City, 1870–1920.* New York: Cambridge University Press, 1983.

Rothenberg, Winifred Barr. *From Market-Places to a Market Economy: The Transformation of Rural Massachusetts, 1750–1850.* Chicago: University of Chicago Press, 1992.

Rothman, Adam. *Slave Country: American Expansion and the Origins of the Deep South.* Cambridge: Harvard University Press, 2005.

Rothman, Joshua D. *Notorious in the Neighborhood: Sex and Families across the Color Line in Virginia, 1787–1861.* Chapel Hill: University of North Carolina Press, 2006.

Rotundo, E. Anthony. *American Manhood: Transformations in Masculinity from the Revolution to the Modern Era.* New York: Basic Books, 1993.

Royall, Anne Newport. *Mrs. Royall's Southern Tour, or, Second Series of the Black Book.* 3 Volumes. Washington: n.p., 1830–1831.

Royall, Anne Newport. *Letters from Alabama on Various Subjects: To Which is Added, an Appendix, Containing Remarks on Sundry Members of the 20th & 21st Congress, and Other High Characters, &c. &c. at the Seat of Government. In One Volume.* Washington, DC: [None given], 1830.

Royall, Anne Newport. *Sketches of History, Life and Manners in the United States. By a Traveler.* New Haven, CT: Printed for the author, 1826.

Ruggles, Jeffrey. *The Unboxing of Henry Brown.* Richmond: Library of Virginia, 2003.

Sale, Roger. *Seattle: Past to Present.* Seattle: University of Washington Press, 1976.

Salerno, Beth. *Sister Societies: Women's Antislavery Societies in Antebellum America.* DeKalb: Northern Illinois University Press, 2005.

Sandoval-Strausz, Andrew K. *Hotel: An American History.* New Haven, CT: Yale University Press, 2006.

Satz, Ronald. *American Indian Policy in the Jacksonian Era.* Lincoln: University of Nebraska Press, 1975.

Saxe-Weimar, Bernard Eisenach, Duke of. *Travels Through North America, During the Years 1825 and 1826.* Philadelphia: Carey, Lea and Carey, 1828.

Scarborough, William K. *Masters of the Big House: Elite Slaveholders of the Mid-Nineteenth-Century South.* Baton Rouge: Louisiana State University Press, 2003.

Schulling, S. Diary, 1824. Historical Society of Pennsylvania, Philadelphia, PA.

Schwantes, Carlos Arnaldo. *The Pacific Northwest: An Interpretive History.* Rev. and enl. ed. Lincoln: University of Nebraska Press, 1996.

Schwartz, Marie Jenkins. *Born in Bondage: Growing Up Enslaved in the Antebellum South.* Cambridge: Harvard University Press, 2000.

Sellers, Charles G., Jr. *The Market Revolution: Jacksonian America, 1815–1846.* New York: Oxford University Press, 1991.

Sheriff, Carol. *The Artificial River: The Erie Canal and the Paradox of Progress, 1817–1862.* New York: Hill and Wang, 1996.

Shipps, Jan. *Mormonism: The Story of a New Religious Tradition.* Urbana: University of Illinois Press, 1987.

Slaughter, Thomas P. *Bloody Dawn: The Christiana Riot and Racial Violence in the Antebellum North.* Oxford: Oxford University Press, 1991.

Slotkin, Richard. *The Fatal Environment: The Myth of the Frontier in the Age of Industrialization, 1800–1890.* New York: Atheneum, 1985.

Smith, Mark M. *Mastered by the Clock: Time, Slavery, and Freedom in the American South.* Chapel Hill: University of North Carolina Press, 1997.

Srebnick, Amy Gilman. *The Mysterious Death of Mary Rogers: Sex and Culture in Nineteenth-Century New York.* Oxford: Oxford University Press, 1995.

Staats, Richard Henry. "Ladies Ticket," in Diary, 1832–1836. New-York Historical Society, New York, NY.

Steele, Margaret. Letters. Southern Historical Collection. University of North Carolina, Chapel Hill, NC.

Steinberg, Theodore. *Nature Incorporated: Industrialization and the Waters of New England.* Amherst: University of Massachusetts Press, 1991.

Stewart, James Brewer. *Holy Warriors: The Abolitionists and American Slavery.* New York: Hill and Wang, 1976.

Stewart, James Brewer. "Reconsidering the Abolitionists in an Age of Fundamentalist Politics." *Journal of the Early Republic* 26 (Spring 2006): 1–23.

Stokes, Melvyn, and Stephen Conway, eds. *The Market Revolution in America: Social, Political, and Religious Expressions, 1800–1880.* Charlottesville: University Press of Virginia, 1996.

Stowe, Harriet Beecher. *Uncle Tom's Cabin; or, Life among the Lowly,* ed. Ann Douglas. 1852; reprint, New York: Penguin, 1981.

Stowe, Steven M. *Intimacy and Power in the Old South: Ritual in the Lives of the Planters.* Baltimore: Johns Hopkins University Press, 1987.

Sutton, William R. *Journeymen for Jesus: Evangelical Artisans Confront Capitalism in Jacksonian Baltimore.* University Park: Pennsylvania State University Press, 1998.

Swett, Philip C. "History of Shoemaking in Haverhill, Massachusetts." Paper read before the Fortnightly Club, n.d. Haverhill Public Library Special Collections.

Tadman, Michael. *Speculators and Slaves: Masters, Traders, and Slaves in the Old South.* Madison: University of Wisconsin Press, 1990.

Tangires, Helen. *Public Markets and Civil Culture in Nineteenth-Century America.* Baltimore: Johns Hopkins University Press, 2002.

Taylor, George Rogers. *The Transportation Revolution, 1815–1860.* New York: Holt, Rinehart and Winston, 1951.

Temin, Peter. *The Jacksonian Economy.* New York: W.W. Norton, 1969.

Throckmorton, Arthur L. *Oregon Argonauts: Merchant Adventurers on the Western Frontier.* Portland: Oregon Historical Society, 1961.

Tocqueville, Alexis de. *Democracy in America.* Trans. Stephen D. Grant. Indianapolis: Hackett, 2000.

Towers, Frank. *The Urban South and the Coming of the Civil War.* Charlottesville: University Press of Virginia, 2004.

Trollope, Frances. *Domestic Manners of the Americans.* New York: Whittacher, Treacher, & Co., 1832.

Turner, Nat. *The Confessions of Nat Turner and Related Documents,* ed. Kenneth S. Greenberg. New York: Bedford/St. Martin's, 1996.

Tyrrell, Ian R. "Drink and Temperance in the Antebellum South: An Overview and Interpretation." *Journal of Southern History* 48 (November 1982): 485–510.

Vickers, Daniel. *Farmers and Fishermen: Two Centuries of Work in Essex County, Massachusetts, 1630–1859.* Chapel Hill: University of North Carolina Press, 1994.

Walker, David. *David Walker's Appeal to the Coloured Citizens of the World,* ed. Peter P. Hinks. University Park: Pennsylvania State University Press, 2000.

Walters, Ronald G. *American Reformers, 1815–1860.* New York: Hill and Wang, 1978.

Warren, Stephen A. "The Baptists, the Methodists, and the Shawnees: Conflicting Cultures in Indian Territory, 1833–34." *Kansas History* 17 (1994): 148–161.

Watson, Harry L. *Liberty and Power: The Politics of Jacksonian America.* New York: Hill and Wang, 1990.

Webster, Daniel. *Writings and Speeches of Daniel Webster.* Boston: Little, Brown, 1903.

Wells, Jonathan Daniel. *The Origins of the Southern Middle Class, 1800–1861.* Chapel Hill: University of North Carolina Press, 2003.

West, Eliot. *The Way to the West: Essays on the Central Plains.* Albuquerque: University of New Mexico Press, 1995.

White, Deborah Gray. *Ar'n't I a Woman? Female Slavers in the Plantation South.* New York: W.W. Norton, 1985.

White, Richard. *"It's Your Misfortune and None of My Own": A History of the American West.* Norman: University of Oklahoma Press, 1991.

White, Shane, and Graham White. *The Sounds of Slavery: Discovering African American History through Songs, Sermons, and Speech.* Boston: Beacon Press, 2005.

White, Wm., *Annual Stageman's Ball.* [Broadside]. New-York Historical Society, New York, NY, 1839.

Wiebe, Robert H. *The Opening of American Society: From the Adoption of the Constitution to the Eve of Disunion.* New York: Knopf, 1984.

Wigger, John H. *Taking Heaven by Storm: Methodism and the Rise of Popular Christianity in America.* Urbana: University of Illinois Press, 2001.

Wilentz, Sean. *Chants Democratic: New York City and the Rise of the American Working Class, 1788–1850.* New York: Oxford University Press, 1984.

William and Maria. Papers (microfilm). American Philosophical Society, Philadelphia PA. Originals at Nantucket Maria Mitchell Association, Nantucket, MA.

Wilson and Hairston Papers. Southern Historical Collection. University of North Carolina, Chapel Hill, NC.

Wilton, John M. *Sketches of the History of New Hampshire, from its settlement in 1623 to 1833.* Concord, NH: Marsh, Capen, and Lyon, 1834.

Wood, Gordon. "Evangelical America and Early Mormonism." *New York History* 61 (October 1980): 359–386.

Wood, Kirsten E. *Masterful Women: Slaveholding Widows from the American Revolution through the Civil War.* Chapel Hill: University of North Carolina Press, 2004.

Wright, Daniel S. *"The First of Causes to Our Sex": The Female Reform Movement in the Antebellum Northeast, 1834–1848.* New York: Routledge, 2006.

Wright, Frances. *Views of Society and Manners in America: In a Series of Letters from That Country to a Friend in England, during the Years 1818, 1819, and 1820. By an Englishwoman.* New York: E. Bliss and E. White, 1821.

Wyatt-Brown, Bertram. *Southern Honor: Ethics and Behavior in the Old South.* New York: Oxford University Press, 1982.

Young, Michael P. "Confessional Protest: The Religious Birth of U.S. National Social Movements." *American Sociological Review* 67 (October 2002): 660–688.

Zakim, Michael. *Ready-Made Democracy: A History of Men's Dress in the American Republic, 1760–1860.* Chicago: University of Chicago Press, 2003.

Index

NOTE: italic page numbers indicate pictures.